Rolling Stones 69

Patrick Humphries

Rolling Stones 69

OMNIBUS PRESS

London / New York / Paris / Sydney / Copenhagen / Berlin / Madrid / Tokyo

Exclusive Distributors
Music Sales Limited
14/15 Berners Street
London, W1T 3LJ

Every effort has been made to trace the copyright holders of the photographs in this book but one or two were unreachable. We would be grateful if the photographers concerned would contact us.

Printed in Malta.

A catalogue record for this book is available from the British Library.

Visit Omnibus Press at www.omnibuspress.com

Contents

Introduction

There are few better examples of the schism that persisted in London society at the end of the 1960s than the film of a recording session that took place in Barnes, south-west London, on the night of March 15, 1969. Mick Jagger appears at the height of his louche, demonic, demi-monde, rock-god phase. Hair cascading around his shoulders, his eyes no stranger to kohl, and the lips... those legendary lips... seemed particularly lascivious. Despite already being renowned for all manner of excess in person, Mick's first film, a drug-fuelled sex-fest, is currently on hold as the distributors shake their heads. Warner Bros. executives wonder, even in these enlightened times, which cinema on the ABC circuit would ever countenance screening *Performance*?

But away from the film set, and his role as 'Turner', the fictional rock-star recluse, the documentary camera catches Jagger hard at work at his day job. As lead singer and principal songwriter of the Rolling Stones, Jagger is fashioning what will become the closing track of the group's eighth UK album of original material, *Let It Bleed*. The song is 'You Can't Always Get What You Want'. The title surely belies the songwriter's own situation: aged only twenty-five, this has to be a man who already has all he could ever want. Michael Philip Jagger must, at this stage, have achieved satisfaction on every level. After six years of hits and idolatry, with a handful of Stones songs cemented into pop history, this is a song he is particularly proud of. But to give the track the gravitas it needs, the Stone decides something majestic is required. Nothing too Satanic though; that particular odyssey, with the release of the album *Their Satanic Majesties Request* in December 1967 – the group's response to the all-conquering *Sgt. Pepper's Lonely Hearts Club Band* – had proved to be a very, very wonky diversion.

This time round, the group needed to pull something pretty spectacular out of the sort of top hat Mick had sported for *The Rolling Stones Rock And Roll Circus*, the concert show filmed just a few months prior. For so long now, the Stones had seemed to be one step behind their only real rivals, The Beatles. The *Rock And Roll Circus*, their imaginative television retort to *Magical Mystery Tour*, could have put them ahead had it not remained unscreened for nearly four decades.

But now the Rolling Stones were once again cloistered, creating what would be their final release of the decade.

Mick Jagger always envisaged 'You Can't Always Get What You Want' as something special. It was *his* song, and it demanded a lavish treatment. From its humble, solo acoustic beginnings, something *big* was required to bring the song to a sufficiently epic climax. It would, after all, be the last word on the final song of this album, and was therefore intended to bring the 1960s to a titanic conclusion.

Mick had always imagined a gospel choir would accompany the track, like the Watts Street Gospel Choir, which had sung at the conclusion of *Beggars Banquet*. The Stones' symbiosis with the blues and R&B was always an essential part of the glue that bound them together. They had already helped to bring black music to a white audience. And a black community choir, singing their soulful hearts out, would appear to be a perfect fit here. Then somebody impishly suggested a classical choir, and it was that collaboration which raised smiles all round. A classical choir buoying the world's most disreputable, debauched rock'n'roll band? The incongruity was just too delicious to disregard.

The London Bach Choir, founded in 1876, is a venerable institution formed with the sole purpose of performing the music of the celebrated composer. It was, and remains, an amateur choir. Member Rosemary Morton Jack sang on the 1969 session for 'You Can't Always Get What You Want', under musical director Sir David Willcocks: "[The choir] was made up of very talented amateurs; they could sightread as quickly as reading a newspaper. I never got paid for the session, but I hope the choir did. I remember it was only a couple of hours – and the general feeling was that it was a fun thing to do. It was a break from doing humdrum jobs, taking part in something outside your sphere. For most of us it was quite exciting to be recording with a notorious pop group! It seemed a bit of an adventure, a bit of a kick. It was a very long time ago, but looking back, it is something I am rather proud of."

Each of the 40-plus members has been squeezed into Barnes' Olympic Studios for the session. There is a visible divide. Many of the male choristers are suited and tied, but even in mufti they look like the sort of harassed bank manager or civil servant that classic English actors Raymond Huntley and Richard Wattis had made a living portraying. The female choristers, some sporting the winged spectacles made popular by Jagger's nemesis, Mrs Mary Whitehouse, smile widely at the thought of being in such close proximity to the world-famous celebrity. The tension is unmistakable. For the occasion, the chameleon Mick puts on his polite, grammar school voice to coax the choir into action. But even that fails to put them at ease and they appear palpably uncomfortable receiving coaching from the 'Devil Incarnate'.

Keith Richards later described the session as "a beautiful juxtaposition". But a further division arises: instinctively, the choir lapses into Received Pronunciation, their 'can't' rhyming with 'aunt', until Mick coaches them to come with something more *American-sounding*. Eventually the session concludes and the choir makes its way out into the night, perhaps eager to be escaping the decadence.

But to everyone's surprise and delight, the combination works breathtakingly well. On completion, thanks to a brilliant arrangement by Jack Nitzsche, the choral voices swell; they ebb and flow, rising like waves on a beautiful moonlit ocean. Bell-clear, voices enunciate and harmonise across odd words about a reception, blown fuses, a cherry-flavoured soda and a fashionable King's Road location... and the end is made complete. After seven years of riotous behaviour while creating classic rock'n'roll, after nearly a decade when they came to epitomise everything the rebellious nature and energy of the sixties had promised, the Stones had delivered. And it has always struck me how strangely apt the final track on *Let It Bleed* is.

Even more extraordinary, half a century on, the band is still performing 'You Can't Always Get What You Want', despite all four members appearing to have precisely everything they ever, needed, desired or, indeed, wanted.

★★★

In 1969, the band knew they needed something a little bit special to see out the year and the decade. But no one, not Mick Jagger, Keith Richards, Brian Jones, Charlie Watts or Bill Wyman; not Meredith Hunter, nor Sonny Barger, nor Allen Klein, nor

Marianne Faithfull... *no one* could have foreseen just what a rollercoaster ride 1969 would prove to be for the Rolling Stones. Revisionist history neatly and conveniently delineates the past into perfect eras and epochs. But, without doubt, few rock'n'roll bands have ever undergone such a turbulent 12 months as did the Stones during that year.

In the wake of the Manson murders, the debacle that was the Altamont Free Concert on December 6, 1969, which resulted in the death of four young concertgoers, drew a line under the heady, hippie optimism of the sixties. Like the rest of us, the Stones were not blessed with foresight; they had no knowledge of rising oil prices, trade union bloody-mindedness, power cuts, financial meltdowns, Middle East hijackings, IRA terrorism... And they did not know that the 1970s were going to be such a long, hard grind.

Only 11 months in, by November 1970, with Jimi Hendrix and Janis Joplin already gone, Lester Bangs was writing in *Rolling Stone* magazine: "The seventies may not have started with bright prospects for the future of rock, and so many hacks are reciting the litany of doom... The form may be in trouble, and we listeners may ourselves be in trouble, so it gets harder each month to even hear what we're listening to."

It was apparent that with the death of sixties idealism something was about to change. Hindsight has it that those who had led from the front – the Stones, The Beatles and Dylan – were bracing themselves for that change. But that was still way over the horizon. Even as the Stones flew away from the Altamont Speedway that night, the full scale of the tragedy was not yet evident. And within days they were back on stage for four London shows to see out the decade.

For all the triumphs of the preceding years, since their sneering breakthrough in 1964, the Stones had spent half the sixties occupying front pages and living lives their fans could only imagine as they pressed their noses up against the glass that separated the band from its audience.

Latterly, the Stones appeared to be spending more time in the law courts than in the studios, but after the psychedelic awfulness of *Satanic Majesties* they had managed to regroup with 1968's *Beggars Banquet*. Under the bright studio lights, brighter than usual because they were being filmed for *One Plus One* (an, if you will, political 'rockumentary'), the Stones laboured over the crucial recordings they desperately hoped would atone for *Satanic Majesties*' sins.

The swaggering 'Jumpin' Jack Flash' marked a welcome back-to-basics approach, but that proved to be just an hors d'oeuvre. "*Beggars Banquet* isn't a return to anything," Graeme Thomson wrote astutely in 2018, on the album's 50th anniversary. "It is, instead, an immersive exploration of the band's bedrock sources. The LP brims with gritty blues, heartfelt country, Dylan-esque diversions, samba fusillades, state-of-the-nation broadsides, and calls to arms from the violent streets..."

Gone was the inflated and phoney grandeur of *Satanic Majesties*; here instead was a band locked into a unique groove. One of the Stones' best ballads is the frequently overlooked 'No Expectations', later hauntingly covered by Johnny Cash. Nobody had heard anything like the pulsing rhythms of 'Sympathy For The Devil', nor the strident call to the barricades of 'Street Fighting Man'. The lewd and lascivious 'Parachute Woman' and 'Factory Girl' played up to those who still saw the Stones as emissaries of the Devil and, heard today, the prowling paedophile of 'Stray Cat Blues' is unsettling. The Stones' blues roots were revisited but now with a sneering, know-all attitude. And each side of the near 40-minute LP ends on a high note. Side One concludes with a call to the outcasts and outlaws, including band members, rounded up on 'Jigsaw Puzzle', while Side Two ends with 'Salt Of The Earth', a timely call to arms. Too often overlooked in the Stones' canon, this is a toast to the band's imagined audience of hard, working-class people and the low-born. Jagger raises a swift glass to what has been, and then plunges on ahead.

The original unsigned *Melody Maker* review of the album was surprisingly harsh: "The Stones have always set their sights on the R&B and blues field for their sources, the criticism levelled against their music is that little bit harsher. This LP fails because, judged by those standards, it is mediocre."

But to most, *Beggars Banquet* stands out as one of a quartet of truly great albums. Critics may have carped that the plain white album sleeve was both weak, and a week behind that of The Beatles' *White Album*, but the inner sleeve was superb. Here were the Rolling Stones as nature intended: Charlie looking simultaneously blasé and bored; Bill, blithely indifferent; Keith keeping Mick fed; Brian at play... The album launch at the Gore Hotel, hard by the Albert Hall, allowed the band's hard-pressed PR Les Perrin to get his sweet revenge as he entered into the pie-flying spirit of things and began hurling cream cakes with gusto at the group that had caused him so much stress during the preceding year.

"I remember Mick at the head of the U-shaped table," *Melody Maker*'s Chris Welch told me, "and we, the invited media, had a grand old time, plenty to eat and drink, served up by comely wenches. It was rather like one of those Henry VIII-themed restaurants that were just becoming popular. Then Mick stood up and said, 'We haven't invited you here just to eat and drink,' and the custard pies started flying. They weren't actually custard, just foam, but still very messy. I remember they were giving out copies of the album, and I got mine signed by all five of the band, but it got stolen a few years ago."

With panache then, the Rolling Stones delivered the majestic *Beggars Banquet* in time for Christmas 1968. This began a four-year run in which the Stones superseded even The Beatles, producing a sequence of albums by which all other bands were subsequently judged. *Beggars Banquet* followed on from a clutch of singles that even today can fill the floor at wedding receptions and retirement parties.

This was the album that reinforced the Stones' status. In its first issue of 1969, *Rolling Stone* magazine devoted four pages to a review of the LP. Jon Landau presciently wrote of it: "The result is the most sophisticated and meaningful statement we can expect to hear concerning the two themes – violence and politics – that will probably dominate the rock of 1969."

Facing up to a new year, the band were all set to see the sixties out with a bang, rather than a whimper. Plans were made and foundations laid. But no one could have imagined just what a tumultuous 12 months would follow for the Rolling Stones.

PART 1

Jigsaw Puzzle

CHAPTER 1

When The Train Come In The Station

"Pop stars have always been loved... or at least liked. They have been romantic or amusing, or brought rough from backstreet beginnings to polished stardom and admired for their success. But they've never been loathed, or jeered at by half the population. That is, not until 1963!"

That was how Pete Goodman (aka Peter Jones) began *Our Own Story By The Rolling Stones*, the first and "only official account" of the band. *Record Mirror* stalwart Jones was the first journalist to get fully behind the band, publishing *Our Own Story* in 1964, and my five-shilling copy is literally falling apart. I bought it in Beckenham when I was twelve and had run out of Beatle things to read about, so I switched to the Stones. I had experienced a frisson when I spotted local resident Bill Wyman, with his then-wife Diane, pushing their young son in a pushchair down Beckenham High Street. This momentous sighting occurred just outside the Three Tuns pub, where, five years later, David Bowie would run the

Beckenham Arts Lab. Today, it is a Zizzi restaurant – which, as my wife pointed out, they should rename 'Zizzi Stardust'.

It goes without saying that the sighting of any celebrity was exciting in 1964. Even though they had relocated to London from Liverpool, the likelihood of me actually *seeing* a Beatle was remote. But spotting Bill had fuelled my imagination. There really was a playground schism back then: were you a Beatles or Stones fan? The Stones generally appealed to those of a somewhat rougher edge, though in truth I preferred the more melodic, singalong appeal of The Beatles – the Rolling Stones sounded to me like they needed their grittier edges sanded off. In retrospect, even on their early singles The Beatles sounded better on record. And they were fortunate to have come under the watch of George Martin, rather than EMI contemporaries of Martin's: producers Norrie Paramour, who worked closely with Cliff Richards & the Shadows, and Ron Richards, who was assigned to produce The Beatles' first session for Parlophone in June 1962, before Martin took over. From the very beginning, George Martin had discerned a certain elusive something in his charges and was willing to follow their lead. On disc, the Stones had had to rely on Andrew Loog Oldham who, by his own admission, could barely produce his way out of a paper bag. "He's an idiot," the Small Faces' Ian McLagan confirmed to Shawn Levy, in Levy's 2002 book *Ready, Steady, Go!* "He has no idea about sound. He couldn't produce a burp after a glass of beer."

However with new producer Jimmy Miller both on board and behind the board, the Stones were bracing themselves for an equally strong-sounding follow-up to *Beggars Banquet*. They were not to know that, at the dawn of 1969, they were about to have the field to themselves – and, within 12 months, they would move to the top of the pile.

12

By 1969, The Beatles had run their course. At the end of 1968, there had been tantalising plans for live shows at the London Roundhouse (never realised), and the weekly music press was filled with rumours of a 'new phase' Beatles LP to follow September's release of *Abbey Road*. However, a desultory 40-minute show on a windy London rooftop early in the New Year, and that was that – and in those days, when a group stopped touring and releasing new material, that really was it.

Today, it seems incredible to recall the permanent, enduring interest in The Beatles, a band that last released new music and played together half a century ago. Equally incredible is the fact that their main rivals are still going strong. The Stones just keep on keeping on. And on. And on. How many times researching this book did I come across contemporary accounts of the Stones returning to the live arena under the headline 'The Last Time'? It's been the same story since the band first entered tax exile, when Edward Heath served as prime minister from 1970 to 1974. The same headline appears under the administrations of presidents Nixon, Ford, Carter, Reagan, Bush Senior, Clinton, Bush Junior, Obama and Trump… the Rolling Stones' longevity is simply unparalleled.

People assume it is huge financial incentives that keep the band on the road year after year, decade after decade. But that theory misses the point. Each of the Stones could retire comfortably to their lavish properties around the globe, but they tour and record incessantly because that's what a band *does*. That's what the bluesmen they so admire did: they played until they dropped. Though when the Stones do finally drop, it will be under far cushier circumstances than their African-American forebears.

As Keith Richards reminded journalist Roy Carr, a mere quarter of a century into the Stones' career: "Nobody ever turned around to Muddy Waters, B.B. King or John Lee Hooker and said: 'Now you have to stop, you're not allowed to play any longer.'"

Diehard Stones fan and rock journalist David Sinclair told me: "The Stones are redefining old age as they redefined youth. B.B. King and John Lee Hooker played sitting down at the end – they were manifestly old men. The Stones make you look at old age in different ways; they have redefined how you look at growing older."

Despite their legendary status, the Stones are mortal. Like us, none of them had the ability to imagine their future. There's that oft-viewed clip of a cherubic young Mick Jagger opining: "I can't imagine myself singing 'Satisfaction' when I'm thirty." And as early as 1968, he was jokingly telling journalist Keith Altham: "We are hoping to make several live appearances shortly from our wheelchairs!"

Or again, speaking to the *Daily Mirror* in 1972: "When I'm 33, I quit... I don't want to be a rock'n'roll singer all my life. I couldn't bear to end up as an Elvis Presley and sing in Las Vegas." Needless to say, in the course of their endless career, the Stones *have* played Vegas, although, true to their word, they have never succumbed to a residency.

Charlie Watts was, as ever, wearily philosophical when talking to Keith Altham at Olympic Studios during a recording session in the late sixties: "All these things go in cycles... The times have changed and it's going to be a long time till they change again. Outside these studios now there are two kids. A year ago there were 10 and the year before that 20 or more!"

David Sinclair, then chief music critic of *The Times*, remembers being called in by the paper's obituary editor in 1998. The newspaper of national record had it on good authority that Keith Richards was soon for that great juke-joint in the sky, and Sinclair was asked to update the forty-four-year-old rocker's obituary. He duly amended it, but sadly the obituary editor died the following year. I don't know what moral is to be drawn from this, save that

Keith motors on and on. The legend persists that he is driven with someone else's blood filling his veins on a regular basis. The Keith who operates with more chemicals circulating in his system than ICI. Keith, with a well-worn face hewn from the granite of a lifetime's real living. The Keith who, like the Dude in the 1998 film *The Big Lebowski*, simply *endures*.

The Rolling Stones defy all logic and reason, their very durability at odds with the 'live fast and die young' expectations of the rock'n'roll culture they virtually created. They are a part not just of our national culture but also our national heritage. The trajectory of events leading up to 1969 is so well known that it needs only to be briefly sketched in. However, it is worth recalling the steps they took and the decisions they made that so affected their path through to that incendiary year.

The Rolling Stones are not, and never were, just a band. They are an institution. They are an industry. They are venerated and scorned in equal measure. They are rock'n'roll outlaws. They are a number of registered companies. They operate as a cohesive whole. They are at odds with each other. Offstage, they can't bear to be in the same room. They are inseparable. And at the end of the long, long day, mention the Rolling Stones and the gnarled faces of two old men will come immediately to mind.

Older today than Churchill was when first elected prime minister, Mick Jagger still maintains pole position on that curious plateau of the ultra-celebrity, his every move, birthday, grandchild and paternity suit duly recorded in print, on film and in cyberspace. Keith Richards, the other side of that glittering coin, is busy outliving all those howling wolves, lizard kings and crawling king snakes. A man indeed, but more legend than mere mortal.

However, it is the dynamic between Mick and Keith that still fascinates, and it is the fulcrum of their partnership that still intrigues. From the outside, Stones fans want to believe Mick is still waiting on a friend. It applies in the same way you want to believe that Edward VIII was happy having sacrificed his throne to marry Mrs Simpson. Or that Paul Simon and Art Garfunkel enjoy each other's company. Or the Everly Brothers. Or the Eagles. Or Lennon and McCartney, when the former was still alive…

Jagger recognised the public fascination in the pair when he talked to *Rolling Stone* magazine's Jann Wenner a full 34 years after their first proper encounter at Dartford railway station, one of the most significant milestones in the band's – nay, rock'n'roll – history: "People like partnerships because they can identify with the drama of two people in a partnership. They can feed off a partnership, and that keeps people entertained. Besides, if you have a successful partnership, it's self-sustaining."

That enduring on-off, up-and-down, in-and-out relationship is at the heart of any appreciation and understanding of the Rolling Stones. For all the many millions accrued and the gallons of water that have since flowed under the bridge, my bargain-basement Freudian belief is that Mick always envied Keith. Mick was, essentially, a well-brought-up middle-class suburbanite with a strong work ethic. Keith was the naughty rapscallion who didn't give a fuck. Keith would always go as far as he could, out on a limb, in at the deep end, under the cosh. But it was the tenacious Mick who was happy to make the business decisions that ensured the band's future. Without Jagger's motivation, it could be that the Rolling Stones would have found themselves bracketed alongside their long-forgotten Decca labelmates. But Mick diligently crunched the numbers and read the small print, while you get the sense that Keith never was a man to be troubled by detail.

Class was always an issue with Jagger and Richards, as David Hepworth wryly observed in 2018's *Uncommon People*: "Michael Philip being academically able and the son of a middle-class family, had gone to Dartford Grammar School, which turned out

Dartford's next generation of doctors and bank managers. Keith, not being academically inclined... had gone to Dartford Technical High School, which turned out the people who fixed the cars of the doctors and bank managers."

Anita Pallenberg, who more than anyone had the opportunity to observe that dynamic firsthand, confirmed my belief, telling Victor Bockris for his biography on Keith: "In many ways, Keith was the man Mick wanted to be. Free and easy in his own skin, not uptight like Mick. Tough when he had to be, had a good time, enjoyed drinking, drugs and carousing. Mick envied Keith."

For all the louche decadence associated with the name 'Mick Jagger', the sybaritic Stone has always been canny on so many levels. Mick's sole mention in a dictionary of 20th-century quotations confirms that dichotomy: "It's all right letting yourself go, as long as you can let yourself back in."

Mick & Keith, the Glimmer Twins, Keef and Sir Mick... they are the old married couple. They are like Groucho Marx when asked if he loved his brother, Chico: "No, but I'm used to him." They are the owners of the corner shop in the nineties BBC comedy *Stella Street*, in which the characters 'Mick' and 'Keith' forsake rock'n'roll to run a corner shop in Surbiton. Phil Cornwell's 'Mick' fusses over details, ensuring there are sufficient quantities of Daz washing powder, dog food and tinned peaches. And all the while, John Sessions's blithely indifferent 'Keith' necks the JD, unconcerned with the rissoles, and mumbles in that gris-gris patois, beneath which the twang of Dartford is still evident.

For Londoners, Dartford in Kent is remote, but not as far-flung as Liverpool. It sits today inside the M25, but perhaps just a tad too close to Essex for comfort. Billericay and Canvey Island nestle the other side of the Thames Estuary. Kent is the 'Garden of England', the county's rolling hills finding room for hops, apple orchards and strawberry crops for the Wimbledon fortnight. Aside from the

Rolling Stones, though, Dartford barely features in the history of these islands, although it does now boast a Mick Jagger Theatre. At the time of writing, there are no plans for a suitable Keith Richards venue; however, in 2015 a plaque was unveiled on the historic railway platform where Mick and Keith reconnected as teenagers. And it is the linking of those two first names that still lends Dartford its status.

Those early lives, chronicled in every Stones book, are now almost embedded in the National Curriculum. Let us focus instead on that epiphanic moment in October 1961, when a teenage Keith locked eyes on the long-playing records from faraway America that an old primary school chum of his clutched under his arm on a windy railway platform, far removed from the bright lights and big city. Much has been made of the moment, but it is worth reviewing, for without it, quite possibly, the 1960s would have turned out very differently.

Mick was dutifully on his way to the London School of Economics, Keith ambling along to Sidcup Art College. But this was no brief encounter on a platform – there was already a history between the two. But, for Keith, it was the treasure trove in Jagger's arms that held him spellbound. On that day, it was Chuck Berry's *Rockin' At The Hops* and a *Best Of Muddy Waters* that sent out the signals. This was an unspoken code, which almost made the need for language unnecessary. We can picture the scene: two primary school friends, now 'grown up', probably each puffing away on the first fag of the day. Scarves wrapped to keep out the autumn chill. An edgy, lifted chin, a mumbled "How ya doin'?" A shake of the still conservatively short hair, the scratch of an acne-scarred cheek, a pout from those lips, yellowing fingers scratching through an uncombed barnet. And then the moment of revelation. A glimmer of recognition...

'Chuck' and 'Muddy' were not names that would have featured in Dartford school registers. Copies of their work would not have been available at the hardware stores where one could purchase LPs by Cliff Richard and Adam Faith. If the area had such a thing as a lending library, it likely would have stocked classical, with – as a nod to Modernism – possibly some 'jazz'.

We all used to do it, carry LPs under our arms, covers outward, to prove to our peers just what cool cats we were. And it is apt that it was music which drew Jagger and Richards together again. It bound them at the hip; it provided them with a future; and it proved to be a lifelong bond. It is hard to convey today, in this age of immediate information, with the entire history of knowledge available at the press of a button or the flick of a switch, just what a parochial world those teenagers inhabited. But, as it happened, the mere glimpse of Muddy Waters and Chuck Berry sleeves was enough: just one look, that's all it took…

Both Mick and Keith were enchanted and entranced by the music that came across the ocean from the distant United States, whether it was the raw Mississippi blues whipping up from the Delta, or the hard-edged electric blues from Chicago's South Side. Part of that appeal lay not just in the distance of its origin but in its mystery. Those haunted African Americans sang of unimaginable suffering and torment, captivating two teenagers whose main concerns were a lack of cigarettes, sexual congress and the presence of pimples.

It was that sense of mystery and exclusivity that fuelled the early Stones. Just obtaining the records was a struggle; no point in popping along to your local record store – that would entail a fruitless sift through the racks of vanilla-clean Bobby Vee albums or endless trad jazz selections. If you had the energy, Dobell's on Charing Cross Road used to stock US folk and blues in an orange box on the counter, labelled 'Race Records'. I remember jazz musician Chris Barber telling me that he and Alexis Korner almost came to blows over a Robert Johnson 78, given that it was the only copy in London!

And was there ever a more mysterious figure than Robert Johnson? *King Of The Delta Blues Singers* was released just six months prior to that brief railway station encounter between Mick and Keith, and Johnson's guitar styling obsessed the latter. And then there were the mechanics of selling one's soul to the Devil to play like that... the tragic early death... the final resting place... Hell, the one photo of Robert Johnson (haunted eyes and unfeasibly long fingers choking the neck of a guitar) only emerged half a century after his death. Try telling that to 'Alexa' today.

Driven by this great sense of mystery, Mick and Keith soon became Little Boy Blue & the Blue Boys, and began making their first flimsy home recordings, which were notably light on heavy blues and R&B. The teenagers tried out Elvis Presley and Ritchie Valens, and went big on Chuck Berry. That tape was eventually auctioned in 1995, selling for £45,000. The purchaser? One M.P. Jagger.

Soon the pair were diving into London's fledgling R&B scene head-on, journeying to the venues where they'd heard tell of similarly minded souls gathering together to see and hear the music performed live. They voyaged all the way to distant Ealing; they went subterranean at the 100 Club on Oxford Street; they paid homage to Ken Colyer at Studio 51; they weaved along the streets of Soho to the Marquee Club. It was in these temples that bonds were forged and groups were formed.

Being in a group was exciting, enticing. It meant you weren't alone. It gave you somewhere to hide. At those early Stones performances, audiences remember Mick as a shy and tentative performer, finding solace and comfort in a group. In her autobiography, Marianne Faithfull wrote of "all that boys' club stuff that makes it so much easier". For Keith, that early bonding and banding came courtesy of a choir, and then the Boy Scouts. Meanwhile, Mick was encouraged by his father to pour his energy into team sports.

Now it was time for Mick and Keith's fledgling group to come up with a more suitable name than Little Boy Blue for their first gigs around London. Legend has the lads alighting on the Muddy Waters blues song 'Rollin' Stone', recorded in 1950. But in October 1970, *Melody Maker* couldn't contain its glee when, after going through back issues (when it was known as *Syncopation And Dance Band News*), journalists chanced upon a 1932 review of a group called 'The Rolling Stones'. These Stones were fronted by Jack Lewis, "an accomplished dancer, a noted athlete and once schoolboy boxing champion of Britain... Because of his terpsichorean efforts... he gives a clever exhibition of ball punching to music." Blues and hillbilly expert Tony Russell went one better, when he discovered the country and western duo Bud Jamison and Jimmy Adams, who, in 1930, recorded and released a single on the Victor label, 'Down By The Old Rio Grande', under the name 'The Rolling Stones'.

But the name stuck and, down through the decades, the Rolling Stones became Mick and Keith's band. But the *Rolling Stones* began with Brian Jones. It is unlikely that either Mick or Keith had the verve to push far beyond being fans. It was Brian who motivated them, who persuaded them that they could be the ones up there, onstage. It was Brian who needed the group – *his* group – to succeed, to escape the stultifying Cheltenham of his youth, to ditch the unmarried mothers and bastard children. To soar angelic...

CHAPTER 2

Cheltenham, A Diversion

Grave V11393 is located near the parish church of St Mary's in Cheltenham, Gloucestershire. As with all cemeteries, St Mary's is a tranquil location, a place for solace and reflection. Overlooked by the Cotswold hills, the grave is surrounded and shaded by trees. Opposite, a bench is dedicated to "the memory of Brian Jones, founder of the Rolling Stones, from members of Golden Stone". Rather sweetly, a memory book is located graveside for visitors to sign, contained in a plastic sandwich box to protect it from the rain.

The headstone simply lists Brian's name and dates, 1942–1969. But it gives pause for reflection: so young, so very, very young. White and clean, the stone stands out from those who share the space with Brian for all eternity. His companions are from a different era, the Victorian age. Their worn and weary headstones speak of a time alien to his. Even the names of his eternal neighbours are rarely heard now: Ethel... Cuthbert... Jonas... Algernon... Percy... Mabel... The inscriptions, too, are drawn from that long-lost era: "fell asleep in Jesus", "in the midst of life we are in death", "no work begun shall ever pause for death", "weep not, she is not dead but sleepeth", "only goodnight beloved, not farewell".

When Brian was laid to rest on July 10, 1969, the hymn chosen was 'The King Of Love My Shepherd Is'.

Perverse and foolish oft I strayed
But yet in love he sought me,
And on his shoulder, gently laid
And home, rejoicing, brought me

The eulogy from Canon Hugh Evan Hopkins, OBE was a lot more sympathetic than perhaps other writers give him credit for. The canon recalled Brian as a chorister at St Mary's, who never dreamed that he and his colleagues "would become known far and wide because of their ability to express in word and song (and dress) the feelings of literally thousands of young people today".

The canon welcomed Bill Wyman and Charlie Watts, and touchingly also offered up "a prayer to Marianne [Faithfull], who is dangerously ill in Australia".

The reading was from Luke 15, the Parable of the Prodigal Son, who "set off for a distant country and there squandered his wealth in wild living". But the son returns to his loving parents, who rejoice because "he was lost and now is found".

The journey Brian undertook had taken him all over the world but it ended where it all began. Cheltenham is a spa town, which in itself suggests tranquillity, gentility, healing. It is a beautiful place to visit but, particularly when Brian was an adolescent, you can imagine its stultifying aura. For a boy on whom conformity sat unhappily, Cheltenham was a perfect place from which to escape. And, in the end, it provided a final refuge to which he could return.

★★★

Lewis Brian Hopkin Jones had spent his adolescence in the family home on Hatherley Road. Named after William Wood, Baron Hatherley, Lord Chancellor in Gladstone's first government, the street is a long way away from the centre of things. The family's pebble-dashed house, set back from the main road, is similar in style to so many suburban properties which gave birth to that generation of rock stars: Bowie, Townshend, the Davies brothers, Lennon, Jagger – all would have recognised the style. Hard by the Jones' house is a postbox, and it is from here that Brian would have posted his communications to *Jazz News** and his pleading letters to the BBC in 1963, begging for an audition for the Stones on the programme *Jazz Club.*

That suburban conformity is confirmed when you visit Dean Close School, which Brian attended until he was eleven. Red brick and Victorian, seagulls dot the playing fields and the chapel looms over the grounds. It is precisely the sort of place you could imagine Mr Chips holding class. But what struck me most while visiting Cheltenham was Brian's birthplace: 'Rosemead' at 17 El Dorado Road, next to Cheltenham Spa station, was a far more prosperous location than Hatherley Road.

Brian's first impressions of life, of his surroundings, of his world, would have occurred at El Dorado Road, and the property exudes Victorian confidence and stability, although its location somehow suggests something more symbolic. El Dorado ('the gilded') was the Spanish city of gold, set deep in the Amazon jungle. But expeditions, including two led by Sir Walter Raleigh, failed to find this fabled location. For Brian Jones, 'El Dorado' came to mean something more, as *Brewer's Dictionary Of Phrase And Fable* noted:

---

* In May 1962, Brian placed an advertisement in *Jazz News* (a Soho club information sheet), inviting musicians to audition at the Bricklayers Arms in Soho for his new R&B group.

"Metaphorically, the name is applied to any place that offers opportunities of getting rich quickly or acquiring wealth easily."

While not exactly run out of town, many of the spa's inhabitants breathed a sigh of relief when Brian quit Cheltenham. Like Mick and Keith, the blues called out to him across class, circumstance and an ocean. Brian left in search of his own El Dorado, and in the company of his suburban Dartford acolytes he persevered.

Of course, back then it wasn't the Rolling Stones as we know them today. Journalist Paula Hammond asked Paul Jones (later of Manfred Mann) if he'd been asked to join the group (then known as the Rollin' Stones, without the 'g'). "Well, I didn't refuse [them]. I refused a band that Brian Jones was forming, which only became the Stones once Mick and Keith were in it. I thought Brian was wildly over-optimistic to think we could make a living from playing the blues."

Following Ealing encounters, and settling on the big-lipped singer and chippy guitarist from Dartford, Brian rolled out his new group, his fluent, fluid, slide guitar acting like a magnet. With Bill Wyman and Charlie Watts locked in as the rhythm section par excellence, and with a little help from Alexis Korner (and Ken Colyer, Giorgio Gomelsky, Cyril Davies, Andrew Loog Oldham, Peter Jones, Dick Rowe, Norman Jopling…), the wheels finally started turning. Once assembled, the nascent Stones began their crusade to alert the UK to the music of the Delta, the authentic R&B sounds of Memphis and Chicago, and to liberate the youth of the British Isles from the sop pop of Craig Douglas and Jimmy Justice.

As 1963 dawned, the Rolling Stones were ready. At the beginning, the band's proselytising was heartfelt; they really wanted to spread the gospel of blues and R&B. No one doubted their enthusiasm, only their abilities. "Boys, I'll tell you what," Robbie Robertson, of The Band, remembers Sonny Boy Williamson telling him in 1964, "those young English cats over there really wanna play the blues bad, but unfortunately that's just how they play it... bad!"

It is hard now to appreciate just how alien R&B was to the mainstream at the beginning of the Stones' career, and how uneasily it must have slotted into the airwaves and sounded to the ears of a pop-mad nation. A 1964 issue of *Pop Star Pictorial* put the Rolling Stones on the cover and helpfully explained R&B to its readers: "The music, because it was full of private Negro jokes and wasn't intended for white people at all, was at first referred to as 'race' music. Then, when Negro artists began to make records of it to sell among their own people in the thirties, it was listed in the catalogues under the heading of Rhythm-and-Blues."

While rehearsing, and marshalling his wayward troops, Brian simultaneously bombarded the BBC with letters begging for airtime for their favourite recordings. ("Rhythm & Blues is a genuine blues style, evolved directly from the earlier, less sophisticated country blues. R&B in turn gave birth to a commercial offspring, universally known as rock & roll...")

A visit to the BBC Written Archives, near Reading, makes for a wonderful trip down memory lane. When I was last there, pride of place in reception was given to a letter from Brian (102 Edith Grove, London, SW10, January 2, 1963) requesting an audition for the BBC Light Programme's *Jazz Club*: "I am writing on behalf of the 'Rollin' Stones' Rhythm and Blues band... Our musical policy is simply to produce an authentic Chicago Rhythm and Blues sound, using material of such R&B 'greats' as Muddy Waters, Howlin' Wolf, Bo Diddley, Jimmy Reed, and many others."

If Brian had tuned into the Light Programme's *Pick Of The Pops* while writing his plea, he would have heard a chart dominated by the Shadows, Chris Montez, Kenny Lynch, Elvis, Cliff, Bobby Vee, Pat Boone and Mark Wynter, all music I heard while doing my homework, and all music I enjoyed. All lightweight, white-sliced-bread pop. Even the ambitious Brian could never have guessed that, within 12 months, not only would the whole pop music landscape have shifted irrevocably, but a disc by the 'Rollin' Stones' would feature in that crucial chart listing.

During the group's beginnings ('groups' didn't become 'bands' until much later), it was Brian Jones who had the determination and musical vision to really drive the group. And it was Brian who motored them, and who monitored the switch from young men playing at being a group to a proper functioning, performing unit. And, of course, it was Brian who laid the foundations of the group's fledgling repertoire.

Yet within months of landing a recording deal, in a power struggle and boardroom coup, Brian's influence had waned. Crucially, he lacked the ability, and the skill, to harness his talents into fashioning three-minute pop songs, or well-constructed LP tracks that bore his solo imprimatur. He was just too busy living the life. Consequently, he suffered, he wilted, and eventually he would pay the ultimate cost.

CHAPTER 3

Little By Little

Chris Welch remembers the visceral impact the early Rolling Stones had on him as a cub reporter. Knowing his local Bexleyheath paper would lack sufficient clout to gain admission to the Third National Jazz and Blues Festival in Richmond, on August 11, 1963, Chris claimed to be representing the far more prestigious *Kentish Times*. "The thing about the Stones back then," he told me, "wasn't them getting 'a girl reaction' – the boys *and* the girls responded. The girls loved Brian Jones, his blond hair, that shy, vulnerable look, and Mick, of course. Even then though, Charlie was looking glum! The boys responded to the sound, that edgy, unfamiliar R&B sound. And at that time, no other English band played guitars like that, and no other group were that loud.

"Acker Bilk was headlining on the main stage, and the Stones were in a tent at the back of a field. As soon as they were announced, everyone – *everyone!* – flocked to see the Stones, leaving poor old Acker playing to an empty field.

"It's funny looking at the bill for that festival now. It was a jazz festival, even though trad was on the wane by then. Acker, Chris

Barber, Alex Welsh and Terry Lightfoot were the big names, and the Stones were bottom of the bill. But then you look ahead to the 1965 Richmond festival and the Stones were too big to appear by then. It was all the acts that came up in their wake: The Who, The Yardbirds, The Moody Blues, Manfred Mann, The Animals, The Spencer Davis Group."

The momentum was finally building: the first write-up came in the form of Barry May's review for the *Richmond And Twickenham Times* of April 13, 1963. The first to appear nationally, and in a weekly music paper, was by Norman Jopling, in the May 11 issue of *New Record Mirror* – a month before any record release: "The Rolling Stones – Genuine R&B". Jopling was a young, diehard R&B fan. He later wrote, "I'd found my mission: to write about rhythm and blues, spread the word in print... One of my opinions, never reflected in print but which I certainly didn't keep quiet about, was that the British so-called rhythm and blues movement was useless." However, Jopling's fervent 1963 feature enthused: "[The Rolling Stones] are genuine R&B fanatics themselves and they sing and play in a way that one would expect more from a coloured US R&B team than a bunch of wild, exciting white boys."

All those early Stones features made mention of the fact that among fans of the group were The Beatles, who had paid court at the Crawdaddy Club. And any blessing from The Beatles was enough to guarantee useful column inches.

Ironically, Jopling's piece included a quote from an unnamed Stone: "After all, can you imagine a British-composed R&B number, it just wouldn't make it!"

Music historian and critic Tony Russell was another early convert: "If you were interested in blues or R&B, of all the weeklies, *Record Mirror* was our Bible. It used to have a section 'The Great Unknown', and that's where you'd first read about Muddy Waters, Howlin' Wolf, Jimmy Reed... There was a regular

'Rhythm & Blues Round Up' column. After the Stones broke through, Pye International began leasing singles from the Chess catalogue, so in 1964, you'd get releases from Chuck Berry, Howlin' Wolf, Sonny Boy Williamson.

"I'm not sure I buy that story about Mick and Keith getting their records direct from Chess in Chicago. The UK blues enthusiasts, like me, got ours from Randy's Record Store in Gallatin, Tennessee. God, it took forever: you had to get an International Money Order then wait six to eight weeks for these records to come from the States.

"Even the LP *covers* were fantastic, they were so thick, laminated, you could cook steak on them! Lightnin' Slim's *Rooster Blues*, bright yellow. Then *Blues Unlimited* magazine was launched in 1963, and you appreciated there were these pockets of blues and R&B enthusiasts in Newcastle, Plymouth, Manchester, Birmingham... And of course the clubs, many of the trad jazz clubs would host blues and R&B acts."

The late George Melly, singer, columnist, cultural commentator and raconteur, was on the cusp of that change. As lead vocalist with Mick Mulligan's jazz band, Melly played the same circuit as the fledgling Beat and R&B groups, but early on he appreciated that change was afoot. He went on to become an acute observer and commentator on that which followed in his wake. Taking a break from singing, in 1970, Melly published *Revolt Into Style*, one of the first books to take a serious look at the burgeoning pop culture scene, exemplified by rock music. It is interesting now to read Melly's commentary about the fledgling Stones, which emphasised just how marginalised Brian Jones had become.

A lifelong devotee of jazz and blues, Melly knew whereof he spoke, and appreciated the benefit a band like the Rolling Stones had brought to the moribund scene of the early sixties. But he could also be critical of his successors: "To start with they were almost grotesquely derivative; blues shouters from the Thames Valley cotton fields; and Jagger's early success was based almost entirely on his sexual charisma [...] Without Jagger, without the Stones, it's possible that Rhythm & Blues might have remained a minority interest, a rather pedantic British homage to a certain aspect of the music; but Jagger was there, shaking away in Richmond. He was the charismatic Moses needed to lead R&B out of the clubs and into the promised land."

Writing from the vantage point of the 21st century, it is worth reinforcing just how much of a pioneering force the Rolling Stones were at that time. It was rare for blues and R&B to gain airplay on BBC radio, although jazz was well accommodated, and *Saturday Club* offered some sustenance. But you were just as likely to hear Chuck Berry on *Children's Favourites*, sandwiched between 'Nellie The Elephant' and 'The Laughing Policeman'!

"I first saw the Rolling Stones in summer 1963, about a month after the release of their debut single 'Come On'," Tony Russell remembered. "A teenage convert to R&B, I was living in the blissful dawn of discovering Howlin' Wolf, Muddy Waters and John Lee Hooker, and I had no purist objection to hearing their music channelled through homegrown bands.

"Like many R&B venues of the time, and some repurposed trad clubs, it was a large room above a pub, the Star & Garter Hotel. I was ridiculously early, and was sitting at the foot of the stairs – probably smoking Gauloises and trying to look as if I did that sort of thing all the time – when the band arrived. No one else was around, so I helped them carry up their equipment.

"I can't remember much about the Stones themselves, that torrid July evening, since I was less interested in them than in their material, which I was pleased to find was mostly covers: Chuck Berry and Bo Diddley, Slim Harpo's 'I'm A King Bee', that sort of thing. I was greatly impressed that they not only name-checked the original artists but, at least once, the original record label. Looking back, I think what was so extraordinary was how quickly R&B became so well known in the wake of the Stones' success. It switched from being a codified group into a national phenomenon."

It wasn't just the music that separated the Stones from their pop-star peers; they soon junked the uniforms required for TV appearances. Groups were expected to appear nicely turned out – the hair might be allowed to dip down below the collar, but it had to be a suit collar! However, from the start, the Stones were encouraged by a manager keen to convert attitude into column inches to grunt their way through encounters with journalists. Andrew Loog Oldham was cut from the same cloth as his clients – young (Oldham was still a teenager), hustling, determined to make waves on the way to his first fortune. On Oldham's watch, it became immediately apparent that the Stones were the other side of the Beatle coin. They had none of the élan needed to find favour with the surly ex-servicemen commissionaires they encountered nightly on tour. Nor was there little in common, either musically or stylistically, with Decca labelmates such as Peter Jay & the Jaywalkers, The Applejacks or Unit 4 + 2.

In 1965, Oldham was categoric, telling *NME*'s Keith Altham: "We realised right from the beginning that we were making our appeal to young people and by making a concentrated effort towards freedom on their behalf we could upset those we neglected. We chose the young instead of the old, that's all. The old resented it. The Stones are still the social outcasts, the rebels. We worked on the principle that if you are going to kick conformity in the teeth, you may as well use both feet!"

Fuelled by the vigour of Andrew Oldham, the group committed to the new type of music for which audiences were hungry. They were developing a look, they cultivated the rebellious image… they were poised. But they still adhered to the rules, and even Oldham's chutzpah needed showbiz muscle, which came in the form of experienced agent Eric Easton, whose other clients included the defiantly non-rebellious Bert Weedon and Mrs Mills.

The initial contract struck with Easton and Oldham allowed the managers to receive 25 per cent of the group's earnings. Oldham, however, had not forgotten the tip he'd received from an encounter with another young hustler. Phil Spector had advised him to form a company and license the recordings to a record label, thereby allowing the manager to retain control of the copyrights.

★★★

The Stones signed to Decca Records in May 1963. Their debut single was a speedy cover of a recent Chuck Berry song, intended to introduce them to a wider, poppier audience. 'Come On' was released on June 7, and thus began a testy relationship with the group's UK label.

However, the single was well received. Already appreciating the group's live appeal, the trade paper *Record Retailer* noted: "New London R&B group on their debut. They take an old Chuck Berry number and give it a group vocal for this commercially slanted disc. Harmonica is included in the backing and the whole thing moves well. But they're not able to capture all their on-stage excitement." *Beat Monthly* called it "A good intro disc from this London R'n'B group. Number is a Chuck Berry opus which could just catch on in a big way."

There were precious few opportunities to promote a new release back then, in the pre-*Top Of The Pops* and *Ready Steady Go!* age. The premier platform was Saturday evening's *Thank Your Lucky Stars*, and it was there, on July 13, 1963, that the Rolling Stones made their TV debut, all in matching suits. Journalist David

Sinclair recalls the impact of that performance: "People talk about Bowie and the 'Starman' moment on *Top Of The Pops*. Well, the Stones on *Thank Your Lucky Stars* was another of those moments. They were unlike anything you had ever seen or heard. It was the length of their hair, which was really long... contrast that with Freddie & the Dreamers! Even in their suits, the Stones were sneering, scowling, chewing gum; they looked like gangsters."

However, for the Stones, real opportunity took a long time to knock. My theory regarding the genuine, sustained success of The Beatles is that they succeeded because they came as a self-contained unit. With their own 'built-in tunesmith team' of Lennon–McCartney, they broke the Tin Pan Alley stranglehold. Unlike Billy Fury, Cliff Richard or Eden Kane, The Beatles didn't need to rely on old-school music publishers hustling songs, or wait breathlessly to become the first UK act to cover a US hit. The Beatles were the signpost to the future. And such was their ubiquity, and the sheer volume of their material, that John and Paul were able to toss off a quickie for the Rolling Stones' second single, the driving 'I Wanna Be Your Man'.

Next came a Buddy Holly cover. "A clean cut beat, plus a prominent harmonica, does much to add to the impact of the group's image...", enthused *Pop Weekly* of 'Not Fade Away'. Then on to a further cover of The Valentinos, before one from Willie Dixon. But it was soon apparent that the well was running dry.

So Jagger and Richards became the beasts of burden. Legend has it that Oldham separated the pair from the pack and locked them in their kitchen, with orders not to emerge until they had written an original pop song. The early songs were dispatched to those in need. George Bean was the recipient of their apprentice efforts. But they did get better...

Something simply fell into place once the Jagger/Richards team had locked in to songwriting proper. Maybe it had always been there, way back in a Dartford primary class, or on a station platform, or in an Earl's Court bedsit. More likely, they found what they were looking for during one of those hundred nights in an English hotel where the bar closed at 11 p.m. and room service, if you were lucky, offered at best a plate of cheese sandwiches.

"Andrew convinced Mick and Keith they could write", Charlie testified in 2004's *According To The Rolling Stones*. "Thank God he did, because without those songs we would have been another Freddie & the Dreamers, remembered for playing 'Going To New York' at Ken Colyer's Club on a Sunday afternoon!"

But the calibre of that early material was almost immaterial. The fact that a Stones single could come as a Stones single with a Jagger/Richards composing credit in parentheses beneath the title, proved liberating. More significantly, with that credit the Stones suddenly had a future, and it lay in their own hands, rather than in the archive of R&B obscurities that had been Brian Jones' domain. It was a quick rewrite of 'The Last Time', a Staple Singers song, credited to Jagger/Richards, that saw the Stones achieve their first UK number one. That was when the tectonic plates in the Rolling Stones really shifted, and when Brian Jones began his drift away and eventual exile from the group. He remained an integral member, a fans' favourite, a focus for the television cameras, that shy, retiring smile beneath a perfect blond fringe, a soft-spoken favourite for the music press... Sadly, already, Brian was nearer his end than his beginning.

Besides being pioneers at the forefront of a musical revolution, the Rolling Stones also influenced the way their audiences looked. *Time* magazine had officially declared London to be "swinging" in 1966. Boutiques blossomed, and it really did seem as though the bomb-scarred capital had switched suddenly from black and white into spellbinding Technicolor. And at the forefront of that kaleidoscopic change were the flamboyantly adorned youth, whom Ray Davies christened the "Carnebetian army".

"As if overnight, it was as acceptable for men to take care about how they dressed as it was for women," wrote Geoffrey Aquilina Ross in his comprehensive account of men's style of the period, *The Day Of The Peacock*. "Even men with what might seem to be impeccable social (and heterosexual) backgrounds were going about their daily lives wearing velvet suits, or jackets accessorised with brightly coloured flowing silk scarves. Their hair was longer too. Until then, all men had been conventional, comfortably wearing the clothes expected of their professions, and visiting their barbers for a precision trim in a fortnightly routine."

For some, the way the Stones dressed was an affront to all that had gone before. Ally that to the unfamiliar sounds they produced and, at times, it seemed as though civilisation may well have been teetering on the brink of an abyss.

Brian had, and kept, 'The Look', but it was the Jagger & Richards tandem, egged on by Oldham, that paved the way for the Rolling Stones – not only to survive the sixties but for the band to enjoy an enduring future. The success of 'The Last Time' not only saw the writing on the wall but, more significantly, the group writing its way into the charts.

In Bill Wyman's 1990 book *Stone Alone: The Story Of A Rock'n'Roll Band*, he confirmed the reasons for Brian's detachment: "First, money and his own greed. Secondly, the Stones' need for a hit songwriting 'machine', which basically didn't interest him. And thirdly, Andrew Oldham divided the band up very quickly once he moved into the same house as Mick and Keith; it immediately became those three on one side, Brian, Charlie and me on the other."

In obeisance to their original blues roots, and Brian's last sustained input to the group, came a Willie Dixon cover, 'Little

Red Rooster', which sounded unlike anything else gaining airplay on the conservative BBC airwaves of the period. It was a slow, weary blues number, quite at odds with the breeziness on offer from the group's peers. Those early half-hour Stones LPs also contained tips of the hat to those that had gone before, a ragbag of R&B, blues and rock. Then the Jagger & Richards juggernaut thundered on, producing a run of singles that, even today, more than half a century on, still bring crowds across the world to their feet in a roar of delighted recognition.

Then came 1964, the group's breakthrough year. Their eponymous debut LP knocked *With The Beatles* off the top slot, and they got their first number one single and their first number one EP.*

For the Stones, of course, 1964 also brought further controversy. It was Maureen Cleave's article in the *Evening Standard* on May 11, 1964 that fanned the flames: "Parents do not like the Rolling Stones... They do not want their sons to grow up like them; they do not want their daughters to marry them."

"Would You Let Your Daughter Marry A Rolling Stone?" or "Would You Let Your Sister Go With A Rolling Stone?" screamed the headlines, testifying to the group's wild public image. Hairdressers, headmasters, guardians of public morals, parents and established institutions... all soon seemed to view the Stones as a major threat to the English way of life.

The papers were full of stories of the group being refused entry to restaurants because of their scruffy look. Even their fans were

---

* People forget just how popular four-track extended players were back in the day. A halfway house between a two-sided single and a 12-track LP, they could be used as a dumping ground, or as a format for experimentation. For all its failings, when the film aired on BBC1 on Boxing Day 1967, one reason UK fans were so fond of The Beatles' *Magical Mystery Tour* album was its novel two-disc EP format.

shocked. Sally Brown, from Brian's hometown of Cheltenham, wrote to *Rave* in 1964: "Considering the amount of money the Rolling Stones fork out on clothes, surely they can look respectable on stage at least instead of looking as though they'd been dragged through a hedge backwards?"

A group appearance on *Juke Box Jury* also led to a fusillade of complaints to the BBC; typical of these was one licence payer from the Channel Islands: "The Stones not only smoked through the programme, but only one of them had the manners to stand when a young lady was shaking hands with them."

Jagger would soon taste full public odium when he began stepping out with singer Marianne Faithfull. For many, she was still the doe-eyed, virginal blonde, wistfully whispering 'As Tears Go By'. But with the vampiric teeth of Mick Jagger sunk into that particular swan's neck, it was as if Marianne had been publicly deflowered. I interviewed Marianne when her autobiography was published in 1994, and she explained: "A story I heard years later was that Mick had really wanted Julie Christie, and when he couldn't get her, he took me instead!"

The group's forward momentum came close to being permanently halted over confusion about dates booked by Eric Easton in the autumn of 1964. This almost led the BBC to issue a blanket ban on the band. The Stones were still rolling, with headline tours and regular airplay. But such a ban could have seriously jeopardised their career, as the bulk of the audience could only hear their singles, EPs and LPs on the BBC Light Programme. A memo from the BBC's light entertainment manager fumed: "One would like to think that we could totally ban this group for a period of, say, six months; that is to say, they would not be seen on television, nor would they be heard on sound radio either live, or by means of the playing of commercial gramophone records."

It really seemed as though the Corporation were using the Stones as whipping boys *pour encourager les autres*. However, the BBC's Patrick Newman recognised that such a ban could not work if the Stones featured on chart programmes such as *Pick Of The Pops* ("we could hardly leave them out if that particular week they were number one on the list").

Grudgingly, after Easton had eaten humble pie, the Stones were back on the playlists. Their diaries filled with tour dates, TV appearances, radio broadcasts… and recording sessions squeezed in during the band's precious downtime.

And then, though it took some time, the States succumbed. There was no 'Stonesmania' when the band landed in June 1964 to step onto the familiar tour–TV–gig treadmill. It was on that trip that the band's members were infamously roasted on national television by Dean Martin. Sensing that change was in the air, and that the glory days of the Rat Pack were behind him, the forty-seven-year-old 'King of Cool' mercilessly ribbed the Stones. (Funny to think that Dino was the same age then as Mick Jagger would be when he performed on the *Urban Jungle* tour in 1990.)

However, there were definite benefits to that first American visit, when an opportunity came to pay homage at Chess Studios in Chicago, and to visit the Harlem Apollo. It really was a dream come true for the lads from Cheltenham, Dartford and Penge.

And in their wake came all the other British bands, inspired by the music of the Land of the Free and the Home of the Brave. Led by The Beatles, bolstered by the Stones, on they came in waves, over the waves, among them The Animals, The Yardbirds, The Who, Them, Manfred Mann, The Kinks, The Zombies, The Moody Blues, The Dave Clark Five and Herman's Hermits. All arrived, wide-eyed at the sheer scale of the USA, marvelling that they were here, in the land from which the music they had listened to as teenagers on transistors or youth club record players had emanated. They had transmogrified it, put a spin on it, made it their own, but its roots were still somewhere deep and dark in America's heartland. It took the British Invasion to remind American audiences just what had inspired them. No wonder Bob Dylan called his 1965 transitional 'acoustic into electric' LP *Bringing It All Back Home*.

As with everyone else around at the time, Mick became fascinated with Dylan's deft wordplay ("... everyone looked up to him as being a kind of guru of lyrics").

Writer Keith Altham testified: "I came from *Fabulous!* to *New Musical Express*, and it was all 'Angela Jones', 'Um Um Um', 'Doo Wah Diddy'. Fine poppy pop songs to dance to; to clean windows to. But it was Dylan who really turned it all around. You simply cannot over-emphasise what a game-changer Bob Dylan was. He made 'pop' more important, and what the musicians said was suddenly of substance, which, in turn, gave the journalists more to do and say than 'What's your favourite colour?'"

Dylan's influence on the Rolling Stones soon became apparent, with the release of songs such as 'Get Off My Cloud' ("a stop-bugging-me, post-teenage-alienation song," said Mick to *Rolling Stone* in 1995). The belief that a pop song could ever say more than 'Our love's gonna grow, oo-wa...' came from Dylan, and later informed 'Heart Of Stone', 'Mother's Little Helper' and 'Lady Jane'. At one early meeting with the group, Dylan boasted: "I could have written 'Satisfaction', but you could never have written 'Mr Tambourine Man'."

Still, the Rolling Stones were only just beginning...

CHAPTER 4

Coke & Sympathy

For the Stones, the majority of the sixties blurred past in the usual whirl of tour–TV–recording session–gig-radio show–tour. In between came the narcotics to help them keep up the pace, and the willing women to soothe their fevered brows. And, gradually, they were embedded into the national consciousness: the stone-faced Bill and Charlie, preening Brian, sinister Keith and prancing Mick.

A flavour of the madness was caught in the Peter Whitehead documentary *Charlie Is My Darling*, a fly-on-the-wall chronicle of the band's 1965 Irish dates. The Stones were always ill-served on film, and this was no exception. No *Hard Day's Night* or *Don't Look Back* this; instead, the Stones gurn at the camera, stare out of train windows and commit to spectacularly unrevealing interviews. Writing years later (actually about The Doors, but nonetheless applicable), David Hepworth captured that mundanity: "They speak like men who have already learned that the filmed rock interview is a new medium in which it is possible to embark on a sentence without the slightest idea where that same sentence might end up. Here they are pioneering the monotonous, affectless ribbon of musing that became the standard way in which... rock acts communicated with their fans and absolutely nobody else at all."

Charlie Is My Darling is, however, good at capturing the monotony and repetition of life on the road the endless grinding routine, be it Dublin, Dallas, Dubrovnik, Dundee or Düsseldorf. Just think how many airport terminals, baggage carousels, stage doors, dingy dressing rooms, grubby toilets and hotel rooms these boys have seen. Riots became a testament to the Rolling Stones' pulling power and the world soon took notice. On and on it went. And they loved it, for a while... There is a great clip of a hysterical Brian as he watches a fan nearly tear Mick apart onstage at the Royal Albert Hall.

The Stones did eventually attract a devotion only equalled by The Beatles – and fan letters to the pop magazines proudly listed their acquisitions, like shavings of the true Cross: "I have half a fag of Keith's and a piece of his chewed gum, also a threepenny piece of Mick's... a piece of Charlie's shirt." Sixteen-year-old Marilyn "had some Coke bottles and a cigarette stub", but she generously passed them on to "less mature fans".

While tarred by the same brush, by virtue of being members of the same band, Bill and Charlie remained rather more 'conservative' in their habits. However, for the remaining 60 per cent of the Rolling Stones, narcotics provided an oasis during the years of hysteria. Mick was tentative in his indulgence, while Keith plunged in, taking it to the limit, but then he was blessed with the constitution of an ox. However, for some the ride was already proving too hard.

Brian was visibly failing and it was, in fact, he who the *News Of The World* fingered in late January 1967. Under the headline 'Pop Stars: Facts That Will Shock You', the scandal sheet was on the prowl. The word had got out to Fleet Street that drugs were in widespread use in pop-star circles. And, here's the dangling carrot: coverage of these popular delinquents would surely increase circulation.

The hacks, however, proved unable to differentiate between the types of drugs in use. For example, the paper ran the unforgettable and physically impossible headline 'I Saw Couples Injecting Reefers'! The *News Of The World* then tracked down a bleary Brian at the Blaises club as he rambled on about drug use. Inexplicably, on February 5, 1967, the paper ran a feature about 'Pop Stars & Drugs' – and attributed Jones' quotes to Mick Jagger, who was pictured in the article!

Jagger himself was out of the country but was shocked to see a photo of himself in the *News Of The World* with a caption claiming he had "admitted to our investigators that he had taken LSD". In fact, Mick hadn't even tripped at that point – all that was to come later, with the infamous 1967 drugs bust at Keith's Redlands mansion. But although the scalps of pop stars were now making the front pages, little differentiation was made over the nature of the drugs. For example, when Mick was convicted after the 1967 bust for the illegal possession of four over-the-counter pep pills, which he'd acquired in Italy – where they were legal – many assumed the tablets to be in the same category as heroin.

NME's Keith Altham frequently witnessed the Stones at work in the studio, but doesn't remember drugs being seen or discussed: "I don't remember drugs on the scene much before 1967. We journalists were drinkers, it was a drink culture. Drink made you more gregarious, more social. But by the time pot kicked in, you were staring at flowers! It made you introspective, it was not a shared experience. It was the same with bands; they were divided into the drunks and the druggies."

Melody Maker's Chris Welch was the same: "There were other bands who were far more druggy, and I always thought that the Stones kept away from drugs because of all the jazz musicians they so admired – they could see what drugs had done to them. Mick was never a drinker though. I remember him saying to me once: 'I can't imagine anyone drinking a pint of anything, let alone a pint of beer.'"

★★★

For UK television viewers in the late sixties, there was no equivalent to the great late-night US chat shows. No Johnny Carson; instead, we had to settle for Eamonn Andrews! There was no denying that Eamonn was amiable and engaging, or that his was the only platform for late-night celebrity chat. However, Eamonn was never one to truly get under the skin of his guests. I remember his interview with the actor Anthony Quinn: "Tony, you told me backstage you were reluctant to talk about your father – why was that?"

However, for star interviews, Eamonn's was still the only sofa in town. His guests that February night in 1967 were the actors Hugh Lloyd and Terry Scott, the singer Susan ('Bobby's Girl') Maughan, and Rose Tobias Shaw, a casting director who had given an early boost to the careers of George C. Scott and Kim Novak. Also appearing on that night was Mick Jagger.

An uneasy guest, he clearly managed to get under the skin of the other guests from the more traditional end of 'showbiz'. But Eamonn's was the platform Mick chose to announce that he was taking legal action against the *News Of The World* for their hack job. The announcement ranked alongside Oscar Wilde's decision to sue the Marquess of Queensberry for criminal libel. But Jagger's comments on the television chat show meant the gloves were now off; the *News Of The World* smelled blood and, within a week, all roads led to Redlands, confirming the public image of the Rolling Stones as decadence personified, as men without morals, as drug-taking corrupters of youth.

The Redlands bust on February 12, 1967 cemented Mick and Keith's relationship. Keith was particularly shocked at the vehemence of the prosecution ("I used to believe in law and order... I fell for the whole shtick"). Jail doors slammed, and Keith faced off the establishment from the dock ("We are not old men. We're not worried about petty morals"). Mick wept at the prospect of prison, and began fashioning a song about being a long way from home.*

When the draconian sentences were announced, even the establishment that had delighted in seeing the pair in the dock was divided. Half reasoned that Mick and Keith had got what was coming to them, while the others felt the prison terms were too stringent. In his famous *Times* editorial 'Who Breaks A Butterfly On A Wheel', arch-conservative William Rees-Mogg came out unexpectedly on their side: "The normal penalty is probation... It is surprising therefore that Judge Block should have decided to sentence Mr Jagger to imprisonment, and particularly surprising as Mr Jagger's is about as mild a drug case as can ever have been brought to the courts." In a letter to *Melody Maker*, a fan called Alan Franklin wrote, "One day the persecuted groups will be seen as the 1960 equivalent of the Suffragettes."

Even the notoriously conservative John Gordon, writing in the *Sunday Express*, unexpectedly allied himself to the singer: "Was Jagger convicted of taking one of the evil drugs like heroin or cocaine? Or LSD... Not at all. Did he smoke marijuana which some experts say is evil but others equally expert say is not so evil?

---

* For more detail on the Redlands bust, the most comprehensive account remains Simon Wells's *Butterfly On A Wheel: The Great Rolling Stones Drug Bust*, published in 2012 by Omnibus Press.

That wasn't alleged against him. He merely had four Benzedrine tablets, legally purchased abroad, which with the knowledge and approval of his doctor he took to keep him awake while he worked."

The *NME* also published letters in support of the the Stones. Bill Smith from Ilford wrote: "Jagger's crime, a first offence, would normally carry a £20 fine, and Richards too should only have been fined. What the law has done is to make martyrs out of two public idols and widen the gap between teenagers and the police."

Judge Block, who had been reprimanded for his summing up at the trial, dug himself into a further legal quagmire when, addressing the Horsham Ploughing & Agricultural Society a few months later, he quoted Julius Caesar: "You blocks, you stones, you worse than senseless things", ruefully continuing, "...Be that as it may, we did our best your fellow countrymen – I and my fellow magistrates – to cut these stones down to size."

The Redlands saga further confirmed the Rolling Stones as being in the vanguard of the 'Us versus The Man' brigade. Talking to Mike Hennessey in *Melody Maker* at the end of April 1967, Mick was quoted as saying: "Everybody knows that Britain is short of police – but they send big groups of them raiding clubs… it's madness.

"The situation is not only becoming ridiculous but frightening. You sit at home and think you are safe because you are not in South Africa or some other police state. But when suddenly the police move in, it's very disturbing and you begin to wonder just how much freedom you really have." On their sentences being lifted, the jail guitar doors were hurled open. John and Paul came on board to help out the Stones, harmonising on 1967's 'We Love You'. Perhaps with the sword of Damocles suspended over their heads, Mick and Keith's Summer of Love single was a more durable effort than its Beatles counterpart, 'All You Need Is Love'.

The Stones played delightfully with language, distorting grammar to a thrilling, pounding piano riff from session man Nicky Hopkins. The harmonies soared, the lyrics spoke of punishment and forgiveness – yet all were suffused with an air of menace.

The promo video for the track drew comparisons with an earlier cause célèbre: Mick was cast as Oscar Wilde (complete with green carnation) and Marianne as the unimaginably beautiful Lord Alfred Douglas, the 'Bosie' who had brought about Wilde's downfall, while Keith was a bewigged and bewildered judge. The symbolism was immediate, the scales of justice and a fur rug clearly visible.[*] Predictably, the BBC chose not to screen the promo. A spokesman commented: "Producer Johnny Stewart received it, looked at it and rejected it as unsuitable. After all – it is for *Top Of The Pops!*"

Upon release of the new single, the music press was treated to full-page ads from 'The Stones' ('We Love You All For The Help From Our Friends To A Happier End'). The Who expressed solidarity by releasing a double A-side single of Stones hits, while The Kinks' Dave Davies happily concurred about the merits of 'We Love You' during his review of the week's single releases (including Traffic's 'Hole In My Shoe', The Jimi Hendrix Experience's 'Burning Of The Midnight Lamp' and The Monkees' 'Pleasant Valley Sunday') in *Melody Maker*'s 'Blind Date' feature, in which guest musicians were played singles 'blind' before being asked to guess who'd recorded them and offer their opinions on the track. Initially mistaking the Rolling Stones for the easy-listening group Sounds Orchestral(!), he goes on to call 'We Love You' "the best thing they've ever done".

---

[*] A further irony was found in the location for Wilde's historic 1895 trial, the Magistrates Court on Soho's Great Marlborough Street; in 1969, Mick would be hauled up before the beak at the same location, during which he was ordered to pay a fine of £200 for possession of cannabis.

The uncertainty over the band's future following the 1967 trial led to an understandable lack of promotion. 'We Love You' peaked at number eight, which meant that, for the first time in four years, the Rolling Stones didn't feature in *NME*'s 'Top 20 Singles of the Year'. The list was compiled from points awarded to chart positions throughout 1967: 30 for number one; one for number 30; and so on. That year, Engelbert Humperdinck dominated the chart, with a score of 1,218. The Stones limped in at 26, though the paper's Derek Johnson was conciliatory: "... bearing in mind their adverse publicity, I reckon this shows them still to be holding their own; if Mick and the boys would only pull their socks up and treat the fans to a few more singles they would go shooting up the table in 1968."

(It is worth noting at this point that one week in November 1967, the *NME* announced that for the first time in its 20-year chart history, the Top 20 was comprised entirely of British discs, such was the musical revolution led by The Beatles and the Stones. But the dichotomy of the period ensured that right up there, alongside fellow pioneers such as Procol Harum, the Bee Gees, The Kinks, Donovan, Traffic and The Who, were staid stalwarts including Frankie Vaughan, Val Doonican, Des O'Connor and the aforementioned Engelbert.)

Earlier in 1967 the Stones had released their best LP to date, the winsome *Between The Buttons*, but it was soon overwhelmed by the incandescent, all-enveloping world created by *Sgt. Pepper's Lonely Hearts Club Band*. The trip down the Beatle rabbit hole began with the album cover itself, a beguiling stained-glass window of 20th-century popular culture. Then – a pop first, this – the lyrics printed on the sleeve, the coloured inner bag, the *Sgt. Pepper* cut-outs... and all this before you even heard a note! What fantastic, magical landscapes 'Lucy In The Sky With Diamonds' conjured up... How cosy 'When I'm 64' sounded... What other third-worldly sounds

'Within You Without You' evoked... How timeless and endless 'A Day In The Life' seemed, with its run-out groove that ran forever... The Stones' camp may have felt some consolation when, after a six-month run as the UK's number one LP, *Sgt. Pepper* was deposed by one of their Decca labelmates, the cutting-edge album *Val Doonican Rocks, But Gently!*

If the Stones won the Summer of Love single battle, they had lost big time in the LP war. Post-*Pepper*, they could never simply fashion a further 14 'pop' songs – the band had to be seen to be in direct competition with The Beatles, to go in a whole new direction and fashion a new dimension. That year had also seen debut LPs from the Velvet Underground, Pink Floyd, The Doors and The Jimi Hendrix Experience. In the States, *Smile* broke the will of Brian Wilson, who was striving to compete with *Sgt. Pepper*. And in Britain, the Stones offered up the pale psychedelic salad of *Their Satanic Majesties Request*.

"Mick felt they were under pressure because of *Sgt. Pepper*," engineer Glyn Johns told music writer Graeme Thomson. "I remember him sitting me down before we started and saying that he wanted me to come up with more innovative sounds."

Diehard fans of the LP argue that *Satanic Majesties* gave Brian Jones free rein to experiment with sound patterns; that the album reflected the vivid and vibrant colours of its sleeve. In truth, along with the pressure of producing themselves, the band were worn down by the drug busts and scandals that enveloped them. The Stones were swathed in the wafts of the dope smoked to bring the album home. The circumstances did not bode well, despite the optimism still present within the band.

"We had just been getting into a nice recording groove," Mick told Chris Welch in August 1967, "when the court thing happened and messed us up. No, I wasn't really scared about the verdict. It was just that it took up so much time both mentally and physically."

When all was said and done, the finished album was light on actual songs and almost willfully designed to emphasise their rebel status. Symptomatic of that dismal album was Mick disingenuously enquiring "Where's that joint?" on what was obviously intended to be *Satanic Majesties'* equivalent to 'A Day In The Life', the formless eight-and-a-half-minute 'Sing This All Together (See What Happens)'. The good songs on the album (the opening of '2000 Man', '2000 Light Years From Home' and 'She's A Rainbow') were swamped by the remaining substandard material – I mean, five minutes of 'Gomper', really! It was a sign of just how desperate the band were that, for the first time ever, they'd included a Bill Wyman song, which surely testified to the album's limp predicament. In hindsight, probably the best thing about the album was its sleeve: "a completely new technique in album covers", the music press breathlessly reported. "A three-dimensional moving colour photograph... an abstract musical experience to visually capture the new dimension in music".

Upon its release, only *Record Mirror* was truly favourably disposed towards the album: "This LP should do for them what *Sgt. Pepper* did for The Beatles. That is, show them as a group capable of appealing as much to the more discriminating and aware record buyer as to the younger fan element." Mind you, *Record Mirror* was part-owned by Decca, the band's record label.

Otherwise, *Satanic Majesties* was savaged, with even loyal comrade Jann Wenner calling it "disastrous... a recording episode as unfortunate as any for any group in the world". *Melody Maker* was withering too: "No great melodies emerge. Nothing is particularly exciting... But extended 'freak outs' like 'Sing This All Together', while superficially impressive, are truthfully tragically trivial."

"There's a lot of rubbish on *Satanic Majesties*," Mick conceded in 2003. "Just too much time on our hands, too many drugs, no producer to tell us 'enough already, thank you very much, now can we just get on with this song?'"

In 2018, Glyn Johns was even more frank, calling the album "A complete crock of shite". But that didn't stop 'The Box Set That No One Wanted' being released in 2017 for the album's 50th anniversary. It should really have come with a sticker boasting: 'Contains *NO* Bonus Tracks Or Outtakes'.

Let the last word lie with 'the Raver' in *Melody Maker*, a month after the release of *Satanic Majesties*: "The Stones should have spent less time on their LP cover and more on the music."

★★★

Free of prison, and chastened by the reception accorded to their latest LP, the Stones braced themselves to face the New Year. Following the fragrant patchouli clouds of 1967, there was a realisation that 1968 needed to be a period of toughening up. It was to be the year of back to basics for many musicians.

It began in January, with Bob Dylan's *John Wesley Harding*. The last the world had heard of Dylan was in 1966, with his 14-minute songs about warehouse eyes, the kings of Tyrus and gypsy hymns. The last they had seen of him was as a coil-headed, hollow-cheeked visionary. The next thing you knew, here was a smiling, bearded Bob, offering up 12 country and western songs that spoke of morality and responsibility at a time when fucking in the streets and never trusting anyone over thirty was the manifesto.

In a similar vein to *John Wesley Harding*, The Band's debut album *Music From Big Pink*, released on July 1 that year, ushered in what we nowadays refer to as 'Americana', or simply mature music, made by adults.

51

As 1968 progressed, The Byrds pushed the country-rock fusion even further with *Sweetheart Of The Rodeo*. The twenty-two-year-old Van Morrison fashioned something extraordinary in the musically dazzling *Astral Weeks*, while whimsy and the spirit of '67 was catered for by Donovan's *A Gift From A Flower To A Garden*, as well as by releases from the Incredible String Band and Tyrannosaurus Rex. Traffic got it together in the country and The Beatles' *White Album* veered far from the colourful landscape of Pepperland – this was the Fabs letting their hair down, while Creedence Clearwater Revival also offered up a gutsy return to roots.

The Stones were facing stiff competition. Their response was to further enhance their bad boy image with the proposition of the now legendary 'toilet cover'* for their next album, *Beggars Banquet*. Unsurprisingly, Decca would not countenance the lavatorial design. In the label's defence, it really was a pretty unappealing image.

A Mexican standoff ensued, delaying the album's release by three months, with neither side willing to compromise. Mick found Decca's reluctance hard to fathom, citing the label's release of *A-Tomic Jones*, with the Welsh singer pictured in front of an exploding atom bomb, as "more offensive than graffiti". Rather half-heartedly, he also defended the decision: "I mean, we haven't shown the whole lavatory."

On the front page of *Melody Maker* on September 14, 1968 (alongside the headline 'Beatles To Play A "Live" Concert?'), Mick fumed: "It doesn't actually show the bowl, which is rude, like they do in the Harpic adverts… There are no swear words at all, nothing obscene. But they've just said we can't use it as a record cover. Nobody who buys our records would object. And there aren't any political slogans, unless you call 'Lyndon Loves Mao' a

---

* The photo of a public toilet adorned with graffiti, including a tribute to the Rolling Stones, was taken by Barry Feinstein at a Porsche repair shop near LA's Hollywood Boulevard.

political slogan. You can't have entrepreneurs making moral judgments. But I'm sure there are reasonable and God-fearing gentlemen at Decca and that a final solution will be reached."

A full-page ad appeared in *Melody Maker* later that month, showing the controversial cover with the caption: "This is the front of our new album which we finished two months ago. Due to religious disagreements, no release date has been set. If you would like a copy write to Decca Records Ltd., 9 Albert Embankment, SE1."

And so *Beggars Banquet* lingered in limbo until the band eventually conceded, and a simple plain cream sleeve, which imitated an invitation to the banquet, wrapped the best Stones album to date. Once again, though, they were seen to come in second, with the invitation cover reaching the shops a fortnight after the release of Richard Hamilton's even more minimalist sleeve for The Beatles' eponymous 1968 release, which of course became known as the *White Album*.

More seriously, Jagger had watched with a keen eye the events exploding around the world, particularly the spectacular anti-Vietnam War protests, during the year leading up to the album's release. The Viet Cong's Tet Offensive of January 1968 proved that America could not hope to win the war, which would drag on for a further seven years. In the same year, Black Power salutes were witnessed at the Olympic Games, France ground to a halt thanks to a rare collaboration between workers and students, Chicago police ran riot at the city's Democratic Convention, smashing hippie skulls, and while the young embraced the new leftist icons of Ho Chi Minh and Che Guevara, Russian tanks rolled into Czechoslovakia to crush the Prague Spring.

Mick's appearance at the massive anti-Vietnam War rally, held in London's Grosvenor Square outside the US Embassy on March 17, 1968, had prompted him to write the band's "most political song" to date, 'Street Fighting Man'. And after that, interviews in the underground press enshrined the group as *the* anti-establishment band. They had snubbed authority and put two fingers up to 'The Man'. But what was needed was a public affirmation of that attitude.

The song became yet another source of confrontation with Decca; at one point, it was considered as a UK single, but Decca considered the song too "subversive". Certainly on its US release as a single, 'Street Fighting Man' was banned by a number of radio networks in the aftermath of the Chicago riots and the assassinations of Dr. Martin Luther King Jr. and Robert Kennedy that spring and summer.

Years later, looking back to 'Street Fighting Man', Mick confirmed to the American music journalist Chet Flippo: "You've always got to have good tunes if you're marching. But the tunes don't make the march!"

Following their acceptance of MBEs, and despite admitting to drug-taking and the experimentation that propelled *Sgt. Pepper*, The Beatles were now seen as part of the establishment. The situation was confirmed by Lennon's indecision about whether to be included 'In' or 'Out' of 'Revolution', the B-side to their August 1968 single.

The Stones ("We piss anywhere, man") were definitely, defiantly, anti-establishment. But even their commitment to the revolution was being questioned. And once again, the band had their own problems to contend with – and this time from within.

CHAPTER 5

The Devil Is My Name

Concerns over Brian Jones' frailty soon emerged within the band's camp. In fact, you can see Brian visibly crumbling, almost eroding, on the film shot during the recording of *Beggars Banquet*. With the film, the Stones thought they could get a jump on The Beatles, and for the first time in five years it seemed possible they would eclipse the Fabs. Cracks had begun to appear in the Beatle façade and, following the death of their manager Brian Epstein on August 27, 1967, at the age of just thirty-two, the band now seemed rudderless. Egged on by Paul McCartney, the ill-conceived *Magical Mystery Tour* film was screened as a BBC TV seasonal highlight, on Boxing Day 1967. But however much notable fans like Martin Scorsese have since claimed *Magical Mystery Tour* a victory, it remains a flawed, self-indulgent, formless fiasco, saved only by the one thing The Beatles could always rely upon: their music.

Here at last, thought Mick Jagger, eager to pounce like a leopard on a wounded okapi, was a chance for the Stones to forge ahead.

The original idea for *The Rolling Stones Rock And Roll Circus* concert was novel: the band were to recreate a whiff of the old sawdust-ring Bertram Mills circus tents that they would have enjoyed as children, as a way to further promote *Beggars Banquet*. Originally, Brigitte Bardot was approached to play ringmaster, though sadly she declined, as did Johnny Cash. The Isley Brothers were unavailable. Steve Winwood was asked to put together a band following Traffic's split, but a throat infection saw him reluctantly step down. Nevertheless, the final lineup was impressive: The Who; an up-and-coming Jethro Tull; a wistful Marianne Faithfull; a gutsy Taj Mahal; and, tying in with the current vogue, a 'supergroup' called the Dirty Mac starring Eric Clapton, John Lennon, Mitch Mitchell and, on bass, Keith Richards – and, of course, space also had to be found for Yoko to do her thing. And finally, topping the bill, the act you've known for all these years... the Rolling Stones.

The concert took place on December 11, 1968 in a replica of a big-top tent on a BBC sound stage in Wembley. However, technical delays, audience restlessness (the performances began at 2 p.m. but went on till 5 a.m. the next morning) and, crucially, The Who just off the road and on blistering form, saw the Stones sadly falter. Reviewing the footage in the aftermath, the band felt eclipsed by Townshend & Co. And so, what could have been their saving grace was shelved.

When, 36 years later, *The Rolling Stones Rock And Roll Circus* was finally seen and heard, few would find fault. The Who were good, but the Stones seemed to be fired up and renewed – though hindsight has, of course, added poignancy to the set, since it was to become Brian's last ever appearance with the group he had founded.

Cinematically, the Rolling Stones never really got off the starting blocks. The Beatles had eclipsed them earlier: 1964's *A Hard Day's Night* was, and remains, a breathtakingly fresh cinéma vérité document, a bridge between the world in which the four

Liverpudlians had grown up ("I fought the war for your sort", "I bet you're sorry you won!") and the one in which they now found themselves ("They've gone potty out there. The place is surging with girls"). Here was youthful vigour and dynamism, the Fab Four at their Dandyish height during Beatlemania. And for capturing the later folly and hedonism of 1965, the capering and colourful *Help!* has much to recommend it.

For the Rolling Stones, though, despite ambitious high-sounding plans – *A Clockwork Orange* (Mick Jagger *is* Alex!)... *Only Lovers Left Alive* (the Rolling Stones *are* the last gang in town!) – the band were under-represented onscreen.

Only Lovers Left Alive was the nearest the Stones got to making a feature film. *Melody Maker* reported in October 1966 that filming of the David Wallis sci-fi novel, dealing with "five men and their girlfriends who are the only humans left alive following a nuclear holocaust", would commence in studios at Borehamwood the following month. In theory, this meant that the Stones would be filming at the same MGM studios where Stanley Kubrick was fashioning *2001: A Space Odyssey*. The screenplay for *Only Lovers Left Alive* would be written by Keith Waterhouse and Willis Hall, well-respected scriptwriters with prestigious titles like *Whistle Down The Wind* (1961), *A Kind Of Loving* (1962) and *Billy Liar* (1963) to their credit. Sadly, though, the project would remain unrealised.

"Ideas about movies," Bill Wyman told me, "people approaching [Mick and Keith] about making a movie of the band. It became, 'Oh no, don't use the band, just me, Keith, Marianne, Anita, Michael Cooper, our friends; forget Charlie, Bill, Astrid and Shirley, Mick Taylor and Rose...' So they had discussions and we never found out about things until sometimes months later when money had been spent, and scripts had been done."

Once again, the Rolling Stones were confident that they could change all that by linking up with a filmmaker whose reputation as a rebel on film matched their own on record.

By 1968, Jean-Luc Godard was the enfant terrible of the nouvelle vague. His run of early movies, *À Bout de souffle* (1960), *Une Femme est une femme* (1961) and *Alphaville* (1965), ditched traditional linear narrative and became famous for their jump cuts, arbitrary action and random storylines. "All my films have a beginning, a middle and an end," Godard memorably explained, "but not necessarily in that order!"

The critics lionised the director: "What Godard basically has done", wrote the acclaimed documentary maker and film historian Basil Wright, "is to codify the various factors which separate the cinema from the theatre. Over and over again in his films, Godard plays tricks on us, stupefies, impresses, irritates us through his manipulation of these space–time relationships."

"At the turn of the sixties", Peter Cowie breathlessly wrote of the maverick movie-mad Godard, "he re-wrote the grammar of film as surely as Griffith, Eisenstein and Welles had done before."

Despite looking "like a French bank clerk" (according to Keith) to his admirers, Godard had a mysterious and mesmerising charisma. Hiding behind a fug of Gauloises smoke and permanent shades, Godard was given to gnomic utterances such as "The cinema is truth 24 times a second" and "My aesthetic is that of a sniper on the roof." And, as the sixties progressed, the director's films became more and more political, espousing revolutionary ideals: stridently anti-capitalist, vehemently opposed to American involvement in Vietnam, pro-Black Panthers – you could see why such a rebel would appeal to that other band of outlaws, the Rolling Stones.

An independent producer had persuaded Godard to make a film in England, and claimed to have The Beatles interested in appearing. But the original subject was to discuss the legalisation of abortion, and with the group sundering and bogged down in Apple business, the Fab Four's interest waned and eventually they withdrew. However, Godard remained intrigued by the possibilities of using rock music and rock musicians as his new puppets. And, eventually, with a budget of £180,000 secured, the Rolling Stones committed to the project.

Godard chose them as the featured players in his first English-language film, best known today as *One Plus One*. Of course, Godard being Godard, it wasn't just his aim to track the Stones in the studio as they routined 'The Devil Is My Name'. Rather, they were to provide a breathing space for his revolutionary manifesto. The fact is, that song went on to become the enduring 'Sympathy For The Devil', easily outliving anything the director had envisaged for his film.

In one of the few interviews he gave on the subject, to Marina Warner in *The Observer* colour magazine of November 17, 1968, Godard said he wanted to "register, to print some British voices" and selected the Stones because "the new music is something specifically British. My film is composed of several people, groups, tribes, talking. There is the Stones' language, and the voice of Black Power [...] I was glad to start shooting the Stones. I like the people they represent, their certain kind of society."

At the beginning, all were enthusiastic. Mick Jagger "has always shied away from any kind of symbol status in society, and has constantly refused the role of leader and figurehead of the drop-out generation that television interviewers, the press and the judiciary have thrust upon him," Warner wrote.

"If he [Godard] supposes one represents a certain part of society," Jagger said, "it's easy to see what part. Uncompromising; the hard line; rebellion against all the established thought patterns. And a lot of background things besides."

Needless to say, the finished result – released on November 30, 1968 as *One Plus One*, though occasionally known as *Sympathy For The Devil* – pleased neither party. "A total load of crap," Keith wrote of it in *Life*, while to Mick, Godard was "a fucking twat."

The director's insistence on intercutting revolutionary agitprop (already creaky and outmoded even at the time of the film's release) with footage of the band recording disappointed both revolutionaries and Stones fans. In the film, the band is needlessly interrupted with random readings from the works of black militants, notably Eldridge Cleaver, Minister of Information for the Black Panther Party. Oh, and chunks of Hitler's *Mein Kampf* are intoned in a porn bookshop, alongside the display copies of *King*, *Duke*, *Playboy* and *Topper*. Then a character called 'Eve Democracy' (subtlety never did figure high in Godard's oeuvre) is interviewed, wandering through woods. Black Power is the key ("the main enemy is whitey"), while misogyny* runs riot alongside jaw-dropping tedium.

Furthermore, Godard's high-minded aesthetic determined that the finished track, 'Sympathy For The Devil', should not be heard in the film – his justification being something along the lines of 'a revolution is never complete'.

Speaking to Lon Goddard (no relation) about the film director in July 1969, Keith had clear memories of the experience: "You can't talk to him because he's busy freaking out. He is hung up on revolution and he was trying to put those revolution scenes on you. I watched the rough cut of the film for a while, then fell asleep… One of these days his revolution thing is going to turn around on him and there will be demonstrations against Jean-Luc Godard. 'Revolution through destruction' were the only words we

---

* I later discovered that one of the hapless white-sheathed, blonde victims was that awfully nice, latter-day star of the BBC1 TV adaptations of *Pride And Prejudice*, *Miss Marple* and *Rebecca*, Joanna David.

could get out of him, and that was totally apt since the Olympic Studios caught fire on the last note of the film!"*

Watching the film again recently took me back to bum-numbing screenings at suburban arts labs, waiting for *Don't Look Back* or *Magical Mystery Tour* to appear – in colour! *One Plus One* was regularly screened, and it was a real treat seeing the Stones in action, since there is surprisingly little footage of the band at work in the studio. And to see the sad decline of Brian Jones so manifest lends the film true poignancy.

In the end, the majestic strut of 'Sympathy For The Devil' dwarfs all Godard's ponderous, pretentious politicking. And if it is thought of at all today, it is surely recalled for the song the band so endlessly laboured over.

One Plus One premiered at the London Film Festival in November 1968. Iain Quarrier, who acted in and produced the film, desperate to claw it into profit, insisted that the version shown at the National Film Theatre contain a complete rendition of 'Sympathy For The Devil'. The director disagreed, called the audience "fascists", and then took a swing at the producer before storming out.

"I was very disappointed in the Rolling Stones," Godard later admitted. "It was very unfair for them to accept being emphasised over all the others in the film… unfair to the black people." Commercially, of course, what drew the few people who constituted the audience for *One Plus One* upon the film's release was the very presence of the Rolling Stones.

Under the headline 'Stones Film A Last Chance To See Brian', in the issue dated July 19, 1969, the *NME*'s Richard Green

---

* To ensure every movement was captured, Godard's crew installed powerful arc lights at Olympic Studios – but, in keeping with the director's revolutionary ardour and the incendiary quality that always dogged the Stones, the heat from the lights caused the studio ceiling to catch fire!

enthused: "The finest possible momento [sic] of the original Rolling Stones, when Brian Jones was still raving with them, is about to be unleashed on the group's countless fans... Fans will also be thrilled by the behind-the-scenes glimpse of the group recording, arguing about, creating and altering 'Sympathy For The Devil'. This is a remarkable insight into how a group like the Stones get down to recording a hit." But then the review hit the rocks... "The main theme is Black Power and long texts of anti-white propaganda are read aloud by Negroes sitting in a car graveyard while white girls are molested and shot."

Keith Altham was also predictably caustic: "I sneaked into a private screening last week and was never certain whether I was supposed to be provoked, disturbed or titillated. So I fell asleep... As far as the Rolling Stones are concerned I would say it is the most criminal waste of talent I have ever seen on celluloid... the film of John Lennon's one-hour smile would seem like a stirring epic in comparison."

In *Disc* magazine, Mike Ledgerwood was similarly scathing: "Complete and utter rubbish... Why on earth the Rolling Stones chose it as a vehicle for their big-screen debut I fail to comprehend. If sitting in a recording studio rehearsing a song is acting, then any pop group in the world could have done the job."

At its US premiere late in 1969, *Sympathy For The Devil*, as it was then titled, also received this raspberry from Marjorie Heins in *Rolling Stone* magazine: "Only in the Stones' recording session does the action seem to move in any direction [...] Godard likes to make frustrating, tedious films. He made it a special point that the song not be sung to completion. It keeps playing and playing, coming and coming. When at the end it finally comes, the tension of the film is released, and there is a sense of achievement, as if all the groping and provoking and sloganeering do reach some goal, and are more than the pathetic gestures of impotent revolutionaries."

Bored with London and frustrated by the Stones' unwillingness to ally themselves to actual revolution, Godard began shooting his next film late in 1968. *An American Movie* continued his fascination with Black Power and once more featured Eldridge Cleaver. Intriguingly, the finished film also contains a sequence of a rock band performing on a rooftop before the cops shut everything down, a full three months before The Beatles' legendary Apple rooftop gig. The band was Jefferson Airplane, of whom Godard commented: "the Jefferson Airplane is the only rock group in the world that is me".

The studio sequences with the Stones in *One Plus One* do, however, remain compelling. James Fox is witnessed loitering; Charlie steadfastly refuses to join in the song's 'woo woo' refrain; Marianne drifts dreamily by… There is a lift around 53 minutes in, as 'Sympathy For The Devil' finds its familiar samba groove. But just seeing the shabby studios as pipe-cleaner-thin Nicky Hopkins works out his piano parts, Mick reworks the song's lyrics, and Keith searches for that elusive riff – those sequences alone are almost worth the price of admission. The Stones operated a pretty tight closed-door policy in the studio, while fashioning the songs that continue to captivate, so for all its manifold faults *One Plus One* did provide priceless footage of the band at work.

Perhaps the most enduring, ghoulish fascination of *One Plus One* is its fly-on-the-wall glimpse of Brian Jones in his last, desperate days with the band. Literally isolated in a booth, at one remove from the band he formed, Brian is plainly struggling to keep up, and failing. It remains a harrowing picture of the decline of a genuine sixties icon. *One Plus One* offers up a Dorian Gray in reverse: at home, in a glossy penthouse is the portrait of Brian as the quintessential rock'n'roll dandy, the lustrous blond hair brushing the eyeline, the mouth petulant and enticing, rake-thin at the epicentre of the demi-monde. On film, the chubby Stone is visibly unable to get it together, suffering the ultimate indignity of not realising his guitar wasn't plugged in. ("Brian spent more time shampooing his hair than he would making a record", was Keith's comment at the time.)

Following in the same vein as *Their Satanic Majesties Request*, and the withdrawn *Rock And Roll Circus*, *One Plus One* was another body blow to the Stones when screened. 'Sympathy For The Devil' was only one of the highlights of their 1968 LP. But despite the undoubted merit of *Beggars Banquet*, when the album was finally released, the winning triple combination of the *White Album*, *The Best Of The Seekers* and *The World Of Val Doonican* denied it the number one slot in the UK album charts.

And so it continued; whatever they did, and however they did it, the Stones were always seen as trailing in the wake of The Beatles. But although the press loved to stir up controversy, the perceived rivalry between the Rolling Stones and The Beatles was pretty non-existent. From early on, as Beatlemania swept the land, The Beatles' opportunities as a live band were thwarted by the increasing hysteria that greeted their every performance. That hysteria would soon embrace the Stones too, but then theirs was music of a more... primitive nature.

From early on, when Andrew Loog Oldham proclaimed himself the Stones' record producer, the band had suffered in the studio. The early singles sounded fine coming out of tinny transistor radios, but even they lacked the depth that George Martin was bringing to his charges at Abbey Road. The Stones lagged far behind The Beatles in the 'long-playing records' handicap race. Take 1966: *Revolver* was a 14-track tour de force, balancing hypnotic rock ('She Said, She Said'; 'Doctor Robert') with some of pop's most plaintive balladry ('Here, There And Everywhere';

'Eleanor Rigby'). And the album concluded with 'Tomorrow Never Knows', a startling glimpse over the horizon and into the future.

And the Stones' contribution that year? Well, *Aftermath* had its moments ('Out Of Time'; 'Lady Jane'; 'Mother's Little Helper';), but was undermined by the misogynistic 'Stupid Girl' and 'Under My Thumb', as well as a brace of unremarkable rockers. Hindsight also has the 11-minute 'Goin' Home' as breaking new boundaries, when in truth it is an undistinguished jam with no clear shape that simply meanders to an unremarkable conclusion.

In 1968, legend has Mick persuading the DJ at a top London club to spin the Stones' new single, 'Jumpin' Jack Flash'. It was well received – which irked Paul McCartney, who happened to be in attendance and also happened to have an acetate, which he then slipped the DJ. It was his band's new single, 'Hey Jude'. And the place went wild...

However, while the music press may have tried to paint a competitive edge between the UK's two leading bands, they were in fact closely allied. Like warring nations, waiting until the harvest was in before commencing hostilities, they liaised and synchronised record releases so as not to clash, at least until 1970, when the Stones had the field to themselves. Both Beatles and Stones acknowledged each other on their album sleeves, and helped each other out singing backing vocals (John and Paul on 'We Love You'), or appearing on TV shows (Mick and Marianne on *Our World*).

Rumours also persisted that the two leading UK pop acts of the time were to merge, and in July 1967 *The People* reported that they were to form a joint company "looking for new studios in London, probably to record unknown pop groups. And they may make films together." The story prompted a swift response from the Stones' PR, Les Perrin: "Mr Jagger states that preparatory conversations of a purely exploratory nature were held between him and Mr Paul McCartney. These conversations have not been resolved and any assumption to the contrary should be considered premature."

In October 1967, a *Melody Maker* front page queried, 'Beatles, Stones To Link Up?' Beatle PR Tony Barrow was quoted as saying, "It's highly possible that the two groups will get together for fresh business ventures but there is no chance of any sort of co-operation on record... There is a possibility of future intriguing schemes, these could include a 'talent school'."

With the band clearly unhappy with the way the *Rock And Roll Circus* had turned out, and with *Beggars Banquet* now denied the number one slot in both the UK and the USA, it seemed that no one in the inner circle was too unhappy to see the end of 1968.

★★★

As 1969 dawned, it became apparent that to safeguard their status, the Rolling Stones needed to prepare a fusillade for the new year. To reclaim their crown and recapture lost ground, there needed to be a return to regular live work and a stonking studio LP. The bad old days had to be dispatched. Old certainties needed to be confirmed. New territories must be conquered. The plans were laid in sleepy London town – in fashionable Mayfair, where their UK office was located; in the borough of Barnes, where the Stones recorded; and at Cheyne Walk, the Chelsea address that gave Mick, Marianne, Keith and Anita a haven of domesticity.

Chelsea has always been an important part of Bohemian London. I can't think why Elvis Costello didn't want to go there, but Thomas More, Carlyle and Rossetti all did. Perhaps because, despite the bustle of lorries thundering west on the Chelsea Embankment, Cheyne Walk remains shielded, and still offers an oasis of calm, affluent isolation in the midst of it all. Cheyne Walk has always been a quiet backwater, though this slice of Chelsea has long attracted rakish residents. Among those in the Stones' SW3 orbit was John Paul Getty Jr., famously remembered as the father of the kidnapped heir. During the late sixties and early seventies, the Getty address at 16 Cheyne Walk was party central, but things soon calmed down after Mick Jagger introduced JPG to the MCC and a love of cricket. *Their Satanic Majesties Request* cover photographer, Michael Cooper, had his studio just round the corner in Flood Street, where he also shot the *Sgt. Pepper* sleeve. Sound Techniques Studios (where Nick Drake, John Cale and Pink Floyd, among others, recorded) and the Chelsea Arts Club nestled nearby on Old Church Street, while way across the river from Penge, Bill Wyman, too, hunkered down in Chelsea, SW3.

"Chelsea was very much removed from the rest of London," the art collector Christopher Gibbs told Shawn Levy. "There were people who hung out in Chelsea who might not go east of Sloane Square for months." It was famously at Gibbs' Cheyne Walk property that Antonioni paid people £30 to come to smoke pot and be filmed for his Swinging London effort, *Blow-Up* ("I remember the word around town," Paul McCartney recalled. "'There's this guy who's paying money for people to come and get stoned'... Everyone was being paid, like blood donors, to smoke pot!")

Of course, for Jagger and Richards, Cheyne Walk really was a step up in the world. A fit man like Mick, and even the slothful Keith, could make their way from their palatial Chelsea mansions to nearby Edith Grove in a matter of minutes. The journey from the Stones' seedy beginnings in Earl's Court[*] to their exotic

---

[*] There was a rare opportunity to relive that seediness when, in 2016, the Edith Grove flat was breathtakingly recreated at the Saatchi Gallery for the Rolling Stones' exhibit, *Exhibitionism*. It was a case of 'Enter at your peril, and marvel at the empty Watney's beer bottles and copies of the *Daily Herald* in which the sustaining fish and chips came wrapped. Then make a dignified exit through the gift shop, with the branded hoodies, T-shirts and phone cases...'

Chelsea location of wealth and taste was a mere few hundred yards, but in a few short years they had travelled so far, accomplished so much and soared so high. Close to Cheyne Walk is the Cross Keys pub, which displays a plaque of its celebrated patrons: Dylan Thomas (few surprises there), Agatha Christie and... Bob Marley. It is tantalising to think of Mick and Keith knocking off early and popping in for a quick pint. A jar with... Jah?

London has always been a magnet for suburban aspirants and metropolitan dreamers. For the Stones, it was from these London locations that debts were settled, grudges were deepened, juices flowed and plans hatched. And by the end of 1968 it was clear just who was who in the hierarchy. While the Rolling Stones may have started out as Brian's band, within five short years it was evident that he was in no fit state to remain in, let alone lead, the band. As principal songwriters Mick and Keith held sway, and so it was time to cast off, sail on or go down with the ship...

It was at the Rolling Stones' office at Maddox Street, Mayfair, during early 1969, that a plaque hung on the wall. Later famously known as 'Desiderata', it was rumoured to have been a 17th-century sacred text, although actually it was a 1927 poem that took on a life of its own in the late sixties, with its calm and placid lyricism. It was also used as an advert for King Crimson's third studio album, *Lizard*, recited with reverence by Leonard Nimoy on his 1968 album *Two Sides Of Leonard Nimoy*, and it gave Les Crane a 1972 American hit. In hindsight, the words could be seen as a roadmap for the Stones' activities during 1969: "Go placidly amid the noise and the haste, and remember what peace there may be in silence. As far as possible, without surrender, be on good terms with all persons... Exercise caution in your business affairs, for the world is full of trickery... "

PART 2

A Storm Is Threatening

CHAPTER 6

Diamonds From The Mine

Over three issues of *Melody Maker* in March 1969, Mick Jagger ("the most controversial and greatest anti-hero of our time along with the Great Train Robbers") opened his heart to Keith Altham. Given that every interview nowadays is designed specifically to sell tickets or shift product, it is surprising to recall just how accessible and candid the Stones were back then.

Altham had begun his career on *Fabulous!*, a teen pop magazine. And with each weekly edition selling over a million copies, Brian Epstein and Andrew Loog Oldham knew that journalists like him were worth cultivating. Keith went on to a fiery career at the *NME* – it was he who suggested to his old mate Chas Chandler that if his client Jimi Hendrix set fire to his guitar it might generate some extra media interest. Later, on quitting journalism, Keith took over from Les Perrin as the Stones' PR.

With hindsight, and knowing what was to follow, what Jagger said on the record at the time to a journalist he trusted makes for fascinating reading.

"I'm not interested in being a shopkeeper, an executive or a capitalist [...] I don't want to do ten weeks touring the States and staying in grotty hotels [...] I don't think I shall live to a very old age anyway – I've always had that feeling [...] I liked the way The Beatles did it with 'Hey Jude' so that the orchestra was not just to cover everything up. We may do something like that on the next album."

That "next album" turned out to be *Let It Bleed*, and the "something like that" was what I believe to be the apogee of the Rolling Stones on record: 'You Can't Always Get What You Want'.

Sessions for what became *Let It Bleed* had begun late in 1968. And somehow, rather aptly, the band started with what would become both the album's final track, and its enduring anthem. 'You Can't Always Get What You Want' was, by any standard, a good start. However, for the band at least, it looked like 1969 was set to continue on the same trajectory as preceding years.

For all the critical acclaim that had greeted *Beggars Banquet*, by early 1969 it had only just breached the Top Five on album charts on both sides of the Atlantic.

And despite the low profile they kept while recording, the Stones were always capable of generating headlines: Rolling Stones barred from luxury hotels over outlandish dressware... Brian Jones' increasing unreliability... Keith crashes his Mercedes and breaks pregnant Anita Pallenberg's collarbone... Five hundred indignant Australians protest at the casting of Mick Jagger as Ned Kelly... Rock's golden couple, Mick and Marianne – the counterculture's Edward and Mrs Simpson – are busted on yet more drugs charges...

The band's every move was duly documented: Jagger's refusal to marry his pregnant girlfriend led to his locking horns on morality with the nation's guardian, Mary Whitehouse, on a David Frost TV show: "I don't really want to get married... I don't feel that I really need it... but if I were with a woman who really did need it, well that's another matter. But I'm not with that kind of woman."

"The dreadful thing about Mick and I", Marianne ("that kind of woman"!) told me, "was living in the public eye. We didn't expect that at all. There must have been something magical about us as a couple that neither of us realised... well, maybe he did, he's awfully clever. But something caught the public imagination."

Then, on May 28, Mick answered the door to his Chelsea townhouse and watched open-mouthed as a platoon of police paraded through with a warrant to search for drugs. Jagger had been stopped earlier by the fuzz while driving along the King's Road (natch), and had refused their request to search his car for drugs. That refusal may well have led to the subsequent home visit a week later. As ever with the Stones, court appearances had to be juggled with recording sessions. And so it was that Mick and Marianne made a 50-second court appearance on May 30, at which Mick's bail was set at £50.

Like The Beatles, the Stones were used to seeing serried ranks of the Old Bill protecting them from overzealous fans. ("The Stones like the police quite a lot", readers of *Rave* were informed in 1965. "They can take jokes and they don't find it beneath them to come in and ask for autographs... And sometimes they give us a fantastic escort into towns.")

But they were unprepared when the gloves came off. In 1967, Caroline Coon founded the organisation Release to help young people arrested on drug offences who had no legal representation. "The police thought they really could do what they liked," she told Simon Wells for *Butterfly On A Wheel*. "They'd walk into a person's house, steal their money, plant them, punch them, be violent towards them... It kind of shocked us all, it shocked Jagger, it shocked everybody who was educated to believe that British justice was wonderful, that the British Empire was the most liberal in the world. It all came crashing down against this police state that the authorities, if not condoned, then certainly turned a blind eye to."

It was during this time that the Stones' PR, Les Perrin, really earned his salary. Les was Fleet-Street-friendly, happy cultivating journalists and feeding them stories. He was belt and braces, old school (Mick fondly called him 'Lunchtime O'Perrin' after *Private Eye*'s archetypal hack 'Lunchtime O'Booze'). Following wartime service (as "the worst rear-gunner in the RAF"), Les began an equally unsuccessful, if less threatening career as a drummer, before switching to journalism, becoming news editor of the *New Musical Express*. Public relations inevitably followed and, working out of a tiny Tin Pan Alley office, Les would travel up from Surbiton to look after a diverse roster of clients, including the likes of Frank Sinatra, Louis Armstrong, bandleader Ted Heath, Matt Monro and Queen Salote of Tonga!

But with the exploding Beat boom of the 1960s, Les was soon looking after Cliff Richard, The Shadows and The Dave Clark Five. His forecast for 1964, before he took the Stones on as clients? "I think there will be a return to 'powerhouse'. The sax and other brass will return." In 1966, the "quiet, courteous" Les Perrin was taken on full time as Stones PR.

NME's Keith Altham knew Les well, and remembered him as "a sweet guy, a lovely man. He would drink with all the journalists in the Fleet Street pubs, dropping them little titbits, but he was also propping up the bar at the Wig and Pen Club, where the police and judiciary used to drink! Les's great thing was he could get things in print, but he claimed he could also *stop* them getting printed!"

As Bill Wyman later laconically wrote, Les was "the best operator in London. He wore a suit, seemed some distance from rock & roll. [He was] softly spoken and shy, but with brilliant tactics.

His appointment came only just in time, as problems away from music that we could not have forecast began to envelop the Stones."

It was Les who steered the Stones through their most turbulent times. He was early on the scene at both Redlands and Cotchford Farm, and organised the *Beggars Banquet* launch. The band trusted him, and he was one of the few people Jagger would listen to ("Don't be silly," was Les's regular refrain when talking to the singer*). Once, when asked about the Stones after a few years in the job, Les replied diplomatically: "They are natural story breakers. Sometimes for better, sometimes for worse."

In March 1969, talking to Richard Green, Les was quoted on his most famous client: "Jagger is an original brain. He's not a 144-point headline in a national tabloid or an enemy of the barbering profession, or a musical anarchist…" Diplomatically, the publicist concluded: "We've had a few incidents that hit a few headlines, a few things that perhaps the Stones would have preferred not to have happened."

Andrew Loog Oldham graciously consented that "Leslie's loyalty to his clients far transcended the income he derived from them, and when the establishment decided they had had quite enough of the Rolling Stones and sought to imprison them, it was Perrin who literally held Mick's and Keith's hands as they ran the gauntlet that left me too terrified to act effectively."**

There was always something to occupy Perrin when it came to his most notorious clients. And as the 1960s drew to an end, the police grew ever keener to harass the pop stars they saw as

---

* Journalist Chris Welch remembers that whenever Les referred to the Stones' singer, it was always as 'Michael Philip'.

** Sadly, Les fell ill in 1973, and he died in 1978. However, beyond his work with some of the biggest names in rock'n'roll history, his name lives on in the Les Perrin PR of the Year award, given annually by the trade paper *Music Week*.

corrupting the nation's youth. Such harassment frequently took place in conjunction with the censorious press emanating from Fleet Street. The 1967 Redlands incident had set the scene, and by 1969 the hunt was on. Leading from the front was the notorious detective sergeant Norman Pilcher (the "semolina pilchard" of Lennon's 'I Am The Walrus'). He had joined the drug squad in 1966, and, as Simon Wells wrote, "[was] the officer who would become the scourge of the London-based rock musicians of the sixties".

Among the scalps Pilcher claimed were those of Donovan, Brian Jones, George Harrison and John Lennon. And to rub salt into the wounds, the detective would always ask his victims to sign LPs for his children. However, Pilcher's luck finally ran out, along with the decade that made his name. He was eventually busted himself, and in 1973 was imprisoned for four years on a charge of perjury.

Despite court appearances from both Lennon and Harrison, it was the drug charges against Jagger, Richards and Jones that confirmed the Stones in the public imagination as bad boys. For the band, it was always a difficult balancing act: on the one hand, they had to convince the underground that they were still the rock'n'roll rebels who flouted authority by not twirling round and waving on the *Sunday Night At The London Palladium* carousel. On the other, they had grown accustomed to a lavish lifestyle, financed by huge record sales and concert appearances. And, as the decade waned, their finances, management and relationship with their record label were all in tatters. They were effectively broke, and desperately needed some cash in hand.

With a keen eye on the lucrative American market, and ever mindful that a drug conviction would torpedo any chances of a US work permit, it was through deft deferrals and objections from his lawyers that Jagger got the trial for his May 1969 bust postponed. It was prevented from reaching court until January 1970, a good six weeks after the Stones returned from those crucial, and lucrative, US dates.

Mick got off with a £200 fine. However, papers released by the Director of Public Prosecutions in 2005 strongly suggested that Jagger had been set up. A confusingly named Detective Sergeant Constable (who had arrested Brian Jones the year before) claimed to have found the dope in a Cartier box. ("You bastard, you've planted me," Jagger had protested.)

"Where is your LSD?" Constable allegedly asked Jagger. On denying that he had any, Mick was told: "We can do something about that." Then the detective sergeant had apparently suggested that a £1,000 bribe would keep Mick out of court. The subsequent papers reveal Mick's pedantic response: "I didn't say 'Marianne, they're after the weed'... I simply wouldn't have said that, or used the word 'weed'. It is the most archaic expression which is never used."

The National Archives at Kew hold a massive number of files concerning the 1969 Jagger bust. Simon Wells, who spent many hours trawling through the paperwork for his book *Butterfly On A Wheel*, has a theory that Mick inflated the police corruption and bribery accusations, as he knew that such a complaint would ensure an inquiry. That meant a delay in the trial, and thus did not affect his eligibility for a visa, which was crucial for the Stones' planned US tour.

Commander Robert Huntley, who oversaw an investigation into Jagger's accusation of police corruption at the time leading up to the 1970 trial, concluded: "At one end are respected law-enforcement officers and public figures, whilst at the other end are the dregs of society." Extraordinary to think that, in 2003, that particular "dreg" was knighted by Prince Charles.

★★★

Keen to prove that there was more to him than the hip-shaking, head-shaking, drug-addled, morality-challenging Stone, sometime in the late sixties Jagger appointed Sandy Lieberson as his acting agent.

From early on, rumours abounded of the charismatic Jagger and his inevitable film career. In October 1967, on the front page of *Melody Maker*, film producer Carl Forman (*The Guns Of Navarone*) cabled: "Mick Jagger press agent Leslie Perrin absolutely correct in saying Mick Jagger will *not* appear in *The Virgin Soldiers* – mainly because I never for one moment considered him for any role and never, repeat never, offered him any part in the film." The Welsh film and television actor Hywel Bennett became the eventual star of that film when it was released in 1969. It did, however, feature Mick's future Live Aid partner David Bowie in a literally blink-and-you'll-miss-him role. "I'm in it for about 20 seconds as an extra," Bowie later confirmed.

The *One Plus One* experience had been dispiriting, but as the years have shown, Jagger is nothing if not determined. The fag end of the year had seen Mick undertake his first dramatic role in the film *Performance*, which continued to occupy him until the end of 1968. Director Donald Cammell had written two forgettable films – *The Touchables* and *Duffy* (both released in 1968) – and was then punting around a script called *The Liars*, or *The Performers*. He came to Jagger's attention because they shared the same agent, and the singer found himself captivated by Cammell's script. Donald's brother, David, whose background was in advertising (with the agency Cammell, Hudson & Brownjohn*), was brought in to produce.

---

*   In one of those fortuitous coincidences that were so much a part of the London scene in the late sixties, the Brownjohn in question (Robert) went on to design the sleeve for *Let It Bleed*.

After Mick had wrapped his part in the film, *Performance* limped on long afterwards. While co-directors Donald Cammell and Nic Roeg were largely unknown quantities, even with a script that could at best be described as half-finished, Warner Bros. was keen to bankroll the film. And the reason for the studio's zeal was simple enough: its star, Mick Jagger.

Warner Bros. knew that with the rock star on board they were guaranteed a best-selling soundtrack LP, and with the film pitched as "a sort of crime movie starring Mick Jagger" they were halfway there. Jagger chafed because, unlike their contemporaries, the Rolling Stones had never made the transition to the silver screen. However, by the time filming began, and with much infamy attached to their star name, Warner Bros. suspected they were unlikely to get a pop star vehicle such as The Dave Clark Five's *Catch Us If You Can* or Herman's Hermits' *Mrs Brown You've Got A Lovely Daughter*. However, the studio was still hoping for something to rival the success of *A Hard Day's Night*.

With the charismatic Jagger cast as the reclusive 'Turner', an equally substantial name was required to play opposite him. The role of the brutal gangster 'Chas' was, intriguingly, initially offered to Marlon Brando. But by the end of the sixties, the American 'Method maestro' was bored, and declined. And so it was that James Fox was persuaded to flex his acting muscles instead. One of British cinema's biggest stars of the sixties, Fox was best known for languid, aristo roles in films such as *The Servant* (1963) and *Those Magnificent Men In Their Flying Machines* (1965).

Perhaps it was as a deliberate antidote to his upper-class background (Fox attended the exclusive boarding school Harrow and was, for a short time, a commissioned officer in the Coldstream Guards) and screen image that Fox chose to immerse himself totally in the role. He bonded with London underworld contacts, and spent two months in a flat over the Thomas A'Becket pub on the Old Kent Road, famous for its boxing connections. Working out daily, 'Chas' was to bring out, by Fox's own admission, his own "nasty, dark side".

At the other end of the *Performance* casting scale was lowlife criminal Johnny Bindon. Later hired as security for Led Zeppelin's 1977 American tour, Bindon was "a nasty piece of work", according to Zeppelin biographer Mick Wall. "A shoot-first-don't-even-bother-asking-questions London 'face'", Bindon was arrested following a backstage assault at a Zeppelin show, where he had tried to gouge out the eye of a victim. He was tried for murder in 1979 but was acquitted, and later died in 1993.

Mick was to receive a fee of $100,000 for his role as 'Turner', plus a percentage of the gross. But what the studio bankrolling the project really wanted was some musical contribution, a soundtrack album that could be released on their own label. Such an album from the film's star would surely include his compadres, the Rolling Stones? But in the end, what they got was Mick performing a snatch of a Robert Johnson blues number onscreen and, finally, only one entire song – the memorable 'Memo From Turner'. As if to rub salt into the Hollywood studio's wounds, when finally screened, there was an awful lot of London gangster business in the movie. This would be of little interest to American audiences – their 'London' films were of the *Smashing Time* (comedy satire) or *Kaleidoscope* (starring Warren Beatty and Susannah York) variety. Even worse, the star name above the title didn't make his first appearance until 40 minutes into the film.

However far she travels, and wherever she goes, Marianne Faithfull's name will always be inextricably linked to the Rolling Stones, but she remains philosophical about that unholy alliance: "I was incredibly jealous of Mick's talent," she told me. "I bit the bullet, I put my ambition on hold and did what was required, which was to be there and give him everything I had. I was proud and honoured to do it. What I didn't like was that I was perceived as the 'rock chick'."

With Jagger committed to the film project, it made sense for his widely publicised partner to appear alongside him. Indeed, Marianne's own film career might have benefited from appearing in *Performance* – in 1966, she was mentioned as testing for the role of Bianca in Zeffirelli's *Romeo And Juliet*, as well as auditioning for a role in the big-budget Peter O'Toole vehicle, *The Night Of The Generals*.*

Neither of those Faithfull auditions was successful. To her credit though, Marianne persisted, with a role in Michael Winner's caustic and thoroughly enjoyable *I'll Never Forget Whats'isname*... Coming late in 1967, it just caught the end of the Swinging Sixties movie boat. And the publicity material helpfully pointed out: "The colourful 'psychedelic' artwork used on posters... is typical of the modernistic, free-thinking contents of this essentially 'with-it' film of today." Way down the credits, and understandably below Orson Welles and Oliver Reed, Marianne was competing with Carol White – the "Battersea Bardot". Pre-publicity breathlessly claimed that "Marianne now intends to break away from the 'pop' world and concentrate entirely on an acting career." Incidentally, she also entered movie history by becoming the first actor to utter the word 'fuck' in a mainstream film.

Scheduled to appear as one of the 'Turner' ménage, it was Marianne's pregnancy that saw Anita Pallenberg take over her role in *Performance*.

The role Marianne eventually did take, in 1968's *The Girl On A Motorcycle*, went on to do her few favours. In the States, the film

---

* In another of those eerie coincidences, the role Marianne auditioned for in *The Night Of The Generals* was taken by Joanna Pettet, the actress who had rented the King's Road flat immediately prior to Brian Jones, where he was busted in 1968.

was released under the more prurient title *Naked Under Leather*. Director Jack Cardiff came with a strong pedigree, but as a cinematographer (notably on Michael Powell and Emeric Pressburger's *A Matter Of Life And Death* and *Black Narcissus*). As a fledgling director, Cardiff was enchanted by his leading lady: "Never since I first saw Marilyn Monroe through the camera lens have I seen such irresistible beauty." *The Girl On A Motorcycle*, however, was deeply flawed: at best, soft porn; at worst, pretentious nonsense: "A motorcycle is closer to you than any human being," Alain Delon's 'Daniel' tells Marianne's 'Rebecca'. "A car is something outside yourself, but a motorbike becomes part of you. You are the sensations, there, between your thighs."

With filming finally underway on *Performance* during the autumn of 1968, it was soon obvious that it was going to be a difficult shoot. Like Jack Cardiff, *Performance* co-director Nic Roeg was best known as a cinematographer, spectacularly so on John Schlesinger's 1967 film of *Far From The Madding Crowd*. But there was palpable on-set tension between Jagger and Fox, which co-director Cammell did his best to exacerbate in order to get the actors to identify more closely with their characters. Even more pressing was Keith Richards' gnawing anxiety at the growing closeness between Jagger and his girlfriend, Anita Pallenberg. Gossip of their increasing intimacy had reached the guitarist, who was holed up in a nearby flat. But after all the unease about the situation, at least one positive thing did emerge: it was there in that flat that Keith came up with the tense and stormy riff for 'Gimme Shelter'.

During filming, Jagger had concerns about his acting ability, echoed by Donald Cammell's own uncertainty about his abilities as co-director. Nic Roeg was a less forceful character, so Cammell ended up calling the shots. Wary of his shenanigans, and viewing the situation from the outside, Keith later referred to Cammell as "the most destructive little turd I've ever met... utterly predatory".

And then there was the film's 'technical advisor', David Litvinoff. In his compelling biography *Jumpin' Jack Flash: David Litvinoff And The Rock'n'Roll Underworld*, Keiron Pim fills out the story. Litvinoff was the link between the true criminal underworld of the Kray Brothers and the Bohemian Chelsea set, which by then had wholeheartedly embraced rock'n'roll. Known to the arts dealer Robert Fraser and "London's most famous antiques dealer" Christopher Gibbs, both pivotal figures on the London scene, Litvinoff was now firmly in the Stones' orbit. The band remained baffled as to who had fingered them over the Redlands bust, so Litvinoff was told to apply pressure on a fellow guest, Nicky Cramer, for information as to who might have tipped off the Old Bill to attend Keith's property that night in 1967. Litvinoff's line of questioning included dangling Cramer by his ankles out of a first-floor window – a scene which, with just a little reworking, made its way into *Performance*.

For many, the Krays were still perceived as 'cool', until their arrest in 1968, when the full brutality of their crimes was revealed. "Nobody had ever spoken to gangsters before," confirmed Chelsea-set member Simon Hodgson, "and they seemed rather chic." Film stars and celebrities flocked to their clubs and pubs to flirt with the Krays. The twins even appeared alongside Lennon and McCartney, Jean Shrimpton and Mick Jagger in David Bailey's 1965 photographic book *Box Of Pin-Ups*.

That spurious notoriety also permeates *Performance*, but it was the sexual chemistry between Jagger, Anita, Fox and French actress Michèle Breton (who plays 'Lucy') that lent the film its real notoriety.

On completion, *Performance* was deemed so shocking that the film processing company – Humphries Film Laboratories – refused even to transfer the film stock. By July 1969, though, Cammell had enough footage to hold a sneak screening. However, the preview audience was unprepared; they were anticipating an early glimpse of the controversial buddy film *Midnight Cowboy* – which went on to become the first X-rated film ever to win a Best Picture Oscar at the 1970 Academy Awards. But when *Performance* was screened, one studio executive's wife was sick on her husband's shoes. And as the audience filed out, the last thing the studio heads heard was, "Even the bathwater's dirty!" Following that first US preview, the studio head was seen striding across the studio carrying cans of film, with a junior behind him toting a spade. "Where are you going?" Ken Hyman was asked. "I'm going to bury these," he retorted, dismissively indicating the reels that contained the "depraved and evil" *Performance*.

With a substantial financial investment at risk, logic dictated that *something* had to be clawed back from Warner Bros.' investment. But by then, Nic Roeg was already in Australia shooting his second feature, *Walkabout*, and so *Performance* was handed back to Donald Cammell, who spent over a year cutting the film into a shape the studio regarded as releasable.

Performance finally opened in the States in 1970, and in London in January 1971. *Rolling Stone* was, predictably, enthusiastic, but even its reviewer's enthusiasm was muted: "*Performance* is a stunning film, stunning in the sense of a body blow," cautioned Michael Goodwin. "[It] is a very ugly film. Hallucinatory though it may be, I would not recommend seeing it while tripping." Even in its highly edited form, *Performance* was reviled by the 'straight' press. From *New York* magazine: "The most loathsome film of all." From *Life* magazine: "The most disgusting, the most completely worthless film I have seen since I began reviewing."

Somewhat surprisingly, the London reviews were a lot more benign, including Cecil Wilson in the *Daily Mail*. Although Wilson found *Performance* "too self-indulgently way-out, too arty-crafty busy, obscure and vicious", he concluded with "Even in the first week of January, I doubt whether 1971 will see a more hated, adulated or hotly debated film this year." He also found Jagger making "a better job of it than [he had as] Ned Kelly", although as "the decadent rock star, he looks remarkably like Brigitte Bardot".

The finished film left its mark, with even co-director Nic Roeg admitting: "*Performance* nearly destroyed us." Marianne Faithfull called *Performance* "a virus infecting everything". Michèle Breton, seeing it years later, called it "a feeling of death".

Of all those involved, the film seemed to have affected James Fox most of all – either because of his total immersion in the role of 'Chas', or the switchover with Jagger as 'Turner'. Fox subsequently quit acting, turning instead to life with a Christian sect. *Performance* was to be his last film for nearly 14 years, at which point he returned, excellent as ever, for a starring role in David Lean's epic *A Passage To India*. But the fallout was to continue: David Litvinoff committed suicide in 1975; Donald Cammell committed suicide in 1996. Poor Michèle Breton, still a teenager while filming *Performance*, drifted into drug addiction, and when tracked down by Mick Brown in 1995 said: "My life was always bad... Nobody wants me."

Jagger, as ever, rose above it all and emerged unscathed. Though, as someone who was close to him at the time, Marianne Faithfull is convinced that *Performance* altered her paramour. She later wrote in her autobiography: "Mick came away from *Performance* with his character. This persona was so perfectly tailored to his needs that he'd never have to take it off again. This is Mick Jagger as far as most of the world is concerned and by this point probably himself as well. He came out of *Performance* with two new characters actually. The one we know and feel whatever it is we feel about it – that Mick – and another, more sinister one: the gangster figure, heart-of-stone type."

Hindsight has once again been kinder to the film than it deserves. Whole books have been dedicated to it. Documentaries have dwelled on its significance. It is frequently cited as the key Swinging Sixties phantasmagoria. But on re-viewing it after 40 years I can categorically state they are *all* wrong. *Performance* is a dreadful film. Today, it stands as a wholly unsatisfactory mix of drug-culture babble, pseudo philosophy and dislocated narrative. Even the highly praised London gangster milieu was superseded by 1971's *Get Carter* and 1980's *The Long Good Friday*. However, watching it back today, the film does have some elements of a certain rococo charm ("You'll look funny when you're 50," 'Chas' tells 'Turner'). Then there is the oft-quoted sneer from 'Turner', the has-been rock star: "I'll tell you this: the only performance that makes it, that really makes it, that makes it all the way, is the one that achieves madness." And Jagger, at least, manages to emerge with some dignity, delivering a wistful, androgynous performance. Though you'd have to kiss an awful lot of frogs to find a prince in *Performance*.

Indeed, the film was so very much of its time that *Performance* now seems like a relic. With its nouvelle vague styles, jump cuts, elliptical dialogue, identity issue and continuity out with the bath water, *Performance* could almost be a Jean-Luc Godard film!

For those of a certain age, *Performance* offers a nostalgic glimpse of a now-vanished late sixties London, complete with Watneys Red Barrel, Talk Of The Town programmes and sophisticated bedside teasmades. And it's funny to see Notting Hill's Powis Square looking so shabby. But there are too many louche hippies at play, and too many fatuous de profundis lines. (Shock: Mick quotes Nietzsche! Gasp: gangster reads philosopher Jorge Luis Borges!) Too much emphasis is also placed on the issue of gender fluidity: the clunky handling of identity crises, the spurious delineation of the thin line between sanity and madness. Throughout, there is the feeling that this is the older voyeur looking at how the young misbehave. To my mind, 1963's *Billy Liar* says a lot more about popular culture, the Swinging Sixties and the lure of London than this tired and pretentious effort. To recall the words of the former film editor of *Vox* magazine: "*Performance* is up there with *Zabriskie Point*, *Blow-Up* and *La Vallée* in the category of unwatchable, self-indulgent, hippie bollocks."*

★ ★ ★

What will survive of *Performance* is the chilling track 'Memo From Turner'. Like so much surrounding this film, the song's origins and genesis are swathed in mystery. Legend has Keith dismissing it, with his guitar part taken by an outsider. All the while Jagger struggled with the lyrics, allegedly calling on Donald Cammell for help. Amid the different versions, was the original mix deliberately wiped? Just who does play on it? (The Stones? Traffic? LA session men?) What remains is a swaggering slice of late sixties seediness. And, without doubt, Jagger's lyrics are among his best, although

---

* For the superfans, here are some *Performance* titbits culled from my re-viewing: Among the listed cast is Ann Sidney, winner of the 1964 Miss World contest.

Appearing uncredited in Anthony Valentine's ruined betting shop is Reg Lye. Five years earlier, the Australian actor had appeared alongside Bob Dylan, who was making his television debut in the BBC play *Madhouse On Castle Street*.

Anthony Valentine himself was only a few years away from finding fame as Major Mohn in BBC TV's *Colditz*, in which he starred alongside David McCallum. McCallum's father was a classical violinist who played on 'A Day In The Life' – and he was also the man who suggested to Jimmy Page that he occasionally play his guitar with a violin bow!

An Otis Redding LP sleeve is visible on the floor of 'Turner''s flat. And clearly visible in the ménage-à-trois bath scene, a packet of Whitworth's soft brown sugar!

To a whole generation of Brits, Anthony Morton, as 'Denny', is better known as 'Carlos Raphael', the chef at TV's *Crossroads* motel.

what San Antonio, Hemlock Road in 1956 and a Coca-Cola Convention have to do with Notting Hill gangsters in the late 1960s still eludes me.

In his November 1970 *Melody Maker* review, Chris Welch called 'Memo From Turner' "better than recent Stones recordings and probably a hit, even if Mick doesn't bother with any promotion". Welch was right; without any PR from Jagger, 'Memo From Turner' limped to number 32 on the UK singles charts.

A letter to *Rolling Stone* from 'Slippery Jack' in San Francisco ran: "Riddle me this: How come 'Memo From Turner' isn't going to get a nomination for Best Song in the Academy Awards?" Of course, as we all know, the Oscar that year went to 'For All We Know' from *Lovers And Other Strangers*. (No, me neither.)

Back in the day, Stones' collaborator Jack Nitzsche was called in to monitor the *Performance* soundtrack, pulling in Randy Newman, The Last Poets* and Buffy Sainte-Marie. Jack also introduced a Los Angeles session player who would leave a mark not only on the film soundtrack but also, bitterly, on the Stones themselves.

Ryland Peter Cooder was still a year away from making his debut solo album when he was pulled into the Stones' orbit. Still in his early twenties, he had already fashioned a spectacular CV. Early on, he was in a group with Jackie DeShannon, before moving on to Rising Sons, a band that was fronted by singer Taj Mahal. He also appeared on the debut LP from Captain Beefheart & His Magic Band. I asked Ry when I interviewed him in 1980 if had he ever been tempted to join the Captain on a more permanent basis? "Nah, hell, he was too weird!"

It was Jack Nitzsche who drew Cooder into the Stones camp: "He's another guy who keeps himself interested by doing oddball

---

* The Last Poets were several groups of poets and musicians who arose out of the civil rights movement in the late 1960s. Its members are credited as early influencers of hip-hop.

things," Cooder told me. "If he rang and said he'd got a job producing an album and did I want to come along, I'd always say 'yes' because I knew it'd always be worth it."

With the *Performance* album in the can, and Brian Jones patently falling by the wayside, Cooder was asked along to Olympic to help out with *Let It Bleed*, which is where the trouble really started...

"The Rolling Stones... weren't playing well and were just messing around in the studio," Cooder raged to *Rolling Stone*. "When there'd be a lull in the so-called rehearsals I'd start to play my guitar... as I found out later, the tapes would keep rolling. In the four or five weeks I was there, I must have played everything I know. They got it all down on those tapes. Everything...! They're bloodsuckers, man."

The guitarist's main beef was with Keith, who, according to Ry, alighted on his open-G tuning, which became the foundation for 'Honky Tonk Women', and was later built into 'Gimme Shelter', 'Brown Sugar', 'Tumbling Dice' and others. The sleeve notes that accompanied Cooder's mid-eighties CD releases were unequivocal: "A legendary session musician, Cooder played with a wide range of artists, from Randy Newman to Crazy Horse to the Rolling Stones. He made notable contributions on the latter's 1969 release *Let It Bleed*, providing the central riff to the group's smash hit 'Honky Tonk Women' in the process."

Like an endless duel between veterans, the debate rambled on, and on. "Who did he nick it from?" Keith asked rock critic Adam Sweeting. "This can go on forever. Ry showed me a few tricks, but I knew about that tuning before."

"My theory is that the only thing you can put on a musician's headstone is 'He Passed It On'," Keith stated. In his autobiography, *Life*, he devotes two pages to his rediscovering the guitar in typically colourful Keith terms: "I tip my hat to Ry Cooder... I started playing chords on the open tuning — which was new ground [...] The minute you've tuned a guitar or any other instrument to one chord, you've got to work your way round it. You're out of the realms of normal music. You're up the Limpopo with Yellow Jack."

Talking to Ben Fong-Torres later in 1970, Cooder was categoric: "Keith Richards didn't like me. Like he left the room when I walked in... We'd pick up an instrument, Mick'd dance around, and we had a good time. I did a mandolin thing and played some jams; just got spaced out and played every note I could think of... Keith Richards must have done a sponge job."

By 2018, and pushing seventy, Cooder was more sanguine, telling Bob Mehr: "I have learned the very hard way to shut up about that... It's not one of those things that matters to me, personally."

Throughout 1969, studio wariness and censorship concerns dogged *Performance*, which was not finally released in the States until 1970. Its UK opening, in early 1971, was intended to showcase Warner Bros.' new flagship cinema in Leicester Square. The poster boasted: "This film was 10 years ahead of its time. Now you're almost ready for... *Performance*."

For all the controversy and studio concerns surrounding the film and its soundtrack, it was the music that preoccupied Jagger and his fellow Stones during 1969, as the band edged further forward with their new album.

Unfortunately, running parallel to this were also major financial worries. Original manager Eric Easton had been unceremoniously booted out once the band were on the up, while a press release in September 1967 announced they were parting company with Andrew Loog Oldham – the consensus among the band being that he had abandoned them when the drug busts started. ("Basically, I lost my bottle," Oldham confirmed when he spoke to Jon Wilde. "Looking back, I'm glad I lost it. They wanted a Joan of Arc figure

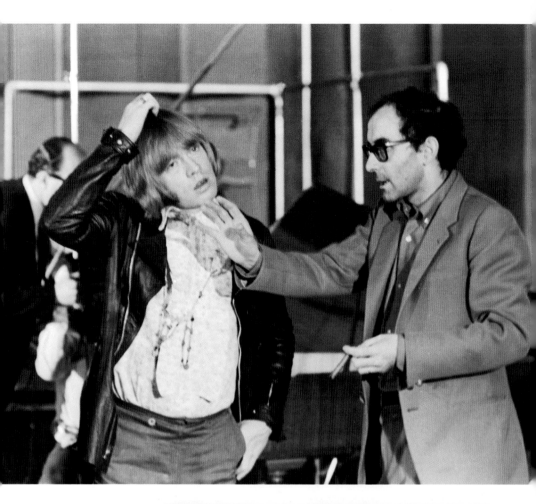

Above: Jean-Luc Godard (right) directs Brian Jones during the shooting of *One Plus One*, Olympic Sound Studios, London, July 30, 1968 [*Keystone Features/Hulton Archive/Getty*]; below: the Stones wait on set of *One Plus One* while Jean-Luc Godard talks to Mick Jagger, June 12, 1968 [*Larry Ellis/ Express/Getty*]

(Opposite page) above: Mick Jagger and Marianne Faithfull appear at the Marlborough Street Magistrates Court for possession of cannabis, May 29, 1969 [Topham Picturepoint/Press Association]; below: The Rolling Stones hold a photocall in Hyde Park to present Mick Taylor as the guitarist replacing Brian Jones, June 12, 1969, (l-r) Mick Jagger, Bill Wyman, Mick Taylor, Keith Richards and Charlie Watts [J. Wilds/Keystone/Getty]; (this page) above: Mick Taylor – the 'New Stone' – is introduced on the front page of *Melody Maker*, June 21, 1969 [TI Media Ltd]

Above: Tom Keylock releases the infamous butterflies onstage at Hyde Park, July 5, 1969 *[Mirrorpix];* below: the Met police and the Hells Angels 'police' converse at Hyde Park *[Mirrorpix];* (opposite page) crowds at the Serpentine join as many as 500,000 people to watch the Stones play Hyde Park *[Mirrorpix]*

(Opposite page) above: Mick Jagger, wearing his Mr Fish dress, and Keith Richards perform at Hyde Park, July 5, 1969 [Mirrorpix]; below: Tony Richardson, director of Ned Kelly, on set with Mick Jagger, Australia, July 1969 [Mirrorpix]; above: Brian Jones's house, Cotchford Farm in Sussex, and the location of his death on July 3, 1969 [Mirrorpix]; below: the front page of the Evening Standard the day Brian Jones was found dead [Evening Standard Ltd]

Above: fans pay their respects to Brian Jones at his funeral at St Mary's Parish Church, Cheltenham, July 10, 1969 *[Mirrorpix]*; below: Brian Jones's family, including his parents, Lewis and Louisa, at the funeral *[Michael Webb/Keystone/ Getty]*

and I wasn't prepared to go along with it… I had no intention of cramping my lifestyle by getting myself arrested.")

To further complicate matters, Easton was locked into a legal battle with the now-departed Oldham over publishing royalties, which saw the Stones' assets frozen. Mick, however, did manage to stump up £50,000 to purchase 48 Cheyne Walk, while Brian, Bill and Charlie had accrued enough postal orders, and were happily settled in manor houses.

Aside from former management woes, by 1969, the Stones were also in a financial quagmire with a stocky, belligerent guy from the Bronx. That man was Allen Klein, the American businessman and record executive known for his aggressive tactics.

Although still only in his mid-thirties, Allen Klein looked considerably older by the time he was manipulating the business affairs of the world's top rock bands, most notably The Beatles. He made no concession to the fluctuating youth fashions of the 1960s. Confrontational from the outset, Klein was nothing like the sort of businessman the likes of Lennon and Jagger would usually deal with.

Tenacious and challenging, Klein had studied accountancy, marvelling at the wool he could pull over everyone's eyes, and the rabbits he could produce from hats by merely studying ledgers, accounts and royalty statements. These were small but vitally important details that left the artists' heads swimming. But Klein was determined. And, when it came to business, he had no 'off' switch. Klein's speciality was approaching performers and – with a Svengali wave of his wand – announcing "I can get you a million dollars!" Grateful acts like Bobby Darin, Lloyd Price and Bobby Vinton looked on amazed as Klein magicked up unpaid royalties from reluctant record labels. Of them all, Klein loved and admired Sam Cooke most, and used him as a template for what a creative artist and an astute businessman could achieve together. Having conjuring up unimagined sums, Klein always felt a 50/50 split was fair.

As the British Invasion crossed the Atlantic, Klein soon found himself negotiating for groups like The Dave Clark Five, The Kinks and Herman's Hermits. All the while, though, the native New Yorker had his eyes fixed firmly on the two acts that swam on a sea of dollars: The Beatles and the Rolling Stones.

Klein first made contact with the Stones in the summer of 1965, wrestling a $1.5-million-plus deal from a shell shocked Sir Edward Lewis* at Decca Records. When he was on your side, Klein fought hard: he advised the band to wear dark glasses and say nothing while he harangued the gentleman executive. Klein also procured the services of a more dynamic booking agency to handle the Stones' US tours and increased royalties from future record sales.

But there was another side to the story. The late David Sandison worked for the Stones' PR Les Perrin between 1968 and 1970. In an unpublished memoir we were working on before his death, he wrote: "the flip side [...] was that the contracts [Klein] wrote up between you and him were tighter than a fish's sphincter. Klein had constructed a labyrinthine group of interlinked publishing and recording companies, bank accounts and accounting systems to take care of the band's international earnings. This meant that *everything* went through ABKCO,** his own holding company."

That was the problem. Believing that Klein could extract seven-figure sums from Decca on their behalf, the Stones were impressed. However, over the year, the band began to appreciate just how tightly Klein controlled them. He used the prohibitive British tax system as the carrot – back then, high earners like

---

* Sir Edward Lewis ran Decca Records for nearly five decades, until his death in 1980.

** Allen & Betty Klein and Company.

George Harrison, who wrote a song about it, fumed as the taxman took over 90 per cent of their income.

Now knowing of Jagger's legendary financial acuity, it is extraordinary to read the band's correspondence with their manager during this period. Here we see the Rolling Stones, the world's number two rock'n'roll band, wailing that electricity in their London office is about to be cut off. Even the normally sanguine Wyman and Watts are frustrated by the American. Transatlantic cables to Klein's New York office went unanswered.

By 1969, the band had become increasingly disenchanted with Klein and his skein of companies. Original manager Eric Easton had settled earlier, which left only Oldham, who was bought out for what Klein's biographer called "the greatest score of Klein's career". A seven-figure sum got the American "a 50 per cent royalty share in everything the Stones recorded up to early 1971, beginning with their first recordings and ending with two tracks on the album *Sticky Fingers*. In between, there were eleven studio albums and EPs, two live albums and numerous compilations."

Phil Kaufman, who worked with the Stones and was close to Gram Parsons, remembers Klein in action in 1969: "He was a little guy with a cigar. He was marching up and down, talking about the Stones and Apple. He delivered a great line. They were arguing about the decision-making process. He said: 'You know, Mick, there were four Beatles and there are only two Rolling Stones'!"

In the long run, Klein got the cream of the Rolling Stones. His companies effectively controlled the bulk of their best-known material. So over the decades, while all those Stones greatest hits compilations were on the market, they were most remarkable for what they did *not* include – basically, anything pre-1969 was Klein. ABKCO also retained three tracks from the *Sticky Fingers* era, too. But it was only in 2002, with the release of the double career-spanning album *Forty Licks*, that the band were able to feature songs from the Klein era in the 1960s alongside material cut for Rolling Stones Records during the 1970s. As the sleeve for that compilation delightedly noted: "For the first time ever! The definitive Rolling Stones Collection."

When Bill Wyman spoke to me about Klein, he explained: "He got us out of a bad deal, put us into a less bad deal... He really abused us, but he was a fool really, he didn't see the long-term view of the band... So he went in there and set it all up for himself, copped all the songwriting, publishing, masters, everything in the period that we knew him, from '65 to '69, probably thinking that was all the band was ever gonna do. He made millions out of us, but if he'd stayed honest and faithful and loyal and true, he could have made billions!"

In a letter to the late Ray Coleman (co-author of Bill's memoir, *Stone Alone*), Sam Cutler, the band's factotum of the time, explained how the Stones began to slip Klein's clutches: "Mick was on 'diplomatic sabbatical' brought on by chivalrous cowardice and someone had to tell Allen, and that someone was Keef... who arrived at the office looking terrible, and I happened to be there and accompanied him to the meeting.

"It was over VERY quickly. Klein said to me 'who the fuck are you?' Keith: 'Allen, we don't want to work with you anymore'. Klein (again to me) 'who the fuck are you?' Keith: 'He just works in the office, we don't want to work with you anymore, can you understand THAT?' Keith then went off to the bathroom to be sick... and that was that. Klein looked daggers at me, stormed into Jo [Bergman's*] office screaming that he wanted 'fucking Mick' to get in touch with him, and then left to sighs of relief all round."

Stone Alone includes pages and pages devoted to the band's inability to squeeze their money from their former manager. In

---

★   Jo Bergman was the Stone's personal assistant between 1967 and 1973.

those pre-fax days, and long before the internet revolution, transatlantic telephone calls were hideously expensive and had to be booked in advance. Telexes flew across the Atlantic with requests for cash for house purchases, record releases, album sleeves...

Klein's agreement with the Rolling Stones ended in May 1970. But he was quick off the mark, and issued a statement two months later: "This development will not alter the rights of ABKCO Industries under existing agreements, including the right to manufacture Rolling Stones records in the future."

With the tenacity of a succubus, Klein adhered to the bulging udders of the cash cow. In 1972, listening to *Exile On Main St.*, and recognising similarities in material cut on his watch, Klein obtained ABKCO publishing for five songs on the double album. In the rock'n'roll equivalent of the Hundred Years' War, Klein and the Stones duked it out over the next few decades. In 1975, a settlement was reached over the release of the *Metamorphosis* compilation. With the introduction of compact discs in the mid-1980s, further legal battles were waged until, finally, in 2002, the release of *Forty Licks* saw the band and Klein reach an understanding about material pre and post his involvement.

Unlike most of us, Allen Klein's dream had been realised: he had been to the mountaintop and secured the world's two biggest bands as clients. As the sixties ended, he turned his attention to The Beatles and the dog days of their Apple empire (a *Disc* headline in February 1969 read 'Stones £sd boss joins Beatles').

In her autobiography, Marianne refers to Klein setting his sights on The Beatles, citing Mick's "fairly diabolical" plan as part of the process: "He would fob Klein off on The Beatles... John, who was susceptible to utopian joint projects such as alliances between The Beatles and the Stones said 'Yeah, what a fucking brilliant idea'. It was a bit of a dirty trick, but once Mick had distracted Klein's attention by giving him bigger fish to fry, Mick could begin unravelling the Stones' ties to him."

It was Lennon who persuaded George and Ringo to side with him and Klein, thus isolating Paul, which effectively, and tragically, sealed the fate of the Fab Four.

There was obviously something about Allen Klein that went beyond the caricature 'Demon King', who "entered the Beatles' story as a villain from central casting and never escaped that role," as Peter Doggett wrote. "Yet we are asked to believe that three of the four Beatles found this 'beady-eyed', 'grossly overweight scorpion' such an attractive figure that they were prepared to trust him with their futures. Clearly the Demon King didn't always exude the stench of sulphur."

Indeed, mention Allen Klein today, and still the terrifying figure of John Belushi as the Rutles manager in 1978's *All You Need Is Cash* springs immediately to mind.

You can understand Klein's appeal to those musicians who lived in a vacuum of sybaritic hedonism and enhanced creativity. Their interest in the big type, let alone small print, was minimal. That's what the men in suits were for: to sit in their dingy little offices, in pressed pinstripes, poring over pages and pages of dry, legal *stuff*. They were there to advise, to steer and to subsidise the flamboyant behaviour of their clients. If you were a Beatle, a Rolling Stone, a Jimi Hendrix, or a Keith Moon, you didn't want to waste your precious time reading contracts. Carrots were dangled, promises made, but like the Eloi in H.G. Wells' *The Time Machine*, these idols' attention span was finite (it "was their lack of interest. They would come to me with eager cries of astonishment, like children, but like children they would soon stop examining me and wander away after some other toy").

In sharp contrast, Klein showed astonishing perseverance in pursuing what he wanted, and once he locked onto a target he never wandered, strayed or deviated. Business nous, chutzpah, determination, intimidation – like layers in a submarine sandwich from a New York deli, the American had it all: "Allen Klein could be the most charming and interesting person you'd ever met," his business associate Allan Steckler told Peter Doggett. "He loved music. And he could have been the most brilliant psychologist of all time, because in ten or fifteen minutes he could get you to do anything he wanted. But he could also be crude, rude and very uncaring. That's a strange mixture of qualities, but it was what made him a brilliant businessman."

Following Klein's death in 2009, Fred Goodman, in his exhaustive account of Klein's life and career,[*] wrote: "It was no surprise that the business didn't remember Klein warmly, but it was surprising that he seemed to hope it would. He was, after all, the hard-nosed realist who'd dismissed business ethics as a canard and whose calling card was the ability to out-think an opponent and then get under his skin. But doing that well is no prescription for popularity [...] Of course, pissing off the two most popular rock stars in the world, Paul McCartney and Mick Jagger, didn't help him either!"

As the Stones' star had risen, so had Klein's percentages, and the band, particularly former LSE student Mick, were looking for ways to loosen themselves from his grasp. It was the aesthete, art collector, antiquarian and former stockbroker Christopher Gibbs who had ushered Mick into the illustrious and glittering world of the demi-monde. And it had been Gibbs (who died in 2018) that suggested 'Beggars Banquet' might make a good LP title. It was also Christopher Gibbs who inadvertently extricated the Stones from their financial mire. He introduced Mick to an Old Etonian

---

[*] *Allen Klein: The Man Who Bailed Out The Beatles, Made The Stones, And Transformed Rock & Roll* (Mariner, 2016).

chum, Prince Rupert Loewenstein, at Jagger's London home during the summer of 1969. It was at a Chelsea party, the night before the Stones' Hyde Park concert, the rock'n'roll equivalent of the Duchess of Richmond's Ball on the eve of Waterloo. "They met at Cheyne Walk," Gibbs told Philip Norman, "and instantly got on well, even though Rupert knew nothing at all about pop music." But, for nearly the next 40 years, it was the Austrian aristocrat who steered the Stones' finances to unimagined heights.

In his memoir, Loewenstein admitted, "Rock and pop music was not something in which I was interested… rhythmic music with lyrics describing trite emotions." Mick, in turn, was scathing about that 2013 memoir. "Call me old-fashioned, but I don't think your ex-bank manager should be discussing your financial dealings and personal information in public. It just goes to show that well brought-up people don't always display good manners." Like most vintage rockers, Mick has gone on record for half a century, happily discussing sex and drugs but, as soon as the subject of hard cash comes up, the lips slam shut.

However, back in 1969, it was the prince who stepped in and saved the Stones' bacon. A thorough trawl through the band's finances during 1969 led Loewenstein to one simple conclusion: the Rolling Stones had effectively gone bust. They had to escape from their contract with Allen Klein, and they needed to land a lucrative new record deal. They also needed to consider moving outside the UK and becoming tax exiles, and they had to get some cash in the bank – pronto. Record royalties took too long to come in, and also sailed too close to Klein for comfort. For the Stones to start making serious money quickly, Loewenstein emphasised, they had to hit the lucrative US concert circuit.

Before then, though, in order to escape the pressure of their grown-up trials and tribulations, Mick, Keith and Marianne hoboed, in style, around South America, sailing from Lisbon to

Rio. And it was on this jaunt that Mick and Keith acquired the nickname that would stick to them for the rest of their career. "Give me a glimmer", a lively American passenger on their ship requested of the pair...

The trip was a long overdue opportunity to draw breath, to reflect and to create. "I read *Naked Lunch* when Mick and I first went to Brazil," Marianne told me, "and I was terribly impressed with that book, but I was too young to know the difference between being impressed by something and having to go out and do it."

Back in Europe, the trio spent time in Italy on the Amalfi Coast. For all the rakish hedonism, the Stones could still be diligent, and after that jaunt Mick and Keith came back with a sackful of songs. But there were still drug busts, wrangles with film censors, management hassles, financial anxieties and declining contributions from the band's founding member. The Rolling Stones needed a retreat, and there was just one place they felt they could escape it all.

CHAPTER 7

You Gotta Move

Located in a leafy south-west London suburb, nestled next to the Thames, Barnes has always exuded a quiet, rather smug prosperity. Today, branches of the exclusive Gail's bakery and Fired Earth shops populate Church Road, alongside the 12th-century church of St Mary's. This was the setting for Olympic Studios, the Rolling Stones' equivalent of Abbey Road Studios. Olympic was their sanctuary from the chaos that surrounded them.

But were the band to visit Olympic today, they would notice several major changes. The building was converted back into a cinema complex* in 2013, though they still retain a small recording studio. During a break between sessions, the Stones might feel impelled to take some of their unwanted stage costumes to the Princess Alice Hospice charity shop next door, or saunter along to the urban oasis of the London Wetland Centre. With time on his

---

* The building had started out life in 1906 as a theatre, housing the Barnes Repertory Company. For most of the early 20th century, it functioned as a cinema, before becoming a TV studio in the late 1950s and being purchased by Olympic Sound Studios in 1965.

hands, Keith could even pop into the nearby Barnes Scout Troop and see if there were any comrades from Beaver Patrol, Seventh Dartford Scouts, to reminisce with.

In later years, the Stones came to favour the Sunset Sound studio in Los Angeles, as well as Pathé-Marconi in Paris, Compass Point studios in the Bahamas, or even Keith's basement. But it was in that unremarkable building, in London SW13, in which was recorded the bulk of the material on which the Stones' greatness was built.

In the years since Olympic opened in 1965, it came to rival Abbey Road as the premier rock'n'roll studio. As such, as well as being the Stones' homebase, Olympic played host to The Who, Led Zeppelin and Jimi Hendrix. Even The Beatles used it to record the backing tracks for 'All You Need Is Love' and the entire track for 'Baby, You're A Rich Man'.

A studio can inspire or isolate you. It is where one goes to work and, if you are lucky, you capture lightning in a bottle. Or it can be a place where you launch a musical revolution.

The Decca Studios in Broadhurst Gardens, West Hampstead, where the Rolling Stones auditioned, is now the rehearsal space for, irony of ironies, the English National Opera. But if you gain access, you can slip down to Studio 1. A poky little space with room today for barely a pool table, it was here, at the end of a recording session on July 13, 1954, that a 20-minute burst from the banjo player for the Chris Barber Band launched just such a revolution. With time to spare at the end of a three-hour jazz session, Lonnie Donegan was happy to replicate the skiffle break the Barber Band took onstage. It was an opportunity for the brass players to take a break, to wander off for a smoke and a hit of lethal Merrydown cider. In the gap, Lonnie led those still onstage through the Lead Belly and Woody Guthrie songbook. To maximise the remaining studio time, one of the songs they cut at

Decca that summer afternoon was 'Rock Island Line'. "Yes, 'Rock Island Line', that was the one!", Chris Barber said, laughing when he told me. "Beryl Bryden on washboard, me on bass, Lonnie on guitar. Recorded at Broadhurst Gardens in July '54 – that's the one that launched a thousand ships!"

'Rock Island Line' was indeed the spark that lit the tinder. The record which, when released a few years later in 1956, marked the breech birth of British rock'n'roll. And all across the nation, teenagers latched on to Lonnie's homemade brand of skiffle: Lennon, McCartney, Van Morrison, Jimmy Page, Mark Knopfler, Pete Townshend, Hank Marvin, Brian May, Elton John, Bill Wyman, Mick Jagger, Keith Richards, and countless, nameless others.

When I started writing the first ever full-length biography of Lonnie Donegan, I spoke to a number of his disciples. Dartford Grammar School spawned the Bucktowns and the Sidewinders skiffle groups. Right before the Rolling Stones' 2003 European dates, Sir Mick Jagger reminisced about the skiffle era, telling me: "The first record I remember was 'Rock Island Line' in 1956... Compared to what else was around, there was something fresh and enthusiastic about Lonnie. I did play guitar in a skiffle group – but I can't remember their name! Skiffle was fun and easy to play, and the lyrics were different from the pop music of the day. Like lots of other kids, I went out and bought 'Rock Island Line' and 'Don't You Rock Me Daddy-O'... Keith and I were both skiffle fans from early on."

Bill Wyman also recalled "Mick trying to form a skiffle band – much later than I did, because he was younger – probably about '59, with a few mates from school. Keith wasn't involved with him then. Brian, in Cheltenham, was in a skiffle band called the Ramrods, and he was also in a couple of little jazz bands, playing saxophone. He was in and out of things, but he was aware of the skiffle thing. Charlie wasn't. Ronnie [Wood] was – he said he made his debut in the interval of a film at the local cinema, when he was nine, with his brother in this skiffle band."

However, recording studios are not all cut from the same cloth. Visiting Sun Studios in Memphis, you are first struck by its size; it's a tiny shoebox of a place, with 'X' literally marking the spot where Elvis Presley inadvertently invented rock'n'roll. Intriguingly, that historic session on July 5, 1954, which resulted in Elvis's debut, 'That's Alright Mama', took place just a week before Lonnie cut 'Rock Island Line'. More recently, it was to Sun that Bob Dylan came one day, knelt down and kissed the spot where Elvis had once stood, nodding to the studio guide and acknowledging, "Everyone's got a hero, man."

Coincidentally, I had been inside Abbey Road's Studio Two just the week before Dylan's visit to Sun Studios, for a press event. It is a cathedral of a space, intended for orchestral recordings until hijacked by The Beatles. That long staircase to the control room* and the coloured lights the Fabs had installed to give the place a bit more of an 'atmosphere' were both familiar to me from photos.

Elvis made the same lighting adjustments to RCA Studio B in Nashville when he recorded his Christmas album there. He also wanted to create 'atmosphere' where there was none. You see, recording studios don't have much atmosphere. They are factories. Rooms to record sound, pristine sound. Pretty much every studio has the same look: the walls are baffled, a Big Brother window overlooks your every move and the room exudes a dead sound. You are cut off from the outside world. Yet you are in a room where you can create your own world.

For the Stones, the worlds they conjured up within the walls of recording studios, including Olympic, were the flat vistas of the

---

* Mick Jagger once told me that his abiding memory of The Beatles recording at Abbey Road was sprinting up and down "that bloody staircase".

Delta or the smoky clubs of Chicago. Later, London streets and distant galaxies grew out of those studios.

So, as 1969 unfurled, the band knew they had to retreat to the security blanket of Olympic Studios. They also knew they had to nail this one. The band had laid the foundations for the future at the end of 1968 with 'You Can't Always Get What You Want', the first session of which was on November 16, 1968, with the choir being overdubbed four months later.

And thanks to Martin Elliott's exhaustive research on the Stones recording sessions, we can trace the evolution of *Let It Bleed* from the get-go. Work on the album proper began at Olympic on February 9, 1969 with the band routining 'Midnight Rambler'. The sessions concluded in Los Angeles seven months later.

★ ★ ★

Looking ahead, things really got cooking in early December 1969, while the band were fired up from their month-long American tour. And, with the paying dates complete, the Stones left their people to set up a free concert. The band then repaired to Muscle Shoals Sound Studio in Alabama to make several guerrilla recordings.

For such a small building, 3614 Jackson Highway has a surprisingly illustrious history. Located in Sheffield, Alabama, the former coffin showroom began life as a recording studio in 1969. But its complex history begins in nearby Florence, just across the Tennessee River. FAME (Florence Alabama Music Enterprises) Studios was opened by maverick songwriter, producer and entrepreneur Rick Hall. The first hit recorded there, in 1961, was 'You Better Move On', a song by Sheffield, Alabama native Arthur Alexander. So there's another Rolling Stones link right there (the band recorded the track for their January 1964 EP, *The Rolling Stones*), and Alexander cements his place in music history as one of the very few writers to have had his songs recorded by the Stones,

The Beatles *and* Bob Dylan. And as if that wasn't enough, Elvis heard Arthur's version of 'Burning Love' and decided to cut it himself!

I visited FAME in 2010, and it is a studio that deserves to be better known. Incredible photos of Bobbie Gentry, Aretha Franklin, Percy Sledge and Otis Redding line the walls, but best of all is Wilson Pickett sharing a joke with Rick Hall's favourite guitarist, Duane Allman, on the day they recorded 'Hey Jude'. A few hours later there were no more smiles: August 4, 1968 was the day Martin Luther King Jr. was assassinated in Memphis.

It was only while in Florence that I learned just how much of a fulcrum that tiny Alabama town was in the genesis of American popular music. Florence was not only the birthplace of Sam Phillips, who went across to Memphis, Sun Studios and rock'n'roll immortality, but W.C. Handy, 'the Father of the Blues', was also born there in 1873.

Handy was the son of a pastor who felt the draw of secular music, only to be told by his father: "I'd rather follow your coffin to the grave than see you as a musician." However, the pastor's son persevered, and it was while visiting Tutwiler, Mississippi in 1903, at a railway intersection "where the Southern cross the Dog", that he later remembered "a lean loose-jointed Negro had commenced plunking a guitar beside me while I slept... As he played, he pressed a knife on the strings of the guitar in a manner popularized by Hawaiian guitarists who used steel bars. The singer repeated the line three times, accompanying himself on the guitar with the weirdest music I had ever heard."

Handy remembered the music, and later wrote it down. He was the first man to document that 'weird' music, and baby, that was the blues. So there's another Rolling Stones link.

By 1969, the four session men Rick Hall had recruited for FAME were tiring of the pressure and routine, so 'the Swampers', as they were affectionately known, opened their own studio,

Muscle Shoals, at 3614 Jackson Highway. It was the Stones who gave the studio its legendary status, and in their wake came Rod Stewart, Cher, Art Garfunkel, Paul Simon, Bob Seger…

Along with *One Plus One*, the film of *Gimme Shelter* offers a rare fly-on-the-wall opportunity to see the Rolling Stones in excelsis, at work in the recording studio. With *Let It Bleed* nailed, the band were looking ahead. The Stones were, however, unable to record in the States. The band's work permits from the Department of Immigration were solely for performance; as soon as Los Angeles Local 47 of the American Federation of Musicians heard that Mick wanted to record at a press conference, sabres were drawn. There was even talk of deportation if any recordings occurred, which explained the undercover activities at the Shoals.

Phoning Chris Welch of *Melody Maker* from Los Angeles while on the US tour, Jagger put the blame elsewhere: "We're not allowed to record here because the English Musicians' Union won't let Americans record in England. We talked to the American Union about it and they say they don't mind us recording there, but they can't do anything, the English Union causes such problems."

Plans were also afoot for the Stones to do a bolt – away from Decca, away from Allen Klein and, finally, away from the UK, which gave the sessions an even more furtive element. It would also later give the Stones (in this case, Mick) an opportunity to sound out major labels to distribute their own Rolling Stones Records label output.

It was Atlantic Records' Jerry Wexler and Ahmet Ertegun* who had arranged for the band to record at Muscle Shoals. Rumour has

---

* Ahmet Ertegun maintained a good relationship with the Rolling Stones over the years. On October 29, 2006, Ertegun attended a Rolling Stones benefit concert at the Beacon Theatre for the Clinton Foundation, at which he fell over backstage, hitting his head on the concrete floor. Sadly, he never recovered from his injuries and died on December 14, 2006, age eighty-three.

it that Leon Russell tried to fix up several session dates in Los Angeles, but word got out, and fines were imposed. Stax Studios in Memphis would have been an obvious port of call – The Beatles had been keen to record there in 1966, but their security could not have been guaranteed. Wexler, Ertegun and the Stones was a dynamite combination: it was Wexler who had coined the phrase 'rhythm & blues', whose work with Ray Charles, The Drifters and Aretha Franklin was legendary. Wexler was a "snake charmer, old school record man … before you knew it, you had signed the napkin and given him your first born", according to pianist Jim Dickinson.

The urbane, jazz-mad Ertegun was particularly keen to court the Stones. He knew the problems they were having with Allen Klein, he knew they were keen to set up their own label and, while money would be the deciding factor, moving Rolling Stones Records under the umbrella of Atlantic would offer some kudos. Both Wexler and Ertegun made the journey south to the Shoals to talk turkey with the Stones.

Of the actual sessions, Bill Wyman told me: "We were on tour – you're on form, your chops are together, you're playing well together… so it's a good time to go in and do a few things. We did three days there and cut a track a day!"

Muscle Shoals gave the band an opportunity to work out the rambunctious 'Brown Sugar', destined to be the debut single on their own label in April 1971. They also cut the beautiful and haunting 'Wild Horses' and a cover of Mississippi Fred McDowell's 'You Gotta Move', both of which would wind up on 1971's *Sticky Fingers*. After endless hours of listening, a final take is apparently signified when Charlie stands up from behind his kit, and walks away.

A Rolling Stones recording session had little of the discipline of their peers. The band would bring in half-formed ideas and riffs and painfully work them up. A lot of patience was required as they felt their way to a satisfactory conclusion. Bill and Charlie would arrive on time then twiddle their thumbs until 'the talent' put in an appearance. Even then, it was a painstaking progress: if Keith had nailed a killer riff, Mick rarely had finished lyrics to hand. This wasn't necessarily down to the all-too-familiar 'distractions' of recording studios across the world during that period; in fact, visitors to the Stones' Olympic sessions recalled little evidence of drug use. There was, however, a lot of hanging round, with high-quality grub on offer (their session men were often amazed at the quality of the catering!).

There's a marvellous moment at Muscle Shoals, captured in the film *Gimme Shelter*, where Keith, lost in a reverie of sorts, listens to the playback of 'Wild Horses'. Director and documentary filmmaker Albert Maysles was particularly proud of capturing that "intangible thing". He told Rich Cohen: "I used to listen to classical music with my father. I'd look at him as he listened, and when the sound was right he looked just like… Keith… in those shots. It's the face of a person in the midst of satisfying a deep-down desire."

However out of it Keith might have seemed to some in the mixing sessions, recording engineer George Chkiantz, who was assisting Glyn Johns on *Let It Bleed*, told author Sean Egan: "I can remember Keith lying across the desk at Olympic, apparently asleep; [Mick] was going on about trying to get someone to play something or other. This one eye suddenly opened like a lizard and Keith said 'No' and suddenly it was all forgotten."

Happy with the results from Muscle Shoals, confidence restored through their negotiations with Ertegun and Wexler, buoyed from their American tour triumphs, it was from the banks of the Tennessee River ('the singing river', the Creek Indians called it) that the Rolling Stones made their fateful way to California.

CHAPTER 8

Something Is Happening

Throughout the early summer of 1969 the Stones soldiered on recording, but as the sessions proceeded it became ever more apparent that Brian Jones was just not cutting it. The musical muscle he used to supply had withered. Never a vocalist, perhaps due to his asthma, as the year progressed, Brian was further marginalised.

Other writers have speculated that it was the earlier knockout blow delivered by 1965's 'Satisfaction' (the Rolling Stones' first US number one) that cemented Brian's downfall. At that moment, he realised he could never compete with the Jagger/Richards axis. From then on, Brian was on the outside looking in. He never claimed a single songwriting credit in his six years in the Rolling Stones. "I've never known a guy with less talent for songwriting" was Mick's withering assessment.

I found Brian's situation within the Rolling Stones analogous to that of Art Garfunkel during the Simon & Garfunkel years. Talking to his authorised biographer Robert Hilburn in 2017, Simon reflected: "Even during Simon & Garfunkel, I realized that people thought Artie wrote the songs and I finally asked someone 'Why do you think he wrote the songs?' and they said 'Because he looks like he wrote songs!'"

As someone on the inside looking out, with a privileged closeness during those Stones glory years (she had, by her own admission, slept with three of the band's members), Marianne Faithfull's observations on the internal dynamics of that formative trio, which she revealed to me in Dublin in 1994, are worth quoting at length.

"I was never surprised when the Stones ended up as an alliance between Mick and Keith because they were the strongest. I think they were very competitive. They saw what The Beatles were doing and the three of them – Andrew, Mick and Keith – said to each other, 'Hey, they're writing songs and making a lot of money, we can do that.'

"Brian had an enormous effect on it all, but he never wrote an actual, real song. It was a technique he hadn't got together. If he hadn't been so fucked up he would have got there, but all those drugs aren't good for that side of your work."

Later, in her second volume of memoirs, Marianne amplified her thoughts: "Brian was unable to write songs. His perpetual… unhappiness and paranoia and low self-esteem all worked against him. It was tragic because he wanted to be a songwriter more than anything else. I've watched the painful process, Brian mumbling out a few words to a twelve-bar blues riff and then throwing his guitar down in frustration."

Or was it something else for Brian? Was that road to exile the first acid trip, which unbalanced his already frail personality? Or was it the subsequent, constant harassment by the drug squad? Or was it the incipient paranoia, which Bob Dylan observed on 'Ballad Of A Thin Man', his 'Mr Jones' cast as the permanent, uncomprehending outsider? Or was it when Keith snatched Brian's 'old lady' Anita Pallenberg on that fateful, post-bust trip to Morocco? Or did it simply go back to the time Mick and Keith were locked in a north London kitchen and not released until they had delivered an original song?

"Brian was just not tough enough," Keith Altham reflected. "He was always charming to me, a gentleman, a gentle man. But he knew I was a journalist. Everyone else hated him. Stu [Ian Stewart, founder and former member of the Stones] couldn't stand him."

Initially, *Melody Maker*'s Chris Welch got on well with Brian: "I remember going to get [him] to do a 'Blind Date'; this was a column where we got the pop stars to talk more seriously than telling readers about their favourite colours – we'd pitch topics like 'Vietnam', 'apartheid' to them. I went round to Brian's flat about nine one morning, and of course he wasn't up. But he was very gracious, he made me a cup of Earl Grey tea, very exotic!

"He was fine, then later on I was doing a feature on 'The Magnificent Seven' – the best guitarists (Eric, Beck, Townshend); drummers (Charlie, Ginger Baker) but I was struggling to come up with 'The Best Seven Rhythm Guitarists', I think I ran out of ideas after the bloke from The Hollies. So I rang Brian and he snapped 'I am not a rhythm guitarist', and slammed the phone down, which ended our friendship. I did see him at *The Rolling Stones Rock And Roll Circus* years later, looking very haggard. I went up and said 'Hello Brian', and he took one look, and ran away."

Only a month after appearing on the *Rock And Roll Circus*, in December 1968, Jethro Tull's Ian Anderson told *Record Mirror*'s Ian Middleton: "Although I'm a great admirer of the Stones, they're poor musicians. They played on their show and they were awful – they couldn't get it together at all... Brian Jones just can't play."

Facially flabby and by then musically inept, the man who had been the driving force behind the nation's second best band was, in the spring of 1969, about to be fired from the group he had founded. Even the steely-hearted Jagger and rambunctious Richards found a fearful irony in the act of separation.

To their credit, Mick and Keith, with Charlie along for ballast, did confront Brian face to face, on June 8, 1969. They drove to Cotchford Farm, the East Sussex property Brian had recently purchased. It had famously been the 13th-century home of Winnie the Pooh creator A.A. Milne. By all accounts, the meeting was relatively cordial, with Brian appreciating just how far the group had moved on from his original vision.

His ensuing statement was diplomatic: "I no longer see eye to eye with the others over the discs we are cutting. We no longer communicate musically... I have a desire to play my own brand of music rather than that of others, no matter how much I appreciate their musical concepts."

Soon after his dismissal, Brian was quoted in an interview with *Disc*: "We started playing authentic rhythm & blues and over a period of time our music progressed at a tangent as far as our separate tastes are concerned. I now feel I want to play my own music – while still appreciating the direction the rest of the group wants to go. It's an amicable split – whether temporary or permanent."

Surprisingly, Brian took his dismissal well, the blow softened by a one-off payment of £100,000, plus £20,000 per annum for as long as the Stones continued. If he could get in shape, perhaps Brian could conceive of himself as a backstage wizard, like the Beach Boys' Brian Wilson, or an *éminence grise*, like Pink Floyd's Syd Barrett, dismissed from the band *he* founded the year before for similarly wayward behaviour.

As the crow flies, Hartfield in East Sussex, where Brian spent the remaining months of his life, is barely 40 miles from London. In truth, it feels a lot further, a chocolate-box picture of a perfect English village, far removed from the fleshpots. Simon Wells knows the area well, and was kind enough to show me round one hot August day. As he pointed out, Hartfield would have had a population barely in excess of a hundred when Brian was living there, yet mustered four pubs!

Simon is convinced it was the increasing police persecution that made Brian seek sanctuary way out in the country. Away from the bright lights, he was less likely to feel the long arm of the law. Local legend has it that Brian was a regular visitor at village pubs like the Hay Wagon, and certainly photos of his bloated appearance towards the end of his life suggest a fondness for John Barleycorn over hard drugs.

It's unclear as to how Brian chanced upon the Milne property. Maybe, like so many rock stars of his generation, he felt his role was to play lord of the manor, and the purchase of a country property was as essential to that role as parading a model girlfriend.

In truth, Cotchford Farm is more a cottage than manor house, or even a farm. It is located at the end of a long lane, so if Brian wanted to visit the village hostelries he would have got there by motor scooter, before teetering back along the quaintly named Jib Jacks Hill and Chuck Hatch Lane. Rumours abound that Brian's outstanding three-figure tabs at local off-licences were posthumously settled by the Rolling Stones office.

The De La Warr family were the local landowners, a distinguished Norman family with close links to royalty, sparking another rumour: that in Brian's day, 'rebel royal' Princess Margaret was a regular visitor, and even enjoyed a tryst with the blond Stone!

Sixty years after A.A. Milne's death, and half a century after Brian's demise, Cotchford Farm is today a magnet for Pooh adherents and Stones conspiracy theorists.*

Brian's parents, Lewis and Louisa, had visited their only son a few weeks before his sacking, in May 1969, and only a few months before his premature death. They called it "the happiest and closest weekend we had spent with him since he was a child". Looking around the home of A.A. Milne, Lewis recalled Brian saying with a wry smile, "Well, I haven't done so bad, Dad, have I?" They never saw him again.

Musically, had he lived, Brian's plans were vague. He was impressed by the fiery electric blues of Johnny Winter and the rootsy rock'n'roll of Creedence Clearwater Revival, then just gaining popularity. He allegedly made contact with John Lennon, Jimi Hendrix's drummer Mitch Mitchell and John Mayall to discuss his musical future.

By all accounts, though, Brian was in poor shape towards the end of his life. In a *Crawdaddy* tribute to Brian a year on from his death, drummer David Montgomery recalled how he'd visited the ex-Stone around the time, with an eye to the drum stool in Brian's new band. However, "he was really smashed... couldn't complete a sentence. He kept giggling... he could barely talk."

One name from the past stood loyally by: Alexis Korner regularly visited Cotchford to advise and offer support. Alexis had fond memories of the blond blues enthusiast crashing on his floor when he couldn't make it back to Cheltenham from Ealing. He also had plans to include Brian in the lineup of his new group. To him, Brian "seemed happier than he had ever been... He talked a lot

---

*   On our way to the Hundred Acre Wood, I was amused to see a sign to the Pooh car park. Out of those making their pilgrimage to the village, Simon tells me that the locals prefer Brian's respectful fans – the Winnie the Pooh lot are far worse behaved!

about the old days." However, the veteran bluesman appreciated that Brian had to get himself together: "He looked like a fat, mummified Louis XIV."

Brian's sudden death on July 3, 1969 – when he was just twenty-seven years old – was front-page news around the world. And, given that it occurred under mysterious circumstances, his passing inevitably left the door open to all manner of speculation and conspiratorial assumptions.

For one, the *Evening Standard*, referring to the fact that Brian had suffered with asthma since childhood, carried an intriguing article on 'Asthma Aid Theory In Jones' Death'. It reported, "the increased used of inhalants for an alarming rise in the number of deaths among asthmatics... In 1966, it was 15 deaths per 100,000 sufferers, compared with only five in 1912." It carried on with a comment from an expert at the Wright-Fleming Institute, which monitored London's pollen count on the cause of Brian's death: "He would have been better off in London. Pollen in Sussex is possibly twice as high." Like Nico fatally falling off her bike, or Jim Morrison drowning in his bath, the death of a rock idol demands more than such a mundane cause. And there appears almost as many theories surrounding Brian's death as those generated nearly six years earlier on that bloody day in Dallas.

With the principal characters all now gone, no one will ever be able to say for certain what exactly happened on that long-ago, drowsy summer night in the heart of the Sussex countryside. Did Brian suffer from an epileptic seizure? Was it an asthma attack? Was it a willful suicide – maybe Brian surmised that, without the Stones, he had no future? Was there a party that 'got out of hand'? Did hijinks lead to Brian's drowning in the swimming pool at his home while under the influence of drugs and alcohol? Did shadowy Mafia types, watching from nearby, have a hand in his demise? Was Brian's 'Grassy Knoll' a builder, jealous of Brian's lavish lifestyle?

In his comprehensive 2014 biography,* Paul Trynka lists 11 possible causes for Brian's untimely death. But in the end, he concludes that death by drowning is the most probable: "As flawed and cursory as the original verdict is, compared to the complexity of most conspiracy theories, this remains the most likely scenario... I believe that Brian's death was most likely a sad accident." Thus, the original coroner's verdict of "death by misadventure" still stands.

Although estranged by the time of Brian's death, leafing through a copy years later of Michael Cooper's collection of photographs from the sixties, *Blinds & Shutters*, Anita Pallenberg was quoted as saying: "The reason he died when he did was that there was no one around who knew what to do when he was starting to overdose and suffering from his asthmatic condition at the same time. He had been in that condition many times before, but there had always been people around to turn him on his side and take care of him."

Following the Stones' Hyde Park gig (more on that later), the *Melody Maker* letters page was full of tributes to Brian – "Thank you... Mick Jagger for your beautiful poem in Hyde Park. God bless Brian, may he rest in peace" – Margaret Adams. "Brian Jones has taken with him the last of the atmosphere of the old Thames-side rhythm and blues. Goodbye Brian" – Laura Hill.

Poignantly, Brian's parents outlived their son – Lewis died in 2009 and Louisa in 2011. Neither spoke in any detail of Brian in public, save for an uncomfortable encounter with Stanley Booth

---

* *Sympathy For The Devil: The Birth Of The Rolling Stones And The Death Of Brian Jones* by Paul Trynka (Bantam Press, 2014).

in Cheltenham, recounted in his *True Adventures Of The Rolling Stones* book.*

Hard-hearted admirers say that Brian's death was the best thing that could have happened to him. To have lived in the shadow of the group he had founded as they soared from triumph to triumph, while he lived off their stipend, would have been debasing and embarrassing. Yet, so much a part of the fabric of the band's history, and with a perverse determination of millions of fans and conspiracy theorists alike to insist there remains more to the circumstances of his death, Brian Jones is unable to be left alone.

In 2005, Stephen Woolley's film *Stoned* was a lamentable stab at unravelling the last months of Brian's life. Unfortunately, actor Leo Gregory lacked the necessary charisma to play Brian, the low budget allowed for no Stones music, and the normally reliable David Morrissey (as Tom Keylock, the band's former chauffeur) looked and sounded like he was a stand-in for Michael Caine. Luca Guadagnino's 2015 rock'n'roll thriller *A Bigger Splash*, with a script by David Kajganich, was equally flawed, though saved by Ralph Fiennes' larger-than-life performance. The fact that the Stones themselves were in consultation with the filmmakers makes it worth a view for anyone with more than a passing interest in sex, drugs and swimming pools.

It is fascinating to speculate a future if Brian had lived. On the back of the UK blues boom, would he have reconnected with his roots? Could he have found success with a British band modelled on the chooglin' sound of Creedence Clearwater Revival? But then Creedence were blessed with the songwriting arsenal of John Fogerty, the one inconsolably deficient musical area of Brian's life.

---

* First published in 1989 by Sphere.

Perhaps if he had managed to clean up his act, Brian could have gone back to his roots. We can playfully imagine fans trickling along to Putney's Half Moon, Harlesden's Mean Fiddler or Barnes' Bulls Head sometime in the post-punk 1970s to see 'The Brian Jones Blues Band', grey heads nodding as the blond produced a blizzard of bottleneck blues. Maybe he would have been happy playing his beloved blues to the small, but equally devoted, audiences in the sort of venues that begat the Stones. In celebration of the band's 50th anniversary, Brian would certainly have been a guest at the Stones' well-received 2012 shows at London's O2 Arena. A mighty cheer would no doubt have greeted the tiny figure, face likely hidden under a hat to mask the blond locks, gone with the wind. Howls of delight at a dazzling display of harmonica virtuosity... sliding through 'Little Red Rooster'... bringing his own musical colourings to 'Ruby Tuesday' or 'Lady Jane'.

That, however, is a diversion, mere fruitless speculation.

"In a way, if he'd lived another 20 years he'd have got worse," Charlie told Rob Chapman for a *Mojo* feature on the 30th anniversary of Brian's death. "He'd have been shuffling down the King's Road, a shadow of his former self. It's better how he went when he did. 'Cos we wouldn't be doing this article if he hadn't."

In the half-century since his death, Brian's bandmates have spoken critically of him ("a very sad, pitiable figure at the end..." "a prick..." "an arsehole..." "a pain in the arse..."). Certainly Jones' blithe indifference to his illegitimate children, and his well-chronicled willingness to lash out at his girlfriends, makes for uncomfortable reading today. His ability to play the nice guy to the press while being a complete drain on his bandmates does not make for sympathetic appreciation.

But for all his many faults, Brian Jones started the Rolling Stones. He pushed, steered and cajoled the unwilling Edith Grove layabouts into a functioning unit. It was Brian's appreciation of, and fondness for, the obscure R&B and American blues that made the nascent Stones stand out. He bombarded the limited media and broadcast outlets of the period to get the Stones a platform, in print and on air. In the end, however, he was too weak, personally and professionally, to sustain that momentum. For many, the best way to remember the frail, conflicted Brian Jones is in the quatrain that appears on the sleeve of *Through The Past Darkly*, the Rolling Stones LP that stood as his epitaph: "When this you see, remember me, and bear me in your mind. Let all the world say what they may, speak of me as you find."

I was drawn to the work of the man who made Cotchford Farm famous, and where he created some of the best-loved children's literature of all time. They may have not worn well with the passing years, but Winnie the Pooh and Christopher Robin were a worldwide phenomenon when first published in 1926. Bloodied and bowed by a world war, the survivors sought sanctuary in the Hundred Acre Wood, in the innocent diversions of Poohsticks at Pooh Bridge, and the search for Woozles. Those stories were written over 40 years before Brian Jones bought A.A. Milne's property, but it is the final story in the last book, *The House At Pooh Corner*, that brings to mind the last time any of the Rolling Stones ever saw Brian, on a Sunday afternoon in June. It could have been, as Milne wrote, an awkward meeting "because it was a sort of good-bye", each standing around waiting for somebody to speak, nudging each other. Then Mick, Charlie and Keith laid out the news, and the terms of separation. They departed, leaving Brian to muse on his future…

Pooh had also been left musing on how to do nothing. Christopher Robin helpfully advised that when you really have nothing to do, you just go and do it. Brian never lived to do nothing. Less than a month after he was dismissed, Brian Jones was dead.

CHAPTER 9

The Stones In The Park

The Stones were in lockdown at Olympic Studios the night of July 3, 1969. The new single was in the can and on its way to the shops; the sessions for *Let It Bleed* were proceeding satisfactorily. The band were recording a cover of Stevie Wonder's 'I Don't Know Why', later to appear on the 1975 compilation, *Metamorphosis*.

However much grief Brian had put the band through, the Stones were shell-shocked when the late-night call came through, almost certainly from Les Perrin. This was the first casualty of the band's inner circle – many more were to follow, but the death of Brian Jones was a line in the sand.

Producer Jimmy Miller remembers the band's reaction on hearing the news: "I had lost the mood for work, but Mick and Keith said 'No, let's finish it.' I was surprised how they took it. I guess, in the tradition of show business, the show must go on."

Journalist Keith Altham was at Olympic that fateful night – he often used to drop by Barnes after a night in town. He was up in the control room observing the Stones at work below:

"I remember Tom Keylock came in at 12, midnight, and they went into a huddle in the studio. It was obvious something was up, and I stayed in the control room just watching. I'm pretty sure it was Marianne who came in, she was in tears, and told me.

"Keith cornered me and told me not to write about it, as the family hadn't been told... The journalist in me was seething, the scoop of a lifetime, but I couldn't, wouldn't, break my promise. Mick was angry. I remember him saying, 'It goes on.' Whether that was the band, or the Hyde Park show, but he was emphatic: '*It goes on!*'"

When the initial grieving was done, the most pressing problem was how to proceed. The Stones were locked into a free concert in Hyde Park the following Saturday, only two days after Brian's death. It was Charlie who suggested the concert should go ahead, not as a triumphant return but as a memorial to Brian.

The band needed to be seen. Their 1966 UK tour had been marked by the mob hysteria that greeted every show, with screaming girls rushing the stage. A series of 1967 European dates kept them in trim amid court appearances, but those were off the beaten path – shows in Malmo, Milan and Cologne buttered no parsnips. The Rolling Stones' only live appearance since then had been a surprise show at the 1968 *NME* Poll Winners' concert at Wembley, on May 12. "You could feel the Empire Pool shaking to its foundations as the roar went up," the *NME* reported. "So who says today's pop lacks excitement? For my money, all we need is the Rolling Stones back as they were on Sunday." As if their appearance wasn't excitement enough, Mick accepted a trophy for Best R&B Group from none other than 'the Saint, Roger Moore'! During the show, the group previewed 'Jumpin' Jack Flash' and delighted with 'Satisfaction'. The occasion marked Brian's last ever concert with the Rolling Stones.

So, with the *Rock And Roll Circus* now shelved, but a strong new single on the racks, and with the Jagger radar as acute as ever, a free concert was on the cards and Hyde Park was the obvious location. Permission had to be obtained from the Ministry of Public Buildings and Works, but with it in place, the Royal Park was selected as the right venue for the Rolling Stones' return to Eden.

Set in the heart of London, Hyde Park has always attracted its fair share of rebels, nonconformists and ne'er-do-wells. It was once a popular location for duelling, while at the top end of the park, by Marble Arch, is Tyburn Tree, where, up until 1783, public executions took place. London's first nude statue, of Achilles, was unveiled near Hyde Park Corner in 1822. Hard by Park Lane is Speaker's Corner, where anyone on a soapbox can hold forth on any subject, outside of anything treasonable, libellous or encouraging rioting. At the other end of the park is the best address in the country – the Duke of Wellington's Apsley House, or 'No. 1, London'. In September 1969, the London Street Commune began what remains the capital's best-remembered squat. The empty property at 144 Piccadilly (right opposite Apsley House) was taken over by squatters before it was eventually demolished and replaced by an anonymous hotel. Number 145 Piccadilly, the childhood home of Queen Elizabeth II, also crumbled under the demolition ball.

However, not since the Crystal Palace was erected for the Great Exhibition of 1851 had Hyde Park witnessed anything quite like the free festival that occurred there on July 5, 1969.

In fact, free rock concerts in Hyde Park weren't a new thing. They began in the summer of 1968: June 29 found Pink Floyd, Tyrannosaurus Rex, Roy Harper and Jethro Tull taking to the stage. On July 27, Traffic, The Nice and Pretty Things appeared. And finally for the year, on September 28, The Move headlined over Pete Brown & His Battered Ornaments, Roy Harper and Clouds. But the one that really did it took place the following summer, on June 7, 1969. That first Hyde Park free show of 1969 marked the debut of supergroup Blind Faith, and Jagger, on a recce to confirm whether or not the park would be the ideal forum for the Rolling Stones to reconnect with their audience, was in attendance.

Cream had split earlier in the year, largely due to the negative press that Eric Clapton's bluesy guitar had generated – *Rolling Stone* magazine's cutting "master of the blues cliché" really stung. Also, Clapton had become enchanted by the back-to-roots approach The Band had ushered in with their debut album, 1968's critically acclaimed *Music From Big Pink*. He wanted his new post-Cream outfit to be tighter and less reliant on those clichéd solos. Steve Winwood was simpatico; Ric Grech was brought in from Family on bass, and the trio rehearsed at Winwood's Berkshire cottage. With that funkier edge in mind, Clapton had in mind perhaps Booker's T.'s Al Jackson for drums, or Winwood's Traffic colleague Jim Capaldi. In the event, Cream's Ginger Baker steamrollered in, and Blind Faith were inevitably doomed from the start to become a pale shadow of the very band Clapton was desperate to move on from.

In fact, that June 1969 Hyde Park show marked Blind Faith's only UK date; rushed off to the lucrative American concert circuit, Clapton grew more enamoured of the supergroup's opening act, Delaney & Bonnie, which led to the next step on his musical odyssey, the formation of the 'anonymous' Derek & the Dominos.

In the event, it was the crowd of 100,000 drawn to Blind Faith's free gig that impressed Mick Jagger more than the music on offer. In recognition, though, of Mick's attendance, the group did include 'Under My Thumb' in their set.

Even peers of the realm were impressed by the enormous crowd's behaviour at the Blind Faith show. The House of Lords debated 'Sleep-in after pop concert' on June 25, 1969. The Conservative Lord Derwent asked if it "was in accordance with the Government's policy to allow entertainments in the Royal Parks which attracted audiences of 70,000 to the detriment of the usual amenities and the peaceful enjoyment of the parks by other citizens?" Lady Llewelyn-Davies replied for the Labour government, "Royal parks are preserved as places where the public can enjoy relaxation and recreation. It has always been customary to allow a very limited number of events with special appeal and these… summer concerts of popular music have been arranged as an experiment. The crowd attracted by these concerts are a measure of their popularity, especially with young people. The behaviour of the audiences has been admirable."

Thus, once the Stones confirmed they would be continuing with their own Hyde Park concert following Brian's death, the music press went into speculative overdrive. The news that the band were rehearsing at The Beatles' Apple HQ led to *NME* breathlessly enquiring 'Beatles In Five-Hour Stones Show?' "There is speculation that the two groups may be planning a sensational 'super-supergroup' appearance in Hyde Park…"

One minor, but nonetheless intriguing mystery remains about that rehearsal location. The Rolling Stones had their own rehearsal space, in the iconic location of Crucifix Lane, SE1, between Tower Bridge and London Bridge. A number of bands, including Procol Harum and The Faces, used the space, so why not the owners, to prepare for their most prestigious gig yet? In their June 21 issue, *Melody Maker* teased that the Stones may not be "actually re-visiting Ken Colyer's Club for Sunday afternoon blues sessions, but by the ghost of Cyril Davies, we can expect a free concert somewhere not one thousand miles from London fairly soon!"

The Rolling Stones' return to live performance was news. The prospect of thousands – probably tens of thousands – of hippies gathering in a Royal Park proved too strong a temptation for the 'straight' television companies. Jagger was happy that a television documentary should defray the costs of the free event. Peter Jenner of Blackhill Enterprises, the company behind the Hyde Park free shows, recalled Granada TV paying to build a higher stage for better television coverage when the Stones announced the show. There's also a lovely letter from Blackhill to Granada on July 21, a fortnight after the show, with a breakdown of costs. These included £10 for the hire of the ambulance that took the Stones to the stage, a whopping £60 for the band's "miscellaneous expenses (food, flowers, taxis, etc.)" and 400 copies of 'Honky Tonk Women', at a cost of £100, for those audience members who stayed behind to help with the clean-up.

Blackhill's costs for mounting the Stones in the Park came to £2,025, and that also paid for the release of several hundred cabbage white butterflies from the stage (£420). According to documents in the late Richard Havers' book, *The Rolling Stones: On Air In The Sixties*, there were 15 lavatories and 10,000 plastic bags (£200). Apart from how ramshackle the Stones sounded, certain memories remain seared into the public memory – Mick's white tunic-dress (£89 from Mr Fish, and originally intended for Sammy Davis Jr.); the reading from Shelley's 'Adonais' to commemorate Brian ("Peace, peace! He is not dead, he doth not sleep/ He hath awakened from the dream of life...") and the aforementioned butterflies (not dead, just resting, and very cold).*

---

* The original plan had been to unleash a flight of brightly coloured parakeets, but the birds had – perhaps luckily for them – proved unavailable. In the case of the cabbage white butterflies, Thomas Frankland, Chairman of the British Butterfly Conservation Society, was disgusted by the turnout. In a letter to *The Times*, he complained of a "trivial gimmick in terms of entertainment and for such a

Equally significant, the Hyde Park show would offer up a preview of the band's latest single, 'Honky Tonk Women', and a taste of the 'new' Rolling Stones, with Brian's replacement guitarist Mick Taylor scheduled to appear for the first time with the group. "Keith says it was my baptism of fire," Taylor reflected when he spoke to music critic Andrew Perry, "but I like to call it my baptism by butterflies."

The show would now, of course, act mainly as a tribute to the memory of Brian Jones. Talking to Granada TV in the lead-up to Hyde Park, and referring to The Band's cover of Lefty Frizzell's 'Long Black Veil', Mick said: "I don't believe in Western bereavement. You know, I can't suddenly put on a long black veil and walk the hills... I want to make it so that Brian's send-off from the world is filled with as much happiness as possible."

The promised spectacle was just too much to resists for fans that had waited over two years for a live outing from their rock heroes. From late on July 4, the faithful began flocking to Hyde Park to light candles for Brian.

By the time the Stones hit the stage the next day, the crowd was estimated at somewhere between 250,000 and 500,000 people – the largest crowd assembled in London since the coronation of Queen Elizabeth II in 1953. ("They were the stars of the show," Keith later marvelled, "like some massive religious gathering on the shores of the Ganges.")

Skinheads, so familiar in the London of the late sixties and early seventies, hovered on the outskirts of the hippie audience. Trouble was anticipated, especially when the Hare Krishna mob chanted their way up from Oxford Street, but the skins, in the end, were overwhelmed by the size of the crowd. They pranced around the

---

meaningless purpose in terms of conservation. I trust Mr Jagger will redeem himself by offering to buy as many again and entrust them to my society so that they can be released throughout Britain."

Krishnas, sang a few verses of 'Knees Up Mother Brown', and drifted off. Future *Uncut* Editor Allan Jones: "There was a marked absence of drunken loutishness... since there was nowhere to buy booze. In fact, there was nowhere to buy anything. There were no facilities at all, including toilets, which I strangely don't remember being a problem."

Sam Cutler was a key figure in the Stones' camp during that tumultuous year of 1969. The same age as the band and originally trained as a teacher, he fell into rock'n'roll by stage managing events at London's Roundhouse and Lyceum, before going on to work for Blackhill Enterprises as "tour manager, booking agent, tea boy, general factotum etc.". Hyde Park was his first gig with the Rolling Stones. In a letter to Ray Coleman, who was working with Bill Wyman on his autobiography, Cutler wrote that "everyone else was too busy working on the Floyd, whom Blackhill were managing and who were HUGE at the time, so the Hyde Park thing fell to me."

The job of introducing the acts onstage also fell to Cutler, the concert bill being very much representative of the contemporary underground scene. The Third Ear Band opened, while King Crimson, after only five months together, went on to dazzle with their imaginative use of Mellotrons. Screw were "a semi underground pop band", who played "as though they were disappearing through a meatgrinder". Alexis Korner's New Church and the ubiquitous Roy Harper were both followed by The Battered Ornaments (Pete Brown had been fired from the band the day before).

The Rolling Stones took to the stage around 5.30 p.m. As well as Jagger's poetic memorial to Brian that Saturday afternoon, onstage was a huge poster, actually a 28-foot-wide and 7-foot-tall reproduction of the inner sleeve of *Beggars Banquet*, with a smiling Brian Jones occupying stage right.

Sadly, for many the abiding memory of that historic set is just how *bad* the Stones sounded. Apparently, tuning the guitars in an air-conditioned caravan beforehand was bad practice when facing the blistering summer heat – as soon as the band hit the stage, the tunings went to pot. "We played pretty bad," Keith remembered a couple of years later, "'Cause we hadn't played for years..." before adding, "Nobody minded, 'cause they just wanted to hear us play again." *Oz* editor Richard Neville confirmed the response: "The group seemed a musical mess – all awkward endings and misplaced cues."

As a live band, the Rolling Stones were always on the edge, a freewheeling gang, welded down by Bill, Charlie and subsequently Mick Taylor. Jagger could always cavort with the best of 'em. And that allowed Keith free rein over those riffs. On a good night, it was that imperial sloppiness, that vaunted arrogance, which made the Stones so compelling. On an off night, you really wondered if you wouldn't have been better off spending your hard-earned cash on a Rolling Stones tribute act.

"Yeah, sometimes we're sloppy," Keith told journalist David McGee years later. "Who isn't? There is a certain amount of unstructuredness about the Stones... We're not the kind of band that goes 'one, two, three, four', you know, and segues into another number. You can't make an SS regiment out of the Stones."

The band's opening number that brilliantly sunny afternoon was a quirky choice, a Johnny Winter song 'I'm Yours And I'm Hers', chosen, apparently, because it was Brian's favourite song at the time of his death. The remainder of the 13-song set, pumped out through a meagre 1,500-watt sound system, featured a cumbersome 'Satisfaction'. The set then drew heavily from *Beggars Banquet*, before the band previewed their new single and part of their work in progress, *Let It Bleed* ('Love In Vain'; 'Midnight

Rambler'). 'Loving Cup' even made an appearance, a track that wasn't released until *Exile On Main St.*, three years later.

Gaining confidence on 'Street Fighting Man', the set concluded with a spirited 'Sympathy For The Devil'. To help Charlie out, Ginger Johnson & His African Messengers came pounding along. That 'Stones sloppiness' was apparent in the performance. "We were dragging. We were off form," Bill Wyman later wrote. "Mick whined at us, 'Tempo! Get the tempo together.' We were not at our best." Of course, the band's apparent awfulness is preserved now on YouTube for all time, for all to see.

In the *Melody Maker* review, Chris Welch called the concert "a nostalgic, out-of-tune ritual that summed up a decade of pop". Talking to Chris half a century after the show, he still remembered it as dreadful: "By that time, bigger, louder music was required – in 1963, The Shadows were louder than the Rolling Stones! By 1969 though, the Stones sounded a lot more ragged. I preferred their original sound, more organised, less leaving it to chance. The Who, in contrast, were beautifully constructed. At Hyde Park, the Stones were struggling to prove themselves.

"There was a sense of anticipation, especially following Brian's death, then on they came, these ragged street urchins. The high drama of Brian's death only a day or so before, and I have to say, I thought Mick was quite courageous to do what he did, reading that poem, in that dress..."*

On the day, though, the summer sun shining through the trees, the calm vibe of hippies relaxing in a Royal Park, the event appeared as timeless as the horses cantering along Rotten Row, as

---

* When the Stones returned to play Hyde Park in 2013 (this time with ticket prices, before they hit the internet, costing between £95 and £300), Mick joked: "I'll try and keep the poetry to a minimum."

calming as the boats on the Serpentine. For the hundreds of thousands in attendance, just hearing the Rolling Stones play was enough.

Geoff Brown, now a well-known writer but in 1969 a fan attending the gig, wanted to be there because "here was a chance to catch them at the end of the decade that had been theirs, that had become ours too... Whenever I hear 'Sympathy For The Devil' I think, in a madeleine moment, of toes splashing in the Serpentine."

Another fan, Helen Lock: "So many of the songs were new to us... We didn't know 'Sympathy For The Devil', but I remember everybody picking up cans and bottles and playing percussion on them, and some people had actually bought tambourines and were playing them."

For writer Lloyd Bradley: "the damndest thing we saw was our German teacher... with a 'chick'... A confirmed grown-up, even though he was probably only about 25, doing a bit of a dance at a pop concert. It's a good thing he had his sports jacket over his arm otherwise nothing would have made sense any more."

Talking to my old friend Bruce Hawkins, I asked him for his memories of the free gig. "Well I went, but I left before the Stones came on." I recoiled, like a Bateman cartoon, at 'The Man Who Went To Hyde Park But Did Not See The Rolling Stones'! "Well," said Bruce, "I had a ticket to see Chuck Berry and The Who at the Albert Hall."

In fact, a number of the Hyde Park crowd decamped to the Albert Hall, too – including Mick Jagger. There were two sets, an afternoon one at 5.30 p.m. and an evening one at 8.30 p.m. Billing arguments ensued about who was to headline, with Chuck eventually agreeing to open the late show, much to the loud disapproval of the rockers and Hells Angels who had also made the journey across to see Berry. For having the temerity to let Chuck

Berry open for them, The Who had beer cans, sharpened pennies and other detritus hurled at them once they appeared onstage.

However, among those who managed to resist the Albert Hall show and who *did* see the Stones perform in Hyde Park were – in the laughably accessible VIP enclosure – Paul and Linda McCartney, actress Marsha Hunt, Donovan, Steve Winwood, Ginger Baker, author Germaine Greer, jazz musician Chris Barber, Mama Cass, David Gilmour and Eric Clapton. MC Sam Cutler's concern for overcrowding in the enclosure acts as a reminder of the attitudes of the time: "There ain't enough room for everyone, so chicks will have to leave!"*

At Cutler's request, Jagger's simultaneous squeeze, Marsha Hunt, grumpily led the exodus of the chicks. Marianne, however, was in an elevated position – she watched from stage left. Oh, and if you still don't think things have moved on over the past half-century, a few months before the Stones Hyde Park show, one weekly was offering a two-page '*Record Mirror* Bird Special!', while the month after, under the headline 'The Many Faces Of Pop', the *Evening Standard* pictured the singer with the caption: "Marsha Hunt, the prettiest golliwog in London."

Outside the VIP section, the backstage medic that day was Samuel Hutt, later known by his stage name Hank Wangford, the English country and western songwriter. In the audience, a besuited young Gilbert & George moved around. I vaguely remember reading a young Irish actor called Pierce Brosnan was there, and I'm pretty sure mega-Stones fan Bill Nighy would have made the trip up from Croydon.

---

* This sort of behaviour was typical of the male chauvinism rampant at the time. The following summer, *Oz* magazine editor Richard Neville published his cultural commentary *Play Power*, which sagely advised: "The way to a girl's mind is through her cunt."

But one young music man was very much not in attendance. In the *Melody Maker*'s 'Pop Think-In' a few weeks later, Bee Gee Robin Gibb came out as strongly against the Hyde Park event: "I don't believe in concerts such as the Rolling Stones had because I think they attract undesirables who always seem to provoke trouble."

Five months later, almost to the day, his words became eerily prescient.

★ ★ ★

Viewing Granada TV's *The Stones In The Park* again is fascinating. Given all that followed, I had forgotten the very Englishness of the event. However, the film suffers from all the usual faults of 'rock on TV' from that period: there are headache-inducing quick cuts and zooms, shots that linger over willowy blondes, the fascination with idiot(s) dancing. And all for a total of £9,000.

However, say 'Stones in the Park' to any music fan, and for many of them the abiding image will be of Mick in *that* dress. Even by the Bohemian standards of Swinging London, and even for someone at the forefront of fashion, a dress was perhaps a Ginger Rogers step too far. Any Greeks in the audience would have been delighted to recognise the style, which was modelled on the uniform of the Greek Army's light infantry unit the Evzones, who today guard the royal palace in Athens!

But then, when it came to fashion, style, call it what you will, Mick Jagger was always leading from the front. The pop groups of the 1960s were allied with the models, actors, photographers and fashion pioneers who helped establish London as the place to be during the sixties. Prior to then, well-brought-up young men like Michael Philip would, like as not, have acquired their first suits from high-street stores such as Burton's, Hepworth's or John Collier. However, after the pop music explosion, which coincided with the rise in outlets that catered for these clothes horses, Jagger was no stranger to the best London boutiques, including Mr Fish, Hung On You, I Was Lord Kitchener's Valet and Granny Takes A Trip, located in that wonderfully named Chelsea outpost the Worlds End. All were vying to be more achingly trendy, extremely fashionable and fashionably extreme. In 1970, the *Evening Standard* created the first ever weekly newspaper column devoted to men's fashion and grooming.

When I was ill as a child, with no afternoon TV and precious few distractions for a bed-bound teenager during that pre-internet era, my mum did everything she could to cheer me up. She'd read about the boutique Hung On You. Their USP was to create any fashion accessory a rock star demanded, no matter how preposterous, and they would always make one other. Thus, the average Joe got the chance to peacock around Swinging London, preening, "The only other person with a jacket like this is John Lennon!" My mum thought this was a great idea, so she got Hung On You to send me one of their unique items. A tie duly arrived – well, I say "tie"; it was more like a piece of carpet, though it had been commissioned by Mick Jagger. "That's all well and good," said my tenacious mother, "but no one will know that Mick Jagger has the other one." So, to their credit, Hung On You sent another tie – this time psychedelic on one side, lime green on the other, and autographed 'Mick Jagger'. Even my mum thought that was good enough...

The only time I ever spoke to Mick was during a phone interview to cover the (surprisingly good) soundtrack he and Dave Stewart had written for the (unsurprisingly poor) 2004 remake of *Alfie*. True to form, Mick had little time for chit-chat, but positively howled with laughter when I mentioned the Hung On You story. "Oh Gawd, that was an *awful* tie..."

Alas, the criticisms that arose from Hyde Park didn't end with Jagger's white dress. The underground press, including *Oz*, the *International Times* and *Black Dwarf*, railed against the band and how they had "sold out". Writing in *Oz*, Germaine Greer⋆ asked why "Mick Jagger did not tell those quarter of a million people to take over the city? Why did they behave so well and pick up the garbage?... No one need be afraid of the Rolling Stones any more."

Their critics may have felt the Rolling Stones' revolutionary commitment was contained but, in fact, the majority of the Hyde Park audience left the park pleased to have seen one of the big players back on the scene – for free. And, those who stayed behind to pick up the litter, of course, were rewarded with that free copy of 'Honky Tonk Women'.

For Keith Richards, "Hyde Park was one of the most abysmal-sounding shows we've ever done, but it was also one of the most important. I guess that day was a turn of the page."

★ ★ ★

Brian was buried just five days after Hyde Park in his hometown of Cheltenham. Perennially sombre-faced, Bill and Charlie conveyed just the right amount of grief. Criticism of Mick and Keith's non-appearance overlooked the fact that, had they attended, the whole thing would have turned into a pig circus.

The young pop star was laid to rest amid the Newlands and the Triggs, his headstone a simple tribute: "In Affectionate Remembrance of BRIAN JONES, born 28th February 1942 died 3rd July 1969 at Hartfield, Sussex". And while he still lives in the

---

⋆   For Keith Altham, his abiding memory of Hyde Park was witnessing one of the few policemen on patrol stopping Greer and asking the archetypal feminist: "Do you have any drugs on you, sir?"

hearts of many, I don't believe Brian's has ever become a shrine to rival that of fellow rocker, Jim Morrison, whose grave lies in the Cimitière du Père Lachaise, Paris.

CHAPTER 10

The Wizard Of Oz

Whether it was because he was staring thirty in the face, or he was just tired of the hounding, drug busts and trouble that always seemed to surround the Stones, Mick Jagger was clearly looking to add new strings to his bow as the 1960s wound down. "Mick was hedging his bets at that time," Bill Wyman wrote later. "If *Beggars Banquet* had failed to cut it then he was considering his solo options. He had, after all, worked on *Performance*, both as an actor and as composer. 1969 was going to be an important year for us."

Criticised for his non-attendance at Brian Jones' funeral, Mick was now off in pursuit of the elusive film career. But that wasn't the only iron in his fire.

Throughout the summer of 1968, an idea had been brewing on the business side of the Jagger brain: to launch a UK version of *Rolling Stone* magazine. Mick would be part-owner, alongside *Rolling Stone*'s founder Jann Wenner.* It was an inspired idea: the

---

* Typically, soon after Wenner launched *Rolling Stone* magazine in 1967, Allen Klein muscled in: "Your wrongful conduct constitutes, at the very least, a

underground press, as represented by *Oz* and *International Times*, with its explosive psychedelic layouts, was – quite literally – unreadable. The London-based music press of the early to mid-sixties, including *Melody Maker*, *Disc And Music Echo*, *Record Mirror* and *New Musical Express* was old-school Fleet Street. They would pay lip service to the emerging underground or progressive scene, but were rarely able to delve too deep.

Chris Welch joined *Melody Maker* in 1964 while it was still in its Fleet Street offices. "The sales were really low; it was always a jazz paper, and had been slow to pick up on the beat boom." Things did begin to shift, though: "The editor Jack Hutton got into the Stones early on, but Ray Coleman, then news editor, was a huge Beatles fan (he got very close to them later on), and Ray would always find a way to put the Stones down with: 'Rolling Stones Flop In US', and front pages like that! Later on, by the end of the sixties, *Melody Maker* was selling upwards of 80,000 copies a week, and you could always multiply those who bought the paper by three or four, so we were reaching a quarter of a million readers a week – every week!"

Keith Altham had joined the *NME* in its Long Acre offices. Along with *Melody Maker*'s Chris Welch and *Disc*'s Penny Valentine, he was part of the vanguard of new rock journalism, which put him in the orbit of new groups like the Stones, The Beatles, The Yardbirds, The Animals, The Who, and The Jimi Hendrix Experience. "Basically, I was a contemporary of theirs, they were mates who happened to play guitars. We'd all hang out in the same clubs – the Speakeasy, the Scotch of St James, the Cromwellian.

---

misappropriation of my clients' property rights in the name *Rolling Stones* for your own commercial benefit." Klein wrote to Wenner in 1968, "It is also a violation of my clients' copyright to the name Rolling Stones." And this, nearly 20 years after the Muddy Waters' song 'Rolling Stone' and three years after Bob Dylan's 'Like A Rolling Stone'…!

There were no minders or PRs hanging around; you'd see Hendrix and he'd know you, so you'd nip over and ask, 'How's it going Jimi?' Any little snippets made it into the *NME*'s 'Alley Cat' or *Melody Maker*'s 'The Raver' columns."

"It was great," Chris Welch said, laughing, when he told me about those days. "The pubs used to shut at 11, so you'd get in the car and drive to the Cromwellian club. I had an old Ford Consul, and you could drive all over London, park where you liked. None of the acts were earning serious money then, I was probably earning more on *Melody Maker* than they were, so I used to give everyone a lift in that car: The Who, Rod Stewart, even Mick Jagger, in 1973, after *Tubular Bells* at the Festival Hall. He was getting hassled by some fans, recognised me, so my wife and I gave him a lift to Trafalgar Square."

However, even then, with that degree of closeness, Altham had to fight to get the weekly inkies to cover 'serious' rock music. There was still an air of 'What's your favourite colour?' in the interviews. A fortnightly paper that took the music and the culture which surrounded it seriously was an enticing and possibly lucrative prospect.

At the time, *Rolling Stone* magazine was the epicentre of the rock'n'roll universe, the Los Alamos of music journalism. It featured long articles in which pop and rock idols were given a platform to express their innermost thoughts. In 1969, it ran Dylan's first interview in three years. Sniffingly dismissing 45s, *Rolling Stone* was presented as "A document of the New America… it publishes the most widely respected reviews of new albums (singles are not reviewed)… Pete Townshend, Mick Jagger [and] Eric Clapton are all subscribers." The impression was that of a turbulent, freewheeling druggy utopia – and to get to the pulsing heart of that utopia, you read, devoured and yearned to be part of *Rolling Stone*.

The UK edition of the magazine could have worked, *should* have worked. The writing was, after all, on the wall: 1968 was the year in which LP sales overtook those of singles for the first time in Britain, and the fans were snapping up albums from progressive and underground bands. Now they were keen to hear them dissect their thought-provoking lyrics rather than whether or not they preferred tea to coffee.

A Decca press release from this period reflects that switch to seriousness: "To learn about the early days of our religions we waited for Moses to descend from Mount Sinai with the two tablets which made up the ten commandments. We look to Shakespeare and Dickens and Chaucer for accounts of other times in our history and we feel that tomorrow we will on many occasions look to the gramophone records of the Rolling Stones... who act as a mirror of today's mind, action and happenings – for albums today are not just 12 songs but 12 stories."

Late in 1969, the pop-heavy *Record Mirror* also issued its resolution to the revolution, proposing a major transition in its editorial direction: "The old order has changed. No longer are the big name groups automatically making the charts. No longer is pop music a strange way-out activity of the hairies. Pop has become a new way of life... The revolution starts next Friday."

To address that new market, the UK edition of *Rolling Stone* was launched in June 1969, with Jagger and Wenner at the helm. Unfortunately, it limped along in a haze of marijuana and soon sank under incompetence (one feature had Bob Dylan appearing as 'Dillon' – heresy to the counterculture). Shocked at such inefficiency being put out under his name, Wenner insisted that the UK edition come under the aegis of its American counterpart, which was based in San Francisco.

But Jagger decided that, in the end, he didn't want to play at being 'Citizen Kane'. "I didn't have that much money at that point," he told journalist Joe Hagan, "because I was in all those disputes with Allen Klein." Less than six months later, in November 1969 *Variety* reported the magazine's closure, claiming a 30,000 circulation, and citing the main reason as "shareholder Mick Jagger's confessed inability to exercise control over the contents". Ironically, the same month UK *Rolling Stone* magazine's closure was announced, *The Beatles Book* (also known as *Beatles Monthly*) was also shuttered after six years in print when it became apparent to its founder, Sean O'Mahony, that the Fab Four would soon be no more.

In a further irony, UK *Rolling Stone* editor Alan Marcuson sent a last, desperate telegram request to Jagger to keep the British edition afloat. The telegram was dispatched on December 6, 1969, but the singer had other things on his mind by then...

★ ★ ★

With *Performance* in the bag, if not actually on the screen, and questing further afield, Mick and Marianne flew to Australia the day after the Hyde Park concert. You could have written the headlines yourself when it was announced that Mick Jagger was flying to Australia to appear in a film about the nation's best-known outlaw, Ned Kelly. The country welcomed the Mephistophelian Mick with less than open arms. Mind you, when a Sydney schoolteacher polled her pupils, asking 'Who Is Ned Kelly?', only 48 per cent got it right – but 84 per cent knew who Mick Jagger was!

Culturally, Australia was still somewhat of a backwater in the sixties, and in 1965, Jean Shrimpton was virtually hounded out of the country for sporting a miniskirt at the Melbourne Cup. For years after Mick left the country, the Australian comedian Barry Humphries could still guarantee a roar of appreciation when he appeared in the scabrous guise of Les Patterson, the lecherous and offensive 'Australian cultural attaché'.

Ned Kelly, however, was an Aussie legend of a different kind. The outlaw, who roamed the outback, rustling and robbing banks, was better known as 'the Australian Robin Hood'. A gun battle with the police eventually led to his capture, and in 1880, when he was only twenty-five, he was hanged. That romantic outlaw element would certainly have appealed to Mick, who had been searching for a role that would take his rookie acting career to the next level.

However, from the moment he and Marianne arrived in Australia, there was trouble. The press was manifestly hostile at the prospect of this limp-wristed Pom playing their great national hero. The papers reported Mick's appearance at Sydney airport with a degree of tongue in cheek: "a white straw boater, long hair swaying in the breeze, a mauve maxi coat, flared trousers, a white Isadora scarf and waving a handbag of Indian leather".

To make matters worse, Marianne overdosed soon after their arrival at the Chevron Hotel near Sydney Harbour, and fell into a coma as she was rushed by ambulance to St Vincent's Hospital in the city. By her own admission, Marianne was in a terrible state ("anorexic, pale, sickly, covered with spots"). Coming off heroin, she had taken Tuinals to help her sleep, only to continue popping "about 150 tablets" while in a haze. Looking into the mirror in the hotel bathroom, "In my drug-induced stupor I dimly recognised the ravaged face of Brian Jones... I was Brian and I was dead... It was all very rational in the way these things are when you're unhinged. I reasoned that since I was Brian and since Brian was dead... I had to take the rest of the pills so I could be dead too."

The accident, which came close to killing Marianne, generated more hostile headlines. Marianne had been due to play Ned's sister in the film. She was quickly replaced by a fresh-out-of-drama-school Diane Craig.

We can only speculate what prompted Tony Richardson to make the disastrous *Ned Kelly*. In the theatre, Richardson was a legend, having directed the landmark production of John Osborne's *Look Back In Anger*. That 1956 premiere was the hobnailed boot kicking through the French windows of prim English theatre: like the Rolling Stones to Terence Rattigan's Cliff Richard. On film, Richardson had won an Oscar for 1964's *Tom Jones*, which in turn opened the floodgates to a bracing new wave of British cinema.

What prompted the director to cast Mick Jagger as the eponymous Ned Kelly was probably nothing more than proximity. In 1969, Richardson was directing the troubled production of *Hamlet* at the Roundhouse, a 'hotspot' of the London underground scene. It featured the titanic Nicol Williamson as the tormented Prince of Denmark and Marianne as a forlorn 'Ophelia'. Also in that eventful production, Anthony Hopkins played 'Claudius' and Anjelica Huston was 'Lady' in the crowd.

Subsequently, Richardson produced a film of the play, starring most of the original cast, including Williamson, Hopkins and Marianne. The film version found the *New York Times*' Roger Greenspun's review very much of its time: "Since the film is shot perhaps 95 per cent in fairly extreme closeup, it is not so much his presence as his head that continually dominates the screen. 'Hamlet' from the neck up (with the occasional Ophelia from the neck down, to acknowledge Miss Faithfull's charming cleavage)…"

Sadly forgotten today, Nicol Williamson was a towering performer ("the greatest actor since Marlon Brando," said John Osborne). But on the opening night of *Hamlet*, Williamson was offended by the chattering audience and quit the stage. For an encore, he came out and sang a song from sixties rock musical *Hair*! But for the esteemed critic Michael Billington, Williamson's was "the undisputed *Hamlet* of the 1960s".

Mick Jagger was a regular backstage visitor during the production's run ("Tony Richardson, like everybody else, was in love with Mick," was Marianne's emphatic verdict), and consequently he won the role in Richardson's new film.

The 1970 version of *Ned Kelly* is not a catastrophe, but it is woefully weak. For all his onstage charisma, Jagger struggles with the role. Onstage with the Stones, Mick is a shaman seen from afar, enticing, provoking, seducing his ardent audience. Onscreen, that charisma is somehow reduced, as every nuance and twitch is projected 20 feet high. And however authentic in character, Mick's stage 'Oirish' is a severe distraction.

And what was Richardson thinking of for the soundtrack? As Robbie Robertson was later to reveal, The Band had wisely declined the opportunity to contribute. A solo Jagger vocal on the traditional 'Wild Colonial Boy' was the main incentive for Stones fans. Shel Silverstein wrote the remainder of the material.

Undeniably, Shel was a great American songwriter, with an ear for catchy, quirky characterisation, epitomised in his best-known songs 'A Boy Named Sue', 'Sylvia's Mother', 'Queen Of The Silver Dollar' and 'The Ballad Of Lucy Jordan' – the latter memorably covered by Marianne Faithfull on her triumphant 1979 album *Broken English*. No doubting, then, Shel's musical merits, although a Chicago-born novelty songwriter might not be your first port of call for a film about one of the Commonwealth's most notorious outlaws. However, having gone down that route, who would you call upon to commemorate in song the history of Australia's best-known outlaw? Why, American country and western legends Waylon Jennings and Kris Kristofferson, of course! In fairness, both contribute their inimitable talents to the material, while remaining horribly incongruous in a film set in the Australian outback.

Karl Dallas interviewed the venerable folklorist A.L. Lloyd, who was a technical advisor on the film: "Of course Jagger is nothing like Ned Kelly to look at. But Jagger is temperamentally suited to playing a social outcast like Ned Kelly." 'Will Jagger's songs be performed Rolling Stones style?' Lloyd was asked. "Not at all. For a start [he] didn't want guitars in it and he is quite wise in that. In Kelly's time, 1867, the guitar was a gentle lady's instrument. One thing that pleased me was Jagger's realisation that he couldn't use the standard pop singer's voice for the songs. I warned him he would have to try to make his style more vinegary and the idea seemed to amuse him."

On release, the film was predictably savaged. "One of the most plodding, dull and pointless films in recent memory," griped Jann Wenner's *Rolling Stone*, a strident supporter of Mick from the magazine's get-go. "Mick Jagger makes a great Ned Kelly," began the *Melody Maker* review, "but he'd make a better Mick Jagger... if he were cast in a more natural role, he could utilise his talents for humour, sarcasm and cheek, for example the role of an East End used car dealer."

Mick himself was dismissive ("It's not worth seeing"). Yet the conservative *Variety* (aka the showbiz bible) was, surprisingly, supportive: "It is a film to which one applies the damning word 'interesting' [...] Mick Jagger is a natural actor and performer with a wide range of expressions and postures at his instinctive command. Given whiskers, that gaunt, tough pop hero face takes on a classic hard-bitten frontier look that is totally believable for the role."

★ ★ ★

As Mick flew halfway around the world to begin filming *Ned Kelly*, 'Honky Tonk Women' was released, which the *NME Encyclopedia Of Rock* later called "one of the group's most swaggeringly debauched singles". It became the Rolling Stones' most successful single to date, with five weeks at number one in the UK and four at the top of the US charts, from where it was ignominiously deposed by the Archies' 'Sugar, Sugar'.

'Honky Tonk Women' did swagger; indeed, it strutted its stuff with reckless abandon. That debauched sound may have carried the song, overriding the lazy rhymes 'ride' and 'mind' and 'fight' and 'mind'. But from the opening, unforgettable cowbell ushering in those sinister, staccato guitars you succumb... And, however many times you hear it, you still picture Mick's lascivious lips detailing barroom encounters, honky-tonk angels and blown minds as he struts from bar to bar, in state to state. An early version, with a verse that occasionally crops up in live performances, had Jagger strolling down Parisian boulevards. But this is the best – a debauched two-verse odyssey, straddling Memphis and New York.

The press, however, were disappointed: "An important single for the Stones, but a disappointing one for us," opined Chris Welch in *Melody Maker*. "The supposedly gritty 'Honky Tonk Women' fails to make much impact and the drum and guitar sound is rather unconvincing. A big mistake is the failure to maintain a strong bass line... What were they thinking of?" In *Record Mirror*, the band's early champion Peter Jones found "Jagger on top form and the tune slightly reminiscent of some of the early Kinks stuff".

The Stones needed to build on the success of 'Honky Tonk Women', and the way to do it was on long-playing record. This was how kings consolidated their crowns. There was also the opportunity to showcase the new material on the band's American tour, their first in three years. With the dates wrapping in early December, the LP would be ready and available for the lucrative Christmas market.

By 1969, it has to be said that the Rolling Stones and The Beatles were seen, in certain sniffy circles, as perhaps (dare it be whispered)... a little old-fashioned? Even after the low-key *Nashville Skyline*, Dylan remained above such criticism. But the number one and number two biggest rock bands had now been hard at it for six long years. They had begun as pop stars, falling in line with the old-fashioned showbiz diktats of the period. But as the sixties came towards their end, newer, edgier groups were beginning to push the boundaries of what was now thought of as 'rock'. The Stones' had pioneered a particular type of R&B, popularising the blues, but their pole position was now under threat from a legion of disciples. The UK 'Blues Boom' was in full swing, led by Fleetwood Mac (in its original Peter Green incarnation), while fresh acts in that vein burgeoned, including the likes of Ten Years After, Taste, Savoy Brown, The Aynsley Dunbar Retaliation, Blodwyn Pig, the Keef Hartley Band, The Groundhogs and Chicken Shack. All relied on a blues-based, powerhouse, steamroller style of playing. All were receiving respectful coverage in the music press of the period.

And then there was Led Zeppelin. For the next decade, the foursome steamrollered across America, shattering box-office records held by The Beatles and carousing in a style reminiscent of the Rolling Stones, although in an entirely debauched league of their own. Intriguingly, in his autobiography, recording engineer and record producer Glyn Johns recalls playing the acetate of that first Led Zeppelin album to both George Harrison and Mick Jagger, neither of whom "got it". Keith was not impressed by the competition either ("the guy's voice started to get on my nerves").

Also, by the end of 1969 Jethro Tull were tipped to be the 'next best thing'. Rumours of their outstanding appearance at *The Rolling Stones Rock And Roll Circus* had leaked. They had enjoyed a number one LP with *Stand Up*, and Ian Anderson was featured in *NME* under a headline that would have raised a wry smile in the Stones camp – 'Would You Take This Man Home To Meet Mum?'

The British blues debate raged on throughout the late sixties, with the genre parodied by the Bonzo Dog Doo-Dah Band ('Can Blue Men Sing The Whites?') and Liverpool Scene ('I've Got These Fleetwood Mac Chicken Shack John Mayall Can't Fail

Blues'), while the editor of *Melody Maker* noted on the letters page in one October 1968 issue: "Mr Piggott's anti-Blues letter drew the largest number of letters in the history of Mailbag."

Elsewhere, bands such as Pink Floyd, King Crimson, Procol Harum, The Nice, Santana, Quicksilver Messenger Service, the Steve Miller Band and The Moody Blues were further advancing the transition from 'pop' to 'rock'. The Who's *Tommy* was hailed as "the first rock opera". In the States, Chicago Transit Authority and Blood, Sweat & Tears were imaginatively fusing jazz and rock, while Miles Davis' *In A Silent Way* was pushing jazz into the rock auditorium. In the UK, whimsical outfits like Marc Bolan's Tyrannosaurus Rex and the Incredible String Band were endeavouring to reconnect to a childhood paradise. Singer-songwriters such as Donovan and John Martyn, folk groups like Pentangle and Fairport Convention, with their landmark 1969 folk-rock fusion *Liege & Lief*, were conjuring up a pre-Industrial Revolution arcadia.

Both in print and on television, there had been seekers of another Eden, including Jonathan Miller's trippy television adaptation of Lewis Carroll's phantasmagoria *Alice In Wonderland*; the first one-volume paperback edition of J.R.R. Tolkien's *The Lord Of The Rings*; Kubrick's other-worldly *2001: A Space Odyssey*; the childhood idyll of *The Wind In The Willows*; Penguin editions of Hesse and Huxley sticking out of jeans pockets… All were out and in the air. On disc, the unclassifiable *Forever Changes* by Love and Van Morrison's *Astral Weeks* were slow-building masterpieces, the latter a particular favourite of Mick and Marianne ("We used to listen to *Astral Weeks* a lot in the sixties," Marianne told me; "it was one of our favourite stoned records").

In concert, solos of the drum and guitar variety were regular features of bands' live performances. These lengthy indulgences were an opportunity to demonstrate instrumental virtuosity. And as for the audience, with the help of herb or calming narcotics, they too could lose themselves in the musical miasma.

Not so the Stones or Beatles: poor old Ringo's drum solo was limited to a couple of fills on the second side of *Abbey Road*, while Charlie Watts would, if possible, have looked even more miserable at being asked to play a lengthy drum solo à la 'Toad' or 'Moby Dick'. Keith Richards had no desire to emulate Jimmy Page, Eric Clapton or Alvin Lee with meandering guitar solos. For the '69 tour, the band did stretch out on some songs, particularly 'Midnight Rambler' and 'Sympathy For The Devil', but the Rolling Stones were renowned for their ability to just about keep it together, and not drift off on self-indulgent solo odysseys.

Charlie Watts was, as usual, looking forward to a long-running Stones tour about as much as root-canal work. In 1991, he told Paul Sexton that "staring at a suitcase the night before a Stones tour is my idea of Hell!" He went on to describe the Stones' '69 jaunt as "'the Led Zeppelin tour' because it was the first time we had to go on and play for an hour-and-a-half. I blame it on Jimmy Page. Led Zeppelin had come to the States, and they would do a twenty-minute drum solo and endless guitar solos. Two or three hours on stage was what we heard… Physically, we didn't know how we were going to feel at the end of 'Satisfaction' if we'd been playing for two hours before we got there… the start, the finish and an encore, because we had never, ever done encores. We used to do whatever it was and go home – which was probably just down to youthful arrogance."

That taint of the 'old-fashioned' affected even the Stones' status as rock'n'roll outlaws. Their very position as arbiters of sedition was under threat. While they were recording in leafy south-west London, on March 1, 1969, after a concert in Miami, Jim Morrison was charged with "lewd and lascivious behavior in public by exposing his private parts and by simulating masturbation and oral copulation". It made Jagger's comments to his Madison Square Garden audience later that year ("I think I bust a button on my trousers... You don't want my trousers to fall down, now do you?") sound more Brian Rix and the Whitehall Theatre than Lenny Bruce and The Living Theatre.

The charges inevitably affected The Doors' earning power as a live act. The release of their fourth album, the distinctly lacklustre *Soft Parade* in September 1969, further diminished the band's standing. In November 1969, Morrison was arrested for drunken behaviour on his way to Phoenix "to lend moral support to the Rolling Stones". And on his charge sheet, the singer was ignominiously listed as a "common drunk".

Of the Miami charge, Morrison was eventually found guilty of the less serious drunkenness and indecent exposure charges in 1970. He appealed in October, but within a year the Lizard King, "the erotic politician", was dead. Once again, the Rolling Stones had seen off the opposition.

And now their rock-behemoth brothers were about to crumble. The Stones were not to know it, The Beatles themselves did not know it, but August 20, 1969 is a day that deserves to be remembered in rock history. That day, all four Beatles came together to supervise a mix for the album that was to be named after those EMI Studios in which, for the preceding seven years, they had made history. The date is significant, as it was the last time that John, Paul, George and Ringo ever convened as a foursome at Abbey Road. Like the Stones before them, from then on the Beatles would become ever more familiar with boardroom battles and law courts.

Despite the sea change in the music charts that year, as the summer drew on, the Stones' confidence began to grow again. Mick Taylor had bled into their first professional lineup change, a lucrative tour was on the horizon, the band's finances looked like getting into some sort of order under the watchful eye of an Austrian prince and the results for the follow-up album to *Beggars Banquet* were encouraging.

Now the Rolling Stones were ready and prepared to take on the world.

Ritchie York spoke to Keith in an interview that ran in *NME* on the eve of the US tour: "It's always been the Stones thing to get up on stage and kick the crap out of everything. We had three years of that before we made it, and we were only just getting it together when we became famous. We still had plenty to do on stage and I think we still have. That's why the tour should be such a groove for us."

The interview eventually appeared in print on a date that will live in rock-music infamy: December 6, 1969.

CHAPTER 11

The Greatest Rock'n'Roll Band In The World

Plans were afoot for the Rolling Stones to return to the concert stage in late 1968, when their PA Jo Bergman wrote to Michael Havers, QC (the lawyer who'd defended Mick and Keith following the Redlands bust) to detail an itinerary for early 1969 that would take in South America, Japan, Hong Kong, Bangkok, India and, crucially, the USA. "The projected world tour is being undertaken not only for financial consideration, but more importantly for the chance it affords, most noticeably, the American public to see the Stones," the letter said.

But there was a shadow hanging over the tour in those early planning stages. Brian Jones had been found guilty of cannabis possession in September 1968, and fined, but the bust meant it was extremely unlikely he would then be able to secure a visa to work in the States. Then, as now, the US government took the issue of work visas extremely seriously. And the press didn't help matters: "Relentless headlines gave the impression that the Rolling Stones were constantly being arrested on drugs charges," Simon Wells wrote, "even though, in reality, several court appearances might result from only one incident."

Following the infamous Redlands bust, Mick's charge had been reduced to a conditional discharge, while Keith's had been thrown out. Mick's May 1969 bust did not come to court until the following year, so the sword of Damocles now hung solely over Brian.

But the Stones needed cash, and quickly. The best way to guarantee an instant cashflow was to hit the lucrative US tour circuit, with a world tour to follow. Brian's inability to obtain the crucial American visa, thus guaranteeing his unavailability, was almost certainly the key factor in the decision to sack him from the Rolling Stones.

With the decision taken to dismiss Brian, Mick Taylor now incorporated, and a rusty return to live performance at Hyde Park, the Rolling Stones were finally ready to return to the Land of the Free. The September 26, 1969 issue of *Melody Maker* led with the story 'Stones To Tour States': "The Rolling Stones' tour of America – their first since their $2 million-grossing 1966 tour – has been confirmed... London Records is expected to launch one of the biggest promotions ever undertaken for a touring act."

As well as promotion, the arena for live performance had altered demonstrably since the Stones' US tour of 1966. Concertgoing audiences were now attentive, savouring the musicianship or wallowing in the communal harmony of a rock concert. Gone were the screaming pubescent girls, moved to hysteria – they were grown now into lace-wearing, soul-bearing, free-loving hippies. Gone were the enthusiastic frat boys, their crew cuts buried beneath lions' manes. All now were keenly embracing the harmonious sex, drugs and rock'n'roll lifestyle.

The spectacle of huge outdoor festivals that sprang up at the end of the 1960s, including Monterey Pop in June 1967, the Newport

Pop Festival in August 1968 and, the Daddy of them all, the Woodstock Music and Art Fair, had alerted the world to the sheer scale of rock'n'roll. What had once been the privilege of the underground community now attracted magazine editors, television documentary makers, columnists, opinion makers and pundits, all attempting to gauge the breadth and substance of these Dionysian times.

For many in the 'straight' world, the Age of Aquarius had begun during the summer of 1969, when half a million music fans descended on the tiny hamlet of Bethel, upstate New York, for a festival the world came to know as 'Woodstock'. By hosting in the vicinity of Bob Dylan's hometown, the promoters were hoping to entice the legend to descend from on high to play.

But, predictably Dylan stayed away, breaking cover instead a few weeks later to make his first live appearance since his 1966 electric tour at the festival held on the bucolic Isle of Wight. Why that festival? "I wanted to see the home of Alfred Lord Tennyson," said one poet of another.

"Come and help Bob Dylan sink the Isle of Wight", teased the advertisements. And they did come, in their thousands – indeed their hundreds of thousands. The only access to the island was by ferry or boat, so this was a rock'n'roll Dunkirk in reverse. Clearly visible in the VIP enclosure were three Beatles (John, George and Ringo), plus Charlie Watts and Keith Richards, who arrived by yacht. Covering the event for *NME* was Keith Altham, who had sparred with the Stones many times in print. On spotting him, Richards barked: "Come over 'ere Altham, I like having the press at my feet." 'Supersession At Isle Of Wight', *Melody Maker* trumpeted, in the issue immediately prior to the festival: "The supergroup to end all supergroups – George Harrison, Rolling Stones, Blind Faith and Bob Dylan on stage together… The Rolling Stones – who except for Mick Jagger who is now filming in Australia, are staying on Keith Richards' yacht off the island, and it is understood they also have expressed a wish to take the stage with Dylan after his performance." In actual fact, Dylan played for a total of 67 minutes, accompanied only by The Band.

With the press eager to confirm these huge festivals as ushering in a brave new world, this was the climate into which the Stones were plunged when they announced details of their US tour at a chaotic press conference in New York, October 1969. The press breathlessly reported that Jagger was clad in "mint green skin-tight pants, a black and white flowered, unbuttoned shirt and a silver and ivory baby elephant tusk around his neck". Journalist Judy Sims called the Stones' visit "[the] biggest event since the moon shot". The best-remembered response of the event came from Jagger when asked: "You sang you couldn't get no satisfaction, are you any more satisfied?" "How do you mean, sexually or other? Sexually satisfied. Financially dissatisfied. Philosophically... trying," he countered.

The press conference was a bunfight, with all questions directed to Mick: his views were sought on Vietnam, revolution, drugs, the changing face of America... and Peggy Lee. Predictably, in the wake of Woodstock and the Isle of Wight, the Stones were asked if they would be playing a free festival. Mick confirmed they would, though not at the Golden Gate Park, as had been mooted. A date, December 6, was set, and San Francisco the location. With no appreciation of the tragedy about to unfold, and in hindsight with a terrible irony, Jagger portentously continued: "It'll create a microcosmic society which sets an example of how the rest of America can behave in large gatherings."

In *Disc*, the magazine's US correspondent Richard Robinson ruefully noted the presence of management and mainstream media, once again emphasising and underlining the esteem in which the Stone were held by the music press, and counterculture at large, yet appreciating that time was not on their side: "The Stones don't belong to us any more. They belong to the mass media." It was a dilemma facing all rock'n'roll rebels. Years later, Joe Strummer of The Clash would sing about "Turning rebellion into money..."

But this was the Rolling Stones' chance to relieve some of the financial pressure that had been tormenting them for years, and they were going to make the most of it.

Prior to the tour, the most collectable of all their albums was released. *The Rolling Stones – A Special Radio Promotional Album* was limited to 200 copies, and made available to DJs in order to further whip up hysteria surrounding the band's breaking cover in the States for the first time since 1966. It ran the gamut across its 14 tracks, from 'Route 66' to the then-unavailable 'Love In Vain', and today copies pass hands for in excess of £2,000.

Details were also announced for a documentary chronicling the tour, and there were plans for a triple live album to commemorate the dates, allowing ample space for the Stones' hand-picked opening acts – B.B. King, Ike & Tina Turner and, on one occasion, Chuck Berry – to be included. To their credit, the band was bringing music that had influenced them to the attention of their young, white hippie audience, to whom American R&B acts weren't necessarily familiar.

There was a lot riding on this tour, and not just financially. The negative reviews for *Satanic Majesties* and the *One Plus One* film, the unseen *Rock And Roll Circus* and the criticisms that had greeted the Stones' shambolic performance at Hyde Park that summer were front and centre. So the band built in two solid weeks of rehearsal, ending up at a soundstage on the Warner Bros. lot in Los Angeles where the entire stage set, lighting and PA was laid out as if in performance. The Jane Fonda film *They Shoot Horses, Don't They?*, a Depression-era drama about the gruelling dance marathons of the 1930s, had just finished shooting on the same lot.

Jagger whipped the band into shape under the film's banner, tantalisingly inquiring, 'How Long Will They Last?'

Sam Cutler was once again on board as stage manager. "My specific duties were never clearly defined, except that it was understood that I would be in charge of the 'lads' on a personal level." He remembered the rehearsals as being like "a kind of phony war period immediately prior to the tour beginning, the lull before the storm". He also remembers stories repeatedly circulating about plans for a free festival. Prior to the opening date, the Grateful Dead's manager, Rock Scully, visited rehearsals (he was a friend of opening act Terry Reid's manager, which gained him entry). Scully painted a glowing picture of free concerts in San Francisco to Mick and Charlie. "As I remember it, there wasn't a massive amount of enthusiasm for the project at this stage," Cutler recalled. "It was left with a tentative 'yes in principle', but 'maybe no in practice' kind of answer. It has always been notoriously difficult to get the Stones to actually say a clear and DEFINITIVE yes to anything!"

During rehearsals, the Stones used Los Angeles as their base, staying in a house on Doheny Drive rented from Stephen Stills, which appeared to have come equipped with a naked blonde housekeeper called 'Angel'. In 2018, she was revealed (by Tom Leonard of the *Daily Mail*, who had tracked her down) to be Leslie Aday, née Edmonds. Leslie had been working as a nanny in California in 1969 when she was recruited by the Stones' management. "Someone would be hired but then they'd complain saying, 'We won't make peanut butter and jelly sandwiches at three o'clock in the morning.' But that was OK by me."

That infamous Terry O'Neill photo, of Keith straddling a motorbike and Mick staring disinterestedly at the naked blonde with her back to the camera, came about when Leslie had emerged naked from a swim ("that's what people did in those days"). As she walked by, Jagger told her, "It would be nice if you would be in the picture. We're just gonna use it for our memories of the tour. It's just personal." But it was to be anything but – *Rolling Stone* got hold of the picture, then the national press...*

When not rehearsing or indulging, the Stones were out and about, taking in gigs by Taj Mahal, The Flying Burrito Brothers and Chuck Berry. Along the way, their every move was monitored. "The Stones [...] were looked on as gods of deliverance in LA," Marianne wrote. "They'd reached mythical status by the time they went on that tour in 1969." The underground press could barely contain their excitement; the straight press was fascinated by the sexual magnetism and political threat the band appeared to pose during those turbulent times.

Once locked and loaded, the band began to play. The opening night at the State University of Colorado on November 7, 1969 was deliberately off the beaten track. It gave the band an opportunity to iron out the flaws, paint over the cracks. The audience response set the tone for the rest of the tour: no screaming hysteria; rather, sheer, unadulterated delight. The set didn't vary; it contained songs that would have been familiar to Crawdaddy audiences ('Carol'; 'Little Queenie') and songs from *Top Of The Pops* ('Satisfaction'; 'Honky Tonk Women'). There was material to remind 1969 audiences of the band's blues roots ('Love In Vain'; 'Prodigal Son') and a Jagger showstopping centrepiece with 'Midnight Rambler'. Finally, there were album tracks designed to showcase the Stones' revolutionary appeal ('Sympathy For The Devil'; 'Gimme Shelter'; 'Street Fighting Man').

On they rolled... through Oakland, Phoenix, Dallas, Illinois, Philadelphia... In Chicago, in light of the contentious trial of activists following the 1968 riots that still endured, Jagger dedicated

---

* Leslie enjoyed a fling with Mick, before returning to Pennsylvania in December 1969, just prior to the Stones finishing their American dates. She went on to marry Meat Loaf in 1979, and remained Mrs Loaf for 20 years.

'Street Fighting Man' to the crowd, "because of what you all did here... you know what I mean".

In fact, wherever they ventured, the Stones were capering across an America that was reeling. The nation was divided over a war being fought in faraway South East Asia. Parents paraded patriotic duty; their children disagreed. The youth were in revolt, with the dread prospect of being drafted to fight in Vietnam hanging over their heads. The hope of Robert Kennedy standing for, and perhaps winning, the presidency had been swept away at the hands of an assassin on June 6, 1968. Two months later, the civil rights message of Martin Luther King was shattered upon his assassination in Memphis. Non-violence and 'We Shall Overcome' were edged out by the militancy of the Black Panthers and the escalating anti-Vietnam protests. Richard Nixon's inauguration of January 1969 set the seal on the potency of the 'silent majority', those who occupied what later became known as 'the flyover States'. Those who had no truck with rebellion, anti-war protests and rock'n'roll. Not for these conservatives the excesses of the liberal elite and their East or West Coast power bases.*

It was a volatile and tumultuous time to be in America, and the Stones were in the eye of the hurricane. The peace and love vibes of 1967 had been blown aside by the violence and hard-edged atmosphere of 1968. The Stones themselves marked those changes on record – 1967 found them galaxy-tripping, '2000 Light Years From Home'. A year later, they were fighting in the streets. By 1969, it was time to reconnect.

King Crimson's Robert Fripp wrote a lengthy, insightful letter to *Vox* magazine, reflecting on the period: "The original impulse of the 'prog rock' genre was the hope that 'we' (and the word was a

---

* A 1969 Gallup poll found that "the three most admired men in America" during that year were President Richard Nixon, Vice-President Spiro Agnew and religious evangelist Billy Graham.

statement of bonding) can change the world'. Sergeant Pepper and the outdoor music festivals celebrating community and affirmation, notably Woodstock, proved it.

"As a young musician and 'hairy' travelling across America in 1969 the connection was unmistakably clear between the peace movement, rock music as an instrument of political expression and the voice of a generation. The demarcation between 'straights' and 'hairies' equally so."

The September 12, 1969 issue of *Time* magazine covered the Isle of Wight festival, with the reviewer marvelling that youth in such large numbers could gather together in peace, and fashion a city free from violence and turmoil, that "in the cool evening air, as evident as the sweet odour of marijuana, hung an almost palpable yearning for some sort of transcendent experience." Elsewhere, though, newspapers were full of the sorrow and division America was feeling. A poll showed 16 inner-city "serious disorders" (riots). Headlines such as 'The Cities: A Failure Everywhere' and 'Can Hijackers Be Halted?' spoke of the state of the nation.

In December 1969, TWA Flight 85 to San Francisco became the 55th aircraft to be skyjacked over America. Of the 71 planes skyjacked during the year, 58 went to Cuba. That same month, the US Supreme Court ruled that four southern states had to end segregation completely, by September 1970 – 105 years after the end of the American Civil War.

The year had begun with the swearing in of President Richard Nixon. His inaugural speech recognised the conflict in Vietnam and domestic turmoil: "We are caught in war, wanting peace. We are torn by division, wanting unity. We see around us empty lives wanting fulfillment... We cannot learn from one another until we stop shouting at one another – until we speak quietly enough so that our words can be heard as well as our voices." Vietnam preoccupied US citizens and politicians alike that year. The USA had already been involved for longer than it had in either world war. By March 1969, over 33,000 American soldiers had lost their lives, already exceeding the casualty count of the entire Korean War. Vietnam was costing the US government $25 billion a year. The fact that the average American could switch on the TV and watch the war unfold on the nightly news gave it a terrible immediacy. Not on the distant beaches of Normandy or the 49th parallel – every night the nation could tune in to see their children fighting and dying in the rice paddies of Vietnam. The national Moratorium to End the War in Vietnam, which saw protestors turn out in their millions, took place on October 15, 1969, a month before the first concert of the Stones' US tour. Vice-President Agnew railed against the protestors: "an effete corps of impudent snobs who characterize themselves as intellectuals".

But it wasn't all bleak. It was in July of that year that mortal man had first set foot on the Moon. For one brief, shining moment, man's reach had exceeded his grasp. As Neil Armstrong took that historic first step, the world held its collective breath, maybe feeling that something could be salvaged as we reached into the cosmos, that we might see beyond the chaos and watch as another world appeared on our television screens, perhaps a better world. However, such scenes were but a transitory diversion. All across a world now united by television images, dread and fear seemed to stalk the planet.

It had begun in a fiery tragedy. Twenty-one-year-old student Jan Palach (who deserves to be better known) set himself on fire that January. The student's self-immolation was not a Buddhist protest against US involvement in Vietnam, however, but a protest in Prague's Wenceslas Square against the Russian invasion of Czechoslovakia the previous year.

Elsewhere, famine swept through Biafra. Ted Kennedy's chances of reaching the White House were doomed when, after

161

accidentally driving off a bridge, he left his passenger, Mary Jo Kopechne, to drown in the car after a party on Chappaquiddick Island. Northern Ireland exploded into sectarian violence, soon leading to 'The Troubles' and its 3,000 eventual deaths. In Leonid Brezhnev's Russia, the authorities clamped down on dissidents, imprisoning anyone who owned a copy of Aleksandr Solzhenitsyn's *Cancer Ward*. The Middle East was as divided as ever. Somehow, John and Yoko staying in bed in Hilton hotels didn't seem to provide the solution.

Beyond the political arena, the Manson murders of August 1969 cast the darkest shadow over the counterculture.

The charismatic Charles Manson was "Rasputin-like", casting "an almost hypnotic spell over his followers, who called him 'God' and 'Satan'". Former Beach Boy Dennis Wilson was interviewed in *Record Mirror* in December 1968: "I told [the Manson girls] about our involvement with the Maharishi and they told me they too had a guru, a guy named Charlie who'd recently come out of jail... when I met him I found he had some great musical ideas." It was those brief relationships with rock stars and Manson's later citing of Beatle lyrics that provided the link between the butcher and the hippies.

The USA had known senseless violence on this scale before, but the five Los Angeles murders of August 8, 1969, and the following night's LaBianca murders, were truly shocking. Maybe because the pregnant Sharon Tate was a film star butchered in the Hollywood Hills, or maybe because the murderers hailed from a 'cult tribe' that was wholly antithetical to established American values, the Manson murders sent shock waves across the country. "It was one of the grisliest, bloodiest and apparently most senseless crimes of the century", *Time* magazine reported, upon the arrest of the suspects.

With his long, hippie hair and beard, and known association with the Beach Boys, Charlie Manson came across as one of us, a member of the counterculture. But the Manson Family murders were rock'n'roll homicide. When it became apparent that Manson espoused the hippie values of free love, drugs and rock'n'roll, it confirmed the very worst that Middle America had suspected all along about rock music and drug-addled hippies: rock'n'roll and narcotics fuelled the basest instincts, culminating in mass murder. *Time* helpfully sealed the deal in their piece 'Hippies and Violence', which stated that "Part of the mystique and the attraction of the hippie movement has always been its invitation to freedom. It beckons young people out of the tense, structured workaday world to a life where each can do 'his own thing'."

The fact that Manson testified to his heinous crimes being inspired by rock music was proof positive of both the culture's destructive power and its alienating effect. In the most tragic misreading ever of any rock lyrics, Manson took The Beatles' 'Helter Skelter' as a call to arms, a clarion call for whites to rise up against black militants. The Tate and LaBianca murders of August 1969 were no pseudo-Satanic event, no well-publicised 'He who sups with the Devil should have a long spoon'. This was not young rebels dabbling in the works of Aleister Crowley; this was no false necromancy. As he was about to begin his butchery at the Tate house, Tex Watson told his victim: "I'm the Devil and I'm here to do the Devil's business."

That was the climate into which the Stones tapped when they began their American trawl, the week the first Manson Family arrests were made.*

---

* Charles Manson was already in police custody for destruction of state property when the arrests took place.

That same week saw the US Army begin its own investigation into the massacre at My Lai in March 1968, where American troops massacred 109 Vietnamese civilians. Of all the carnage that occurred during Vietnam, the My Lai massacre brought home the bloody futility of war. For *Time* magazine, My Lai "sears the generous and humane image, more often deserved than not, of the US as a people". If America had gone to war to save the country from the brutality of Communism, how could it justify such brutality from its own troops against the very people it was there to save?

In Paris, peace talks between American and North Vietnamese negotiators ground to a halt. "We are at rock bottom now in these talks," one frustrated American delegate complained, "so it doesn't really make any difference who sits around that table."

At the same time, in Chicago, police raided an apartment, leaving two Black Panthers dead. Like a tour itinerary, the media reported the gun battles between police and the militant Panthers that raged across Kansas City, Denver, Seattle, Los Angeles, St Louis, Sacramento... In the same city, the trial of radicals charged with conspiring to incite riots during the previous year's Democratic Convention continued. Among the defendants were Yippies Abbie Hoffman and Jerry Rubin. Black Panther Bobby Seale was ordered bound and gagged in court by the judge, causing his counsel to declare, "I feel so utterly ashamed to be an American lawyer at this time."

Over a five-month period during 1969, militant revolutionaries the Weathermen (who took their name from a Dylan lyric) bombed six buildings in Manhattan alone. A Gallup poll found nearly 13 per cent of American students classified themselves as "revolutionary" or "radically dissident". The very air itself was polluted by 140 million tons of grime each year. 'Gimme Shelter',

'Midnight Rambler', 'Let It Bleed'… all seemed to throb to the pulse of such unsettling times.

Like filings to a magnet, the children of the 'silent majority' clung to the Stones and the life-altering power of rock'n'roll. Festivals and gigs like theirs offered an opportunity for the tribes to gather, to coagulate, to discover they weren't alone. Huddled over the records, the lyrics took on a talismanic power, which they could now celebrate in unison. While in 1967 there had not been enough power to 'levitate' the Pentagon, there was undeniably something elevating about witnessing the Rolling Stones in concert, in control, in power during 1969.

Maybe we read too much into it all. Perhaps Charlie's wife, Shirley, was right. As the Stones' plane flew into Los Angeles one night during that eventful tour, she shrugged and said to the band's chronicler, Stanley Booth: "It's just a tour, after all, just a group of people going around getting up on stages and playing music for kids to dance."

And just getting the Stones on to the stage presented its own problems. Promoters had been presented with a 40-page contract and concert rider. The Stones' management played hardball. Allen Klein's nephew, Ron Schneider, who was handling the business end of the tour, approached individual venues. They were obviously keen to host the hottest ticket in town, to have the band play after their three-year absence. But to get the Rolling Stones, there was a demand of 75 per cent gate receipts. This meant the venues worked harder than anticipated to guarantee successful shows, as even 25 per cent of a sold-out show was enticement enough. And to help with the setting-up costs of the tour, they were required to pay 50 per cent of the projected gate up front. By now, the tour and its accompanying melodrama was becoming Byzantine.

Tour manager Sam Cutler was just one person baffled by the band's choice of Schneider – why would they plump for the nephew of the very man they were so publicly keen to disassociate themselves from?

In his memoir, legendary concert promoter Bill Graham recalled negotiating with Schneider. Graham was kept waiting while Schneider walked his dog and witheringly recalled: "That's what he did in the mornings. He walked his dog. It was something he was really good at and something he actually knew how to do."

All the ingredients were there and in place: primarily the messianic power of the Rolling Stones in performance. But already attaching to the tour were rumours of illicit thrills – of backstage sex and drugs and assorted bacchanalia, with a cast of the shadowy figures who, two years later, would become familiar through *The Godfather*.

Footage and photos from that tour are revealing in capturing the times – the empty KFC containers, the crushed cigarette packets, Winsome blondes floating around backstage, ministering to all needs, the endless backstage corridors, the anonymous hotel rooms, the desultory interviews and press conferences, the jaded, faded conversations... and all for 90 minutes of onstage bliss and magic...

Onstage and in performance, every night, however, the Stones were playing a blinder. The reviews were as enthusiastic as the audiences. Albert Goldman's cumbersome review in *The New York Times* drew immediate parallels with the Stones' Madison Square Garden gig and a Nazi rally at Nuremberg.

But, for the band it took until halfway through the tour for them to hit roadworthiness. "We didn't really get it on till Detroit," said Mick, uttering the words that would later become the title of the controversial bootleg album, featuring an audience recording from the Stones' gig at the Detroit Olympia on November 24.

"It's simply amazing the way the audience responds, clapping hard with the beat of each number as if they'd trained avidly for that moment," Greil Marcus enthused. His review of the Detroit bootleg captured the oneness that the underground felt with the band: "Because of their sound and the fury of the Stones themselves, this set is in its way a permanent document of what can happen when a rock and roll band and a rock and roll crowd move in such a way as to create the music and its glory together as a performing unit."

Bootlegs had appeared on the underground scene the year the Stones hit the States. As ever, the dubious honour of the first went to Bob Dylan and the double LP *Great White Wonder* – compiled from hotel room performances and bits of the *Basement Tapes*. From then on, any major act was fair game: there were over 90 hours of Beatle performances culled from the *Let It Be* sessions. Led Zeppelin's legendary live shows were captured on bootleg. The Who; Crosby, Stills & Nash; Pink Floyd... and pretty well every other headline act were immortalised on illegal vinyl.

The Stones were no exception. In fact, it became a badge of honour for an act to be bootlegged, a testament to their appeal. Radicals argued they had already bought everything official anyhow, so pirate recordings of their favourite acts were fair game. As fans, they had been at the mercy of the avaricious record labels for too long; a bootleg was a rebellious two-fingered retort to the corporations. Here, once again, the fans were sticking it to The Man.

To date, there had never been a live LP to capture the Rolling Stones' concert magnetism, so diehard fans felt hard done by. That was soon rectified following the second show at Oakland, the Stones' third stop of the tour, on November 9. *LiveR Than You'll Ever Be* was hailed by Lester Bangs in *Rolling Stone* as "one of the finest albums of 1969... The band is hard, with so much metal in their sound they might be some sort of long-haired construction crew… All qualifications aside, it is the ultimate Rolling Stones album."

Equally enthusiastic about *LiveR Than You'll Ever Be* was Greil Marcus: "The sound quality is superb… The turn-around violence of their sound, the ripping hardness of the guitars and the energy of the rhythm section is all here… It is the most musically exciting record I have heard all year, fully the equal, in its own way, of *Let It Bleed*, and in some ways better."

For his 2003 book, Clinton Heylin tracked down the person responsible for the bootlegs, known as 'Dub' Taylor (identified in court as Michael Taylor), one of the pair who founded Trade Mark of Quality, a bootleg record label in LA. 'Dub' and his partner Ken Douglas were the bootleg industry's Year Zero, punting out Dylan's *Great White Wonder* to record stores around Los Angeles in the summer of 1969. On the back of the success of the Dylan bootlegs, and the anticipation aroused by the upcoming Stones dates, Dub splashed out on state-of-the-art equipment, including "a Sennheiser 805 shotgun microphone and a Uher 4000 reel-to-reel tape recorder".

Such was the stellar quality of the *LiveR Than You'll Ever Be* recording, many assumed it came from a Stones insider rather than a member of the audience. The band's disquiet over their relationship with Decca (and its US equivalent, London Records) was public knowledge. Theories abounded that *LiveR Than You'll Ever Be* was the Rolling Stones' attempt to get revenge on their old label, by cutting Decca's profits. Legend has Sam Cutler buying six copies of *LiveR* while in San Francisco – one for himself, five for each of the Rolling Stones.*

---

* In a further irony, the bootleggers had the album illicitly pressed at the same plant used by the Stones' American label, London Records!

The late sixties and early seventies saw a plethora of bootlegs – studio outtakes were harder to come by, but following the precedent set by *LiveR*, concert bootlegs of top acts who had hitherto refused to sanction live albums (notably Led Zeppelin) soon filled the racks. In a statement to *Rolling Stone* in 1971, the Warner Bros. vice-president, Joe Smith, was eerily prescient: "If bootlegging were to continue indefinitely the entire structure of the music business as we know it would be absolutely destroyed. There would be a chaotic period of nobody willing to pay for anything." In fact, that nightmare scenario had to wait until century's end and something called Napster...

Talking to Roy Carr, Keith conceded that the Stones were relatively sanguine about the bootlegs, citing Ian Stewart: "He always said that our official 'live' records were often over-produced and most of the time he was right. Stew always went for the 'moment' and didn't care if it had a rough edge. Anyway, you know my attitude towards bootlegs – they're an indication of interest above and beyond what you'll find in the charts and that fans will go to great lengths to seek out such things."

LiveR Than You'll Ever Be made it into the shops in time for Christmas 1969. The Stones official souvenir, '*Get Yer Ya-Yas Out!*': *The Rolling Stones In Concert*, wasn't made available until September 4, 1970.[*] Upon its release, the critics drooled. "I'm beginning to think *Ya-Yas* might just be the best album they ever made," enthused Lester Bangs. "I have no doubt that it's the best rock concert ever put on record." In Britain, *Disc And Music Echo* were baffled by the album's release and, indeed, the concept of a live album: 'Stones Give New Vitality To Some Old Numbers', ran the dispassionate headline.

---

[*] The title is taken from Blind Boy Fuller's song 'Get Your Yas Yas Out', meaning to 'let off steam'.

The band clearly remained unloved in their homeland. In *Melody Maker*, Michael Watts was dismissive: "At first sight it is difficult to see why this album has been released, inasmuch as all these numbers have been recorded before on one album or another and were out on a bootleg in circulation a few months ago... It may be something of a 'knock-off' but it serves to fill the gap until the group gets its own label and starts putting out some more original stuff."

The delay in the release of '*Get Yer Ya-Yas Out!*' was due in part to the band's initial decision for a three-LP concert souvenir. That was then modified and cut down to a double album, but neither of those sets ever did happen at the time. It took four decades, until 2009, for a 40th-anniversary edition of '*Get Yer Ya-Yas Out!*' to emerge. Included in the deluxe packaging was "a disc of five previously unreleased Rolling Stones tracks recorded at the same shows and a disc of unreleased performances by the shows' stellar openers B.B. King and Ike & Tina Turner".

The existence of such a package confirmed that the Stones did have the best intentions for that tour, that they really were keen to have their rock audience appreciate the blues and soul power of their contemporaries.

★ ★ ★

While the Rolling Stones were creating mayhem across America, rumours abounded that their only real rivals were in danger of splitting. The Beatles hadn't played before a concert audience in three years. Though no one knew it at the time, a one-off appearance on a windy London rooftop at the end of January 1969 had marked the end of The Beatles as a performing act. It would be only a matter of months before the split was finally confirmed.

Since their previous US tour in 1966, the Rolling Stones had survived the death of Brian Jones, drug busts, lacklustre LPs, a summer of love, a summer of riots... and yet, unlike their Liverpudlian counterparts, they still pushed on, even with renewed vigour. The '66 shows had been routinely interrupted by screaming teenagers and adolescent riots, the youth of America desperate to take home a piece of their favourite Stone as a souvenir. Three years on, the audiences were mellowed by marijuana, a fug of smoke floating over the auditoria. A Rolling Stones audience in 1969 had come to get high and party. But crucially, they had also come to listen.

But not before they had done a lot of whoopin' and hollerin'... The Stones had the hauteur of royalty. Not for them the prison of time; every show started late under the presumption that keeping 'em waiting kept 'em hungry. Then, Sam Cutler's introduction – inadvertently creating the byline by which the group are still known today – would ring out from the PA: "Ladies and gentlemen, here they are after three years, the greatest rock'n'roll band in the world – the Rolling Stones!" The band's name would drown under roaring cheers.

So now they were lumbered with "the greatest rock'n'roll band in the world". Could have been worse. But at the time Mick "hated it. It's so Barnum & Bailey." Since then the tour has been overshadowed by the catastrophe at Altamont, the successes of preceding dates often overlooked. In their 20th-anniversary issue, released in 1987, *Rolling Stone* magazine looked back on 'Twenty Concerts That Changed Rock & Roll', with the Stones US tour justifiably taking its place in the rankings – "During the crazed month of November 1969, the Rolling Stones truly were the greatest rock'n'roll band in the world..."

Rolling Stone's David Fricke pinned down Jagger for his memories of that tour, nearly two decades on. Mick spoke with some fondness: "I was so energized by it, I thought I could hit the roof of Madison Square Garden. I really felt like I was gonna leap out of the fucking dome. The band played really, really together at that point. It was actually the best tour of America the Stones have ever done."

The band had by then been at the coalface for six years. The days of matching stage uniforms and cornflakes adverts were long gone. The band who took to the stage for the first time in three years at the Moby Arena in Fort Collins, Colorado, two days after Guy Fawkes Night, were revolutionaries, grizzled survivors, hardened veterans.

Standing unsmiling and stock still, Bill Wyman resembled more than ever an Easter Island statue, as he let his bass lay the foundations. Slightly elevated on a riser, Charlie Watts pumped it up. While he would likely have been manifestly happier playing behind pianist Pete Johnson, Charlie – ever the professional – matched every Jagger gyration with a nailed-down rhythm. Barely twenty years old, no wonder Mick Taylor looked baffled and uncomprehending at the hysteria that greeted the group at every show. And stage left: the 'Human Riff... the Walking Corpse...' Keith Richards. Between 1969 and 1972, it was Keith who personified all that was right and wrong with rock'n'roll. For all the junkie chic he came to embody, Keith was a workhorse. With a bottle of favoured bourbon never far from reach, Keith fuelled the band with his riffs, his guitar signatures curling like the smoke from the fag stuck in the neck of his guitar.

Years later, rock journalist and author Kris Needs appreciated how Keith just nailed it on that tour: "Richards ripping at his National Steel, displaying the piratical image that launched a thousand looks: bone-earring swinging over his death's head skull and snakeskin boots tapping time."

And from Stones' loyalist Roy Carr, writing in 1991: "You'll have to get in line with all the rest. From Johnny Thunders, Joe Perry and Mick Jones, through to the tousled-haired guitars of

Guns N' Roses, the Quireboys and the Black Crowes, they swagger and stagger to the extent that their self-conscious fixation with duplicating Richards' emaciated renegade stance has become rock's most recycled image."

It's a mistake they all make: they emulate Keith's partying, his hairstyle, earrings, boots… They live by the Tao of Keith, without appreciating that by the time he had become rock's most "elegantly wasted" human being, Keith had been responsible for half a dozen classic singles and at least four timeless albums! You do the drugs *after* you've reached the Pantheon. If the Rolling Stones were the *Titanic*, while Mick was cavorting on the bridge, Keith was slaving away in the engine room, stoking the monster. "Lots of kids leave the cradle thinking that's precisely what you've got to do," Keith laughingly told Roy Carr. "That's all there is to it – sticking a cigarette out the corner of your mouth, bending your legs… which is maybe my fault, but don't blame it all on me!"

While the band had altered irrevocably, the audiences had also changed beyond recognition. Bill Graham's Fillmore audiences had become famously attentive – like jazz fans of old, they dutifully applauded every standout solo from the likes of Mike Bloomfield, Jerry Garcia and Duane Allman. Now they were willing to pay attention, not howl or scream at their idols.

Greil Marcus' review of the first show of the tour makes for intriguing reading half a century on: "We were… judging the music, not responding to it, and this too must have been new to the Stones […] The first thing that hit you when the Stones came out on stage was the evidence of the years in Mick Jagger's face. It seemed to have fallen into place for good. His features were no longer supple and loose; they were hard and thick, like the marble ridges of a statue. But that's a long way from the House of Wax. He still looked beautiful. Dylan doesn't tour, the Beatles don't tour, and it's been three years since any of us have seen Mick

Jagger. So we had to look at him to make sure he was really there. The giant TV screen up above the stage held images that in an odd way were more real than the show itself – somehow it made more sense to see a picture of Mick Jagger than to see Mick Jagger himself."

The Band and Pink Floyd favoured anonymity in performance. Blind Faith were falling apart. The Grateful Dead engendered a sense of community. Out front for the Stones was rock's most charismatic showman. Robert Plant may have had the Greek God image, Ian Anderson had perfected the tramp-most-likely-to look, Jim Morrison may have cornered the market as shaman, but for the thousands who flocked to see the Stones that autumn, and for the untold thousands who couldn't get tickets, it was Michael Philip Jagger who personified the very embodiment of all that was rock'n'roll. The lips, of course, had it. But also the sinuous onstage movements; the coiled sexuality; the threat posed. Up there, he was the tantalising, unattainable demon.

Throughout the tour, Mick favoured a black Anthony Price T-shirt, a mysterious white symbol across the front ("Naaaaaah," Jagger said dismissively to Danny Eccleston, "there's no Satanic reference. It's a sign for Leo [Mick's birth sign]."*

But the Jagger costume didn't stop there. He sported (ironically) a red, white and blue Uncle Sam top hat and a blood-red scarf draped over those surprisingly slight shoulders. Then, as now, Jagger commanded the stage as convincingly as Colonel Kurtz his compound.

It's worth noting that 1969 was the same year that Elvis returned to live performance after an eight-year absence. Those inaugural Vegas shows marked a triumphant return to the concert stage for 'the King', before the concert stage became as much a treadmill as

---

* It also resembled the symbol for omega, the last letter of the Greek alphabet, literally meaning 'great', although omega is often used to denote the last, the end.

a Hollywood film studio. However, it was impossible to miss the vast gulf between the Las Vegas audiences who thrilled to 'All Shook Up' and 'Love Me Tender', and the Stones' stoned disciples. Those who filled the Vegas showroom represented the past – the Stones, the future. While both showmen had the same trick up their sleeve, mind you, Mick *kept* the scarves he wore rather than distribute them like shavings of the true cross à la Elvis.

Jagger knew how to work the crowd, even if his onstage between-songs wisdom was largely limited to "Awright... Y'awright?" There was no denying the sheer voltage, the undiluted charisma the twenty-seven-year-old Jagger generated as a performer. And the music... probably the second-best back catalogue in rock, pumped out with a ferocious energy. It all combined to create something certainly messianic and, let it be whispered, also something slightly... Satanic.

Reviewing the footage now, you are struck by the zealous expectation of the crowd. Here was an audience connecting with their leaders. There was a laughable lack of security – excited girls still managed to get close to Mick onstage before being cursorily ejected. Funny to think of those wide-eyed, Age of Aquarius blondes staring devotedly at their idols as matronly grandmas today.

While the US tour of 1969 will forever be blighted by the tragedy that ended it, it deserves to be remembered for other reasons. It demonstrably upped the ante for rock bands in live performance. It took them out of high-school gyms or halls more suited to classical music. Bringing their own state-of-the-art PA, monitors, lights and video screens, the Stones could expand their act into auditoria. This was the Rolling Stones, clearly visible, in an arena that could comfortably accommodate 20,000 fans. Critics marvelled at "the chance to see, from wherever you were sitting, closeup views of the performers. The live shots, projected from three TV cameras onto an 11 x 14 screen high above the stage." A crew of 20 hung

30-foot drapes and carpeted the stage, ensuring that the sound went out to the audience. It was the first step to the band moving out of venues with a roof and into the open-air stadiums we now associate them with. The tour not only demonstrated how rock bands could reach out to their growing audiences, but it paved the way for the seismic rock concerts of the 1970s.

"The real watershed was the 69 tour," Mick remembered, "a tour of arenas only, with the sound hung from the ceiling. The Volkswagen van was gone forever [...] It was the first time that I exercised and stretched and everything!"

In their 20th-anniversary issue, *Rolling Stone* magazine detailed just why that tour was such a landmark: "On a practical level, the Rolling Stones' 1969 US shows ushered in a new age of rock & roll touring. For the first time, a major rock act hit the hockey rinks in full control of its concert presentation[...] The Stones designed their own stage, handpicked their opening acts, travelled with their own lighting and PA rigs and used sound monitors onstage to hear themselves – luxuries most bands now take for granted but which was almost unheard of then... 'I'd never heard the band onstage before,' Jagger says, 'I was used to singing totally blind. And this was one of the most exciting things, to actually hear the Rolling Stones myself.'"

In all, the show ran for maybe 75 minutes. The stage was designed for Jagger to be comfortable. The effects were in the lights, and the rose petals Mick sprinkled over the audience at show's end. There was no vast inflatable penis, nor a pumped-up monster – the show was the *band*. This time round, there were no backing singers sheathed in skin-tight black skirts, shimmying a cigarette paper away from the Jagger loins.* Not even the

---

* No backing singers, but a hulking Ian Stewart hovered round the back of the amps.

companionable horns of Bobby Keys and Jim Horn. Back then, there was no Keith solo spot, because Keith had yet to have a solo vocal featured on a Rolling Stones LP. But there was still the same buzz. Literally, the buzz... as the lights went down, the amplifiers throbbed and electricity filled the air. There remains something magic about that anticipation, however many gigs you attend, as the pre-show tapes finish, and the lights in the auditorium dim, and all that fills the air is the audience's banshee expectation and the pulsing of the amplifiers, throbbing like World War II Lancaster bombers setting out on a night raid. Then the pencil torches make their way across the darkened stage, leading the band into the Colosseum. The first chords are struck, the darkness splits, the lights explode, and there they are...

That same pulsing excitement can still have that effect, whatever your age. I think that is one reason why the tragedy that befell the Ariana Grande show in Manchester on May 22, 2017 was so affecting for so many people. The youngsters who were wounded or killed were almost certainly attending their first gig; they were experiencing those same sensations, were alive to the tangible excitement, were filled with just that same sense of anticipation.

★ ★ ★

And that sense of anticipation followed the Rolling Stones circus everywhere it went. The critics were delighted; the audiences grew more enthusiastic; the set became more coherent. Mick Jagger revelled in it all. Here, perhaps, was the moment the seesaw finally tipped in his direction. No longer would his band play second fiddle to The Beatles, who were by that point effectively split – George was on the road with Delaney & Bonnie, Paul and Ringo were busying themselves with their debut solo LPs and John was up to his white-suited neck in the Plastic Ono Band. Elsewhere, Bob Dylan was holed up in Woodstock, Led Zeppelin were still testing the waters and Pink Floyd was still perceived as an 'underground' outfit. So, as they blazed across America during the autumn of 1969, the Rolling Stones had the world at their feet.

On November 28 and 29, the band hit New York for three sold-out shows, and were the town's hot ticket. Seven hundred fans camped out overnight to guarantee seats. On opening night at Madison Square Garden, Simon & Garfunkel were also playing across town at Carnegie Hall. Paul Simon told the audience that it was "a true test of faith with the Stones in town". In tribute, he even inserted a quick snatch of 'Satisfaction' during the show.

Other celebrities got to the Garden to pay their own tributes, including Leonard Bernstein, Janis Joplin, Jimi Hendrix, Woody Allen, Leonard Cohen and Andy Warhol. A pre-fame Carly Simon was also there ("an unnamed girl wearing a hat with fox fur lining and a tattered raccoon coat over a pantsuit"). In her autobiography, *Boys In The Trees*, she writes glowingly of her first encounter with the man to whom she was often linked. "Mick entered the room with utter ease. I found him sexy not just from the get-go, but way before the get-go. Charisma is an overused word. It's different from beauty, and it's not the same as cuteness [...] There was no question that seeing Mick was the birth of something powerful in me."

The famous faces were part of the 20,000-strong crowd, who waited patiently to see the band in action. *Record Mirror* reported that "the Rolling Stones crowd were very much the underground scene, eighteen–mid-twenties and a sprinkling of trendy scene seekers using the gig like the first night of a Broadway musical – a place to see and be seen."

However, punctuality was never the band's strong point.

The doyen of US critics, Robert Hilburn, was about to begin his 35-year stint as rock critic for the *Los Angeles Times*, but remembers seeing the Stones in 1969 as a fan. "I did attend their show at the LA Forum," he told me, "the one that lasted all night. They did two sets, one due to start (from memory) at 7.30 and the second at 10 or so… But they pushed them so the first one didn't start till 10! The delay was that the arena had hosted a hockey match in the afternoon, and they had a hard time getting the ice from the floor. Still one of the greatest shows I ever saw."

Record Mirror noted: "The Rolling Stones are still doing good business in their American tour. But they are also running into criticism. For lateness. The Madison Square Garden Friday concert started one and a quarter hours late. The Oakland, California show had resulted in a 45-minute wait for the fans following a wild, exciting act from the Ike & Tina Turner Revue… The Stones were apparently just waiting for the crowd to calm down after the Tina Turner onslaught. There are some things the Rolling Stones can't follow – immediately."*

If it had all ended there, in New York, on the back of a month of ecstatically received shows, the Stones' 1969 US tour would have been seen as a triumph. It would have been remembered as a game-changer in the way bands approached live performances, and the group would have basked in a warm, critical glow. For the Stones themselves, it would have set the seal on the 1960s, ushering them into a new decade and an even bigger stratosphere. It would have seen them elevated to 'leaders of the pack'.

However, even before Altamont, the 1969 tour concluded on a downbeat note, with the band's appearance at the first Palm Beach International Music and Arts Festival, held on November 28–30 in Florida. It was to be the sixties' music festival's swansong.

For a fee of $100,000, the Stones topped the bill over, among others, Jefferson Airplane, Janis Joplin, Johnny Winter, Spirit and

---

* At times, it appeared that Tina's high-energy brand of erotic soul put the Rolling Stones on the back foot – of the Los Angeles Forum show, *Variety* wrote, "Saturday's event was more like a rhythm & blues revue than a rock show."

Iron Butterfly. With inevitable delays (the Stones had to wait for President Nixon's Air Force One to land before they could), by all accounts the crowd of 50,000 had dwindled to a mere 5,000 by the time the group took to the stage in the early hours of the morning. Despite the Palm Beach location, it was also bitterly cold. "I wish I was down there with you," Mick told the crowd, "because I bet it's warmer."

Overshadowing all else, however, was the still-thorny question regarding the Rolling Stones playing an open-air festival. For free. That last element was crucial.

Unlike The Beatles, the Rolling Stones did get to play a rock festival. Mick told David Fricke in 1987: "I remember going to see John Lennon and explaining to him what it was like. The Beatles always said, 'Well, we don't tour because we can't hear ourselves.' I said, 'It's not like that anymore. You can go out there and play – people will listen and applaud at the end.' But for them, it was already too late."

Things really had changed. Robert Santelli, in his *Aquarius Rising: The Rock Festival Years,* cited "Nineteen sixty nine [as] the year it all came together [...] After two years of rapid maturation, the rock festival came of age. No longer was it deemed just a weekend outing for hippies. Instead in 1969 the rock festival became a sociological and musical phenomenon."

Millions attended live music events across America, from Rhode Island to Texas. But there was a price to pay: promoters pushed up their artists' fees and record companies relished the increased sales that stemmed from their acts strutting their stuff before six-figure audiences.

Festivals were groovy and, if not free, affordable for the predominantly white, middle-class crowd. Many forget that Woodstock started out as a ticketed event; only the sheer volume of punters, which forced the organisers to make the event free of charge, turned it into the Woodstock Nation that has since gone down in history. The Florida festival was also intended as a money-making event, with tickets costing $20 a piece.

But rising ticket prices soon had their detractors. In fact, the knives were out for the Rolling Stones even before the US tour, when ticket prices were announced to the public. To one important critic, the band were pricing themselves out of their audience's reach.

Ralph J. Gleason ("the trench-coated conscience of San Francisco rock") was music critic for the *San Francisco Chronicle* and, along with Jann Wenner, co-founder of *Rolling Stone* magazine. According to Joe Hagan, Wenner's biographer, Ralph Gleason "looked like a Scotland Yard detective: deerstalker cap, curled mustache, pipe clenched in his teeth and horn-rimmed glasses on his nose". But Gleason's fogeyish look disguised one of the most erudite of all music critics. By the late sixties, the jazz-mad Gleason had not only interviewed Louis Armstrong and Miles Davis, but also Hank Williams, Elvis Presley and Ray Charles. He initially dismissed Dylan, before becoming one of his loudest advocates. Gleason was the moving force behind the San Francisco scene, an early champion of the Grateful Dead and Jefferson Airplane. His work might not have reached the widest audience, but it mattered.

So, when details of the Rolling Stones' US tour were announced, it was Gleason's *Chronicle* column of October 19, 1969 that particularly stung. He admitted that the Stones "put on a good show" but railed at their financial guarantees ($25,000 a night plus percentages). "Can the Rolling Stones actually need all that money?... How much can the Stones take back to Merrie England after taxes anyway?" He went on to say: "Paying five, six or seven dollars for a Stones concert for, say, an hour of the Stones seen from a quarter of a mile away because the artists demand such outrageous fees that they can only be obtained under these circumstances says a very bad thing to me about the artist's attitude towards their public. It says they despise their own audience."

Gleason also went on to take issue with the (never proven) allegations that the Stones were underpaying their black opening acts, overlooking the debt the band owed the black musicians that had so inspired them. As Philip Norman was to later point out: "Ike & Tina Turner and B.B. King, far from being exploited, were receiving their biggest career boost in years."

So, ticket prices were still a contentious issue in the wake of Woodstock, and there was a perception that rock'n'roll, the music of rebellion, should be open to all. By comparison, a ticket to see Mick, Keith and cohorts may well have cost only a dollar or so more than what The Doors were charging, but this was the Stones' first tour in three years. And they were the *Rolling Stones*. By today's standards the price was laughably low: even taking inflation into account, in 1969 a top-dollar Stones ticket was the equivalent of three pounds, 10 shillings (£3.50).

Pressure continued to mount for the Stones to perform a free concert. Ralph Gleason devoted another column to the band's iniquitous ticket prices: "I personally have very little sympathy for the Devil who is simply charging as much as the traffic will bear. Like any dealer."

In answer to the criticism railed against them, the Stones decided that they would end the US tour with a free concert in San Francisco, a kind of 'Woodstock West'. Under the headline 'Stones US Tour Breaks All Records', in the December 6, 1969 issue of *Rolling Stone*, Mick was quoted as saying of the concert: "It will be free, because we want to do a free concert, except that Ralph Gleason has to pay $50 to get in."

With the decade edging to an end, and with the country on what appeared to be the verge of a violent revolution, maybe the

Stones' free show might be just the tonic American needed. Maybe an hour and a half of rock'n'roll could salve a nation's wounds; 90 minutes of 'Satisfaction' might erase the Manson nightmare, curb the hijackers' need to flee to Cuba, pacify the Black Panthers, defy the Nixon presidency. But then, it was the sixties, and idealism was the common currency...

Even following the desultory Florida appearance, the band's 1969 return to the American concert stage was deemed a triumph. For those who hadn't made it to one of the shows, they could capture the magic on bootleg. And at tour's end came the salivating prospect of a new Rolling Stones LP. But before the Stones could begin their ramble home, there was the overriding issue of that free concert. The free show was designed to absolve the Stones, to thwart the criticism that they had become too elevated. It was an opportunity for the band to prove their commitment to a kind of revolutionary idealism. For them, it would also provide a glorious swansong to the sixties.

For those who could not make the biblical trek out West, the Stones had kindly ensured there would be a film of the event to be enjoyed later. For all the right reasons, a free concert hosted by the Rolling Stones in December 1969 would be the cherry on the cake. A rock band playing at its imperial height; an audience gagging to rekindle the magic of Woodstock; a sunlit Californian location... What could possibly go wrong?

CHAPTER 12

Dancing With Mr D

The road to Altamont was fraught with pitfalls from the outset. With the tour concluded by the end of November, the Stones slotted in some illicit studio time in Alabama. Meanwhile, the date for the free concert was announced: December 6 in San Francisco's Golden Gate Park, the traditional venue for Bay Area bands such as the Grateful Dead, Santana and Jefferson Airplane. The show would feature those acts, along with the added enticement of Crosby, Stills, Nash & Young, who had played relatively few shows following the release of their debut album earlier that year. It was a glorious lineup. The Rolling Stones would be the surprise headliners. Escorted to the stage by a Praetorian band of bikers, it would be the ultimate triumph.

But even without the Rolling Stones, clearly Golden Gate Park could not accommodate the anticipated crowds. And anyhow, no permit had been granted by the city.* So with time pressing, another location had to be quickly sought.

---

* Sam Cutler is convinced that Bill Graham, a titanic figure of the San Francisco music scene, blocked the Golden Gate gig. It followed an onstage dispute with

Even with San Francisco cancelled, the Stones were now struck by the opportunity of headlining the free concert as the perfect conclusion to the year. It would reconnect the band with their underground audience, the Rolling Stones playing "real good, for free". It would rekindle memories of Hyde Park. Finally, in Mick's mind, he could envisage the band playing as the sun set. A massive, passive crowd, united by a love of music, stretching as far as the eye could see to the horizon. Harmony. Energy. An Aquarian Last Night of the Proms. All played out beneath the starlit skies of California. The event would act as the perfect climax to the documentary the Maysles brothers had been filming throughout the US tour.

The brothers (and their co-director, Charlotte Zwerin) had been brought on board almost as an afterthought, given a bare 12 hours' notice to begin shooting the project provisionally entitled 'Mick Jagger's Home Movie'. They did, however, have pedigree when it came to the field of 'rockumentary' – they were there for the inaugural Beatles Stateside trip in 1964, capturing some of the madness of Beatlemania in the documentary *What's Happening?* Their fly-on-the-wall documentaries on Bible salesmen, Marlon Brando and the 1960 presidential election had also been critics' favourites.

In the Stones' mind, a performance before a vast, biblical crowd in a desert would provide a breathtaking cinematic finale. It was the same sort of hubris that led The Beatles to look for a similar climax to their own film project, the *Let It Be* (aka *Get Back*) film. The documentary was originally to conclude with the band making their first live appearance in three years at a Roman Colosseum in Tunisia. From sunrise, crowds of every race, colour

---

the Rolling Stones in Oakland near the beginning of the tour – Jagger was furious with Graham, while the promoter seethed at the Stones' arrogance.

185

and creed would flock to the show, a cross-section of humanity serenaded by the world's most fabled band. In the end, the Fabs said 'fuck it', and grudgingly climbed up on the Apple roof in central London, one windy January day.

Chip Monck, who had done such a spectacular job stage-managing Woodstock and was fresh off the Stones' tour, was appointed to build a stage for the free show, now scheduled to take place at the Sears Point Raceway in Sonoma, California. The raceway's slopes formed a natural amphitheatre, meaning the stage could be built on a slope and therefore needed to be just 3 feet high. But when the location was switched at short notice, that paltry stage was to be the first in a series of cataclysmic errors.

Built to deal with large, enthusiastic crowds attending road-race meetings, Sears Point appeared perfectly suited to cope with the anticipated audience numbers for the Stones' Woodstock. There was parking for an estimated 100,000 vehicles, running water on tap, proper toilet facilities, electricity on site, and it was conveniently located around 35 miles from San Francisco. However, the perfect venue soon fell out of favour. The raceway's owners were a film company who, on learning of the Stones' plans, demanded a seven-figure fee as well as distribution rights for any movie made of the event. But the film was the final, key element in the plans, a fitting conclusion to a triumphant return – the band weren't prepared to share that triumph with a bunch of drag racers. So Sears Point was out, and that left barely 48 hours to find an alternative location.

With increasingly hysterical radio announcements and details in the underground press, the 'Woodstock of the West' was an ideal opportunity for the thousands of fans who had been unable to get tickets for any of the band's four California shows to see the Rolling Stones in action. Plus, with the year's end in sight, and for those who hadn't made it to Woodstock or Florida, the Rolling

Stones somewhere in California was the last date on 1969's festival calendar. By Wednesday, December 3, from all across the nation, the tribes were on the move…

With the clock ticking on the venue, Jann Wenner put the Stones in hasty touch with a lawyer. Melvin 'Mel' Belli had defended Lee Harvey Oswald's assassin Jack Ruby, stood for Lenny Bruce at many of his obscenity trials and had represented various celebrity clients. He can be seen in the film of *Gimme Shelter*, a colourful character, fluently working the phones.

Finally, a space was made available. Sixty miles from San Francisco, the Altamont Speedway was an unprepossessing location, but site owner Dick Carter was only too happy to let the festival go ahead – without charge – on his property. All he wanted was the publicity; by the end of the weekend, Carter reckoned, everyone who mattered would know the name of Altamont.

A veritable caravan transported the PA, lighting rigs and thousands of dollars of equipment across California, from Sears Point to Altamont. The new location meant that, standing alone without any gradient, Chip Monck's 3 foot stage was totally, visibly unsuitable. There were concerns over the lack of basic facilities, that the estimated crowd would clog every road in the area, that the tiny police force would be literally overwhelmed. But by the time the stage had been erected, held together with string, a crowd of thousands was already gathering a day before the concert was scheduled to start.

Chartering a helicopter to view Altamont, Grateful Dead manager Rock Scully had been joined by another figure who would feature heavily in the story. Afro-haired Michael Lang had co-created and organised the Woodstock Music and Art Festival with Artie Kornfeld. The sheer volume of the crowds and the ensuing legend had turned the event into the world's best-remembered 'free' festival and Lang into the 'Wizard of Woodstock'.

Even though it was only four months after the event, everyone, from *Time* to *Rolling Stone*, agreed that Woodstock had become a byword for all that was good about the counterculture. Lang could rest on his laurels, anticipating not just a three-hour documentary but also a three-LP souvenir of the festival, scheduled for release in 1970. Looking down at Altamont from the helicopter circling over the proposed site, Lang (the man who *was* Woodstock) put everyone's minds at rest: "This is perfect. We can do it here."

Not everyone was so enthralled. "To my undying regret," said Sam Cutler later, acting on Scully and Lang's thumbs-up, on viewing the location he called it "a fatal error of judgement". On his first sight, Albert Maysles was disappointed by "the grubby, desolate nature of the place". LSD purist Owsley Stanley called the site "a moonscape of crushed auto bodies... We looked over to the left and saw this place that looked like a skull. It was the actual arena in which they held all these demolition derbies... This place smells of death. I thought 'This is the worst possible place to hold something like this.'"

By then it was too late, the word was out, the flood was underway. An estimated crowd of 50,000 was, on the night of Friday, December 5, snaking to a dilapidated speedway in the middle of a desert. They trudged there looking for a new beginning. Unwittingly, all were making their way to the end.

★ ★ ★

Keith Richards' horoscope in the December 6, 1969 issue of the *Daily Mail* read:

> Sagittarius: Plans may not go as scheduled, you would be wise to postpone anything of importance. Travel is possible, there will be new and exciting faces around you tonight.

Again, with the benefit of hindsight, perhaps we read too much into the runes, the omens, the boiled guts of birds, the entrails sifted through for portents... but *The Times* crossword on the same day did include the following clues – "9 Across: There's no holding a worker in stone... 5 Down: They're subject to Beelzebub".

An ocean, two time zones and a continent away, it was immediately apparent that the access, toilets, concert stage, backstage facilities and medical coverage at Dick Carter's Altamont Speedway were wholly inadequate for a crowd that, on the day, was now anticipated to number in the region of 300,000. Chip Monck was already on the phone to Bill Graham, pleading for access to his experienced Fillmore crew: "We've got a disaster on our hands... We can't build the stage, the power lines aren't in, there's no sanitation and no medical, there's no water. We're in a sandpit. It's not good."

While Graham had his own issues with the Stones, as an experienced concert promoter he could see a sea of problems. Graham was also canny enough to appreciate that any disaster could backfire on the whole rock community. He begged Monck to cancel. But it was too late. Like the inflexible railway timetables that led the European dynasties inexorably into the Great War, Altamont had taken on its own terrible momentum. Mick Jagger himself had promised that the Stones would play a free show at the climax of their 1969 tour... the San Francisco media were saying it would happen... top bands had agreed to play somewhere – anywhere – on December 6...

Whole books have been written about Altamont; its failure has been endlessly chronicled and dissected. Its symbolic nature is hard to overestimate. Yet, at root it was a good idea, very much in keeping with the spirit of the times. However, it was hastily pulled together, at an inappropriate location, and poorly organised. And that's before you add the Hells Angels to the mix.

The Stones had been delighted with the way the Hells Angels had policed the event in July in Hyde Park. But there was an ocean of difference between the UK branch of the Angels and their fearsome American counterparts. I remember seeing the UK Angels queuing for buses, or settling for motor scooters rather than mighty Harley choppers. As Philip Norman wrote, the real Angels bore "as much resemblance to Hyde Park's pimply faux Nazis as White Lightning does to orange Fanta". *Melody Maker's* Chris Welch dubbed them "Hell's Herberts!" The Stones' tour manager, Tom Keylock (the man who unleashed the infamous butterflies – from boxes of Smith's 'Chicken Fry' crisps), was scathing about their presence at Hyde Park: "Mickey Mouse Angels... Teddy Boys from Penge. I don't even remember seeing a motorbike, apart from the copper's one – there was only one copper assigned to the gig!"

The Grateful Dead were particularly close to the Angels' San Francisco chapter, and manager Rock Scully was equally withering about their English 'counterparts': "There was a chapter of real Hells Angels in London. But there were also these other ones, who had just written 'Hells Angels' in chalk and whitewash on the back of their leather jackets... They were riding around on mopeds!"

For the hippies, the Hells Angels retained an outlaw chic. They were Billy the Kid on a chopper. The name had come to popular attention via Howard Hughes' 1930 film about World War I flying aces. However, they soon became a symbol of nihilism, which spread with the 1953 film *The Wild One*, in which a motorcycle gang terrorises a small Californian town. The film gave Brando his best ever onscreen line: "What are you rebelling against Johnny?" "Waddya got?"

In his exhaustive account of Altamont,* Joel Selvin's research into the Angels found their California membership as unlikely to have been more than 100. But that century of members "boasted a record of 874 felony arrests (300 convictions) [...] The outlaw gang had struck a nerve with the public as some kind of contemporary equivalent of old-time western bank robbers, like the James brothers or Butch Cassidy and the Sundance Kid [...] These were real hard men who lived by their own code."

The Hells Angels were happy cultivating their outsider image. After the Hollister riot, which raged at the Gypsy Tour motorcycle rally from July 3 to 6 in 1947, the American Motorcyclist Association allegedly insisted that 99 per cent of their members were law-abiding, decent citizens. This led to the Hells Angels wearing their own patches that read simply '1 per cent'!

It was this type of flagrant rebellion that intrigued members of the counterculture. Hunter S. Thompson spent a year with the Angels and recounted his experiences in his first book, *Hells Angels: The Strange And Terrible Saga Of The Outlaw Motorcycle Gangs* (1966). The Bay Area rock'n'roll bands were particularly close to the Hells Angels' San Francisco chapter. Bands like the Grateful Dead, Big Brother & the Holding Company and Jefferson Airplane courted the Angels, who were often seen at their gigs around the city. As well as a fondness for dope, the hippies and Angels were united in their antipathy to cops. Ken Kesey's renegade Merry Pranksters forged an alliance with the motorcycle gang – largely, it appears, because the LSD Kesey was so enthusiastic about was even more potent than the Angels' favoured wine and weed.

Rock Scully had been the moving force behind the December 6 free concert, and it was on his suggestion that the Angels police it.

---

* *Altamont: The Rolling Stones, The Hells Angels And The Inside Story Of Rock's Darkest Day* by Joel Selvin (Dey Street Books, 2016).

Joel Selvin quoted him as telling Keith, "The Angels are really some righteous dudes. They carry themselves with honor and dignity." It was Scully who took the Stones' Mr Fixit, Sam Cutler, to meet the Angels to discuss security for the event, which, at that point, was still scheduled for the smaller Golden Gate Park. One idea kicked around was that the Angels would greet the Stones at San Francisco airport, and escort them to the park. It would be the nearest rock'n'roll got to a Roman triumph.

In principle, the Angels agreed – they'd be there wherever they were needed but with one proviso: that something was to be laid on to drink. As Joel Selvin later wrote: "In what would become one of the most famous financial transactions since the Dutch bought Manhattan from the Indians for $24, Cutler agreed to provide $500 for beer."

★ ★ ★

In the ensuing half-century, there has been a lot of buck-passing and denial over what unfolded at Altamont. It did not begin altogether ominously. Chip Monck and his crew, working through the bitterly cold night, had managed to fashion a stage, albeit low-slung. Towers were constructed, with rigs for the lights and PA. Among the thousands who had arrived in the pre-dawn hours, fuelled by cheap red wine and weed, huddled round the blazing bonfires, there was a feeling of bonhomie. Keith Richards, who had spent the night before on site with Sam Cutler, was not the only one beguiled by the mood as the sun rose on the morning of Saturday, December 6.

But the feeling wasn't to last. And the trouble began long before the music started. High on acid and fuelled by beer, the Hells Angels amused themselves by driving their choppers through the crowd. There had been a paltry chain-link fence protecting the stage, designed to keep the crowd out and the Angels in. However, someone in the Stones camp decided to put the press in there, and once the concertgoers saw civilians right in front of the stage, the fence came down, which left the Hells Angels roaming free.

As the morning developed, and with no musical distractions, it seems as if anyone even looked at the Angels the wrong way they were scheduled for a beating. Sawn-off pool cues were their weapon of choice. And heaven help anyone who dared stumble and touch one of the Angels' prized motorcycles.

Chris Hillman of the The Flying Burrito Brothers recalls: "I had to argue with the Hells Angels to get onto the stage with my bass, they were so out of their minds [...] It was a day that was oppressive and dark, the sky was dark, the mood was dark, and the ending was the worst scenario you could imagine... I thought that day was the end of the sixties – it had come from the wonderful innocence of the Beatles and Gerry & the Pacemakers to this."

It was, indeed, an ugly scene. The combination of poor security and hastily made arrangements were soon overshadowed by what could only be called 'bad vibes'. As well as the Angels, the audience appeared determined to be wholly blitzed and out of it before a single note was played. They guzzled cheap red wine and mixed it with potent psychedelics. By all accounts, even the LSD at Altamont was ropey, and cutting acid with amphetamines was a recipe for disaster. People were swilling, sniffing, popping, guzzling *anything* that came their way. The peace and love aura of Woodstock was supplanted by an atmosphere of threatening menace. They came to Altamont in their thousands expecting peace and love, but they were confronted with violence and hostility. Even the crowd at Altamont was ugly – one recurring image was of an obese, naked fan dancing. The Angels found him funny, so they beat him up too.

"In a way, the grotesqueness of his nude body and the pictures of him that were printed in the newspapers... symbolized the gruesome and sordid atmosphere that prevailed at Altamont," Robert Santelli wrote. "Grossly overweight, with womanly breasts… he wasn't demonstrative of the pictures of youth and beauty that had been expounded by the press after the Woodstock story made international headlines. Then *Time* and *Life* printed photos of seminude girls with wholesome bodies bathing… in a lake of idyllic purity. At Altamont, an entirely different glimpse of the counterculture was brought to the surface."

Having only just arrived on site, Albert Maysles was unaware of the chaos that was developing. Observing a cameraman getting shots of a clearly tripping, visibly disturbed naked woman, he advised: "Don't shoot that. That's ugly. We only want beautiful things." The cameraman, who had already spent hours watching the hostility unfold, replied: "Everything here is ugly."*

Finally, with the crowd and the Angels already riled up, the music began.

Woodstock favourites Santana kicked everything off, and played a blistering set. But by mid-afternoon, even the music couldn't take the edge off the malign atmosphere. The Angels thought the hippies dancing to the weedy rock of Crosby, Stills, Nash & Young and The Flying Burrito Brothers was laughable. They began beating back the crowd from the stage with motorcycle chains and pool cues.

Over the years, Jefferson Airplane felt they had developed a bond with the Angels, so when vocalist Marty Balin saw one of them laying into a concertgoer during the band's set, he stepped in, only to have the shit kicked out of him. "Woodstock was a bunch of

---

* The Force was most definitely not with another cameramen that day. Twenty-five-year-old George Lucas, with a Galaxy far, far away still eight years in the future, is listed on the *Gimme Shelter* credits. However, his camera jammed and none of his footage made it to the film.

stupid slobs in the mud," said the Airplane's Grace Slick; "Altamont was a bunch of angry slobs in the mud."

Crosby, Stills, Nash & Young couldn't wait to get out of there and split soon after four cursory numbers. On arrival, the Grateful Dead's Jerry Garcia was greeted with the news that the Angels were running riot, and that the bikers had just beaten up the singer of Jefferson Airplane. Garcia's response, captured on film ("Oh, bummer..."), came nowhere close to addressing the growing chaos.

It was a tragic irony that the Grateful Dead did not play at Altamont. The band bottled it. It was their apparent closeness to the Angels that led to them advocating the bikers handle security. That closeness withered and died in a whirlwind of pool cues, fists and blood. If the Dead had appeared, there was a faint possibility that it might have alleviated the violence; the Angels might have listened to the band that had been their early champions. But we shall never know; stoned and terrified, the Grateful Dead huddled behind the stage hearing tales of the carnage out front, grateful not to be dead themselves. The band that had been a crucial conduit to Altamont fled without playing a note or making any attempt to reach out to the Hells Angels running riot. Bummer.

From the photos and footage that exist of the event, one can clearly see the Angels' overt, sneering hostility towards the crowd they had been tasked with policing. Testosterone oozing from every beery pore, the Angels patently, potently, loathed the hippies. They were equally less enamoured of the headline act.

"Mick Jagger had no idea who these men were," Joel Selvin reflected later, "to him, they must have seemed like some kind of colourful centurions of the hippie realm [...] These hard men could be ruthless in the protection of what they perceived as their territory. And now, they were the flimsy line between the massing crowd and the musicians who would soon be onstage."

As the sun sank, if possible, things got even worse... There was nowhere you could go to escape the Angels' wrath. The Stones were cloistered in a trailer with one non-Angel bodyguard in tow. As Mick ventured outside, he was greeted by a daemonic fan who confronted him with "I hate you, you fucker", before punching him in the face. It was far from encouraging. Rumours spread of the ugly vibes emanating from the pathetic stage; it was like the Hells Angels were running the show, with the Stones as their guests. Used to being in complete control, the Stones were watching it all unravel. But they were convinced their show, which had enchanted cities across America over the preceding month, would have the same calming effect on this restless crowd. So confident were the band that they chose Altamont to premier a new song, 'Brown Sugar', which would alone guarantee sales of 300,000 when it became their next single. Music was, after all, the balm.

The Stones were determined to milk the atmosphere. As the magnet that had drawn the crowd to this godforsaken spot, they wanted to assert their power by holding off on appearing till after dark. By then, after a long wait, with the edginess of the stewards apparent, with the heady mix of anticipation, drugs and wine, the stew was boiling. "Getting a bit hairy, Keith," Ian Stewart remarked, as the band made their way to the low-slung stage.

Future Bruce Springsteen manager Jon Landau started out as a critic. A Stones fan, the year before Altamont he had eerily observed, "The Stones live... If the violence of their music was cathartic, how to describe their concerts? The Rolling Stones are violence. Their music penetrates the raw nerve endings of their listeners and finds its way into the groove marked 'release of frustration'. Their violence has always been a surrogate for the larger violence their audience is capable of."

As they made their way to the stage, the Stones themselves were calmly coasting on soothing drugs, anticipating nothing but good vibrations. But once they reached the tiny platform, the Angels were reluctant to vacate it. The band and a harassed Sam Cutler had to jostle their reluctant guards offstage. The Angels' venom was most apparent when Mick finally began his caped capering. The Maysles' documentary shows the poisonous stares from the robustly macho Angels. All looked like their idea of a good end to the evening was applying pool cues to the prancing person of the flamboyantly androgynous Jagger. You can feel their hostility as Mick launches into a powerful 'Jumpin' Jack Flash', with 'Carol' keeping the crowd buoyant. With its infectious 'Whoo-whoo…' chorus, 'Sympathy For The Devil' had proved a guaranteed crowd-pleaser at every gig. It worked at Altamont, too, as the crowd pushed forward to get closer to the spritely singer.

Barely elevated from his audience, Jagger soon sensed that something was wrong. It was hard to see. The awestruck faces he *could* see didn't stretch far beyond the first few rows of the crowd, but faraway fires gave a sense of the throngs that stretched beyond. Within a few minutes, that feeling of brooding hostility seeped out from the darkness and reached the stage. Mick stopped 'Sympathy For The Devil', pleading: "Hey people… brothers and sisters… why are we fighting?… Is there anyone there who's been hurt? Okay, I think we're cool. We can groove. We always have something very strange happen when we start that number." Keith took the mic: "Either those cats cool it, man, or we don't play. Keep it cool! Hey, if you don't keep it cool, you ain't gonna hear no music." The Angels were not there for the music. They were not there to dialogue. One grabbed the mic from Keith: "Fuck you."

For many years, it was one of the demonic myths of Altamont that the Stones were playing 'Sympathy For The Devil' when the murder of eighteen-year-old Meredith Hunter occurred. In fact, they were performing the rhythmically gentler, misogynistic 'Under My Thumb' when the black teenager was cut down and killed by members of the Hells Angels.

A full picture of Meredith Hunter emerged in Joel Selvin's comprehensive 2016 book on Altamont. The background was all too familiar for a poor African American: abandoned by his natural father, his mother was forced into prostitution by her abusive partner. Much of Meredith's adolescence was spent in juvenile hall or prison. He did like his music, though, taking his girlfriend, Patti, to see The Temptations, as well as attending the 1969 Monterey Jazz Festival.

The temptation to see the Rolling Stones – for free – was irresistible, so with two other friends, Meredith and Patti squeezed into a brown 1965 Ford Mustang. The traffic was backed up long before Altamont, so they dumped the car and followed the crowds. About 2.30 on the afternoon of Saturday, December 6, Meredith paused and told his friends: "I've got to go back to the car. I forgot my gun."

Just why did Meredith Hunter need to take a gun to a free concert? Until Altamont, all the reports from the big festivals were of peace and love, the air filled with 'good vibes'. Stage announcements rarely contained menace, only the odd warning to stay away from the 'brown acid' (Woodstock).

Perhaps Hunter was conscious of the fact that there were very few black faces amid the huge crowd, since big festivals tended to attract predominantly white, middle-class audiences. Maybe he was packing for protection. But, true to the spirit of the times, surely he was caught up in the belief that everybody got together and loved one another, regardless of race, creed or the colour of a man's skin?

Self-preservation could have been a motivation – he was, after all, a young black man accompanying his white girlfriend to a busy concert. That in itself would have likely pissed off the Angels, being a red rag to their bullish intolerance – few African Americans ever got to wear the Angels' urine-soaked colours.

All the cool hippie pleas from the stage ("Brothers and sisters... everybody just cool out... I think we're cool, we can groove") could not control the carnage. By all accounts the Angels were picking on Hunter, whether because he was black or he gave them lip. Or maybe they were taking their role as guardians seriously, protecting the band they were there to guard?

Of the many accounts of the murder, there were tales of the Angels hassling Hunter, and him pulling his gun in a show of self-defence. Another theory has Hunter determined to go down in the record books. Was he there to become the first rock'n'roll assassin... *The Man Who Shot Mick Jagger* (also the title of a tacky seventies novel)?

Onstage, Sam Cutler was convinced he had heard shots fired. On verbal evidence, and as can be seen when those awful moments are freeze-framed in *Gimme Shelter*, the teenager did have a gun and it was in his hand, just before the knives plunged in.

'A Witness' in Bill Wyman's *Rolling With The Stones* recounted: "He tried to run and four Angels jumped him. He ran into the crowd... The Angels were hitting him and stabbed him in the back. The kid pulled out a gun with a long barrel... One of the Angels grabbed the gun and stabbed him in the back. Then they hit him."

A young doctor, Robert Hiatt, was the first medical aid to reach Meredith Hunter: "It was obvious he wasn't going to make it... He had a wound in the lower back, a wound in the back near the spine, which could have severed a major vessel, and a fairly large wound in the left temple. There was no equipment there to treat him. He needed to be operated on immediately." This revealed the most cataclysmic failure of Altamont – the scant medical facilities available. Sure, there were doctors and clinics on site to talk people down from their bad trips, but not to save the life of the victim of a stabbing.

Only Meredith Hunter knew what made him take a gun to a free festival, and he died before he could be questioned as to his motives. His murder provided the awful, bloody climax to Altamont. So was he a martyr to the vindictiveness of the Hells Angels and the egocentricity of the Rolling Stones? Or a man intent on murder himself, just a shot away from pulling the trigger he knew would guarantee him celebrity?

Onstage, Keith was told there was "a guy out there with a gun". It was evident something was going horribly, horribly wrong, quickly spinning out of control. Both Mick and Sam Cutler appealed for calm, as well as a doctor and an ambulance. But, such was the pervasive chaos, no one really knew what was happening. A snap decision had to be made: did the Stones continue their set, dimly aware that out there in the darkness something serious was going down? Or did they immediately split, thereby causing the crowd of 300,000 to riot?

Despite the ensuing bedlam, the band persevered; splitting early could have made an ugly scene even uglier. But the final decision was made when, according to Wyman, "helicopter pilot Jan Vinson came onstage and told us in no uncertain terms that his was the last helicopter and he was leaving, with or without us. We played 'Honky Tonk Women' and ended the show with a stupid choice – 'Street Fighting Man'."

Swiftly, the Rolling Stones and Gram Parsons, and far too many others, crammed into Vinson's helicopter. It was intended to carry eight passengers but when it took off there were 17 on board. Like the last choppers leaving Saigon half a decade in the future, the departure from Altamont was a sad and shameful exodus. As the helicopter flew over the festival site, fires blazed below. Huddled round them were a crowd who had come anticipating another Woodstock, and instead were left scavenging at Golgotha.

Writing of Jagger in 1989, and drawing comparisons with Robert Johnson, Steve Grant conjured up a breathless portrait of the head Stone: "Robert Johnson represents that dark, violent, cocksmith side of black music which Jagger moulded with androgyny, Crowley, crowd-control, whiplash athleticism and camp self-worship into something faintly wonderful becoming finally something very weird and unpleasant, blowing back in his face that cold and windy Altamont night 20 years ago. Then grown-up Evil took over and we had the aspect of a frail, scared kid not knowing what he'd done."

Talking to Tom Hibbert in 1987, Jagger admitted, "Altamont was... tough... I didn't see the guy with the gun until I saw the movie and that was a horrific moment. It was one of those hell situations... At that point, one became very afraid. You were just waiting for the next one. What's going to happen now?"

Meredith's wasn't the only death to have occurred at the Altamont Free Concert – two people died in a hit-and-run accident and another drowned in a nearby irrigation canal after taking LSD. Countless more were injured or beaten up. But the full scale of the tragedy did not become apparent until some days later. Due to deadlines, and the problems getting off site to phone in copy, many of the early accounts of Altamont didn't feature the details of the Stones performance or of the tragedy on site. The Sunday edition of the *San Francisco Examiner*, for example, noted that "the record-breaking crowd, probably the largest in the history of Northern California, was for the most part orderly but enthusiastic".

The *Variety* edition of December 10, 1969 reported: "The largest gathering of people in Northern California history, needing no advertising or formal promotion [...] Given the crush of people, the day was peaceful and orderly [...] Those who were on hand for last summer's famed Woodstock Festival in New Yorked labeled Saturday's (6) gathering as an equal."

But by the following Monday, it was apparent just how horribly wrong it had all gone. Across the Atlantic, the *Daily Mail* carried the headline: 'Stoned – 4 killed, 4 born, thousands drugged at the Rolling Stones wildest concert'. Inside the broadsheet, under the picture of a naked hippie, the caption ran: "The concert, the last of the group's US tour, was free. It turned into a free-for-all".

Altamont was also front-page news in *The Times*: 'Births And Deaths As Stones Sing'. Inside, Michael Leapman detailed "a chaotic afternoon and evening [...] The Rolling Stones refused to appear at the original site, a racecourse, after a dispute over film rights for the concert." The report continued, stating that there were "19 doctors and six psychiatrists engaged by the Rolling Stones for the occasion". It pointed out that security was handled by "the Hells Angels, an international motorcycling gang".

At *Melody Maker*, Chris Welch recalled: "Press day was on a Monday, so we got the news of Altamont, printing on Tuesday at Colchester. I do remember Altamont spreading a dark mood over the music business. The Manson trial earlier had cast a pall over 1969, and after the optimism of 1967, the hippie idealism of rock'n'roll, I felt there was a hint of it at Hyde Park, with the Hells Angels. But certainly, following Altamont, suddenly came the darkness."

Talking to the *Evening Standard*'s Ray Connolly a fortnight after the festival, Keith Richards was widely quoted speaking about the differences he perceived between UK and US audiences: "In Hyde Park everyone had a good time and there was no trouble. You can put half a million young English people together and they won't start killing each other. That's the difference."

Nearer to the scene of the crime, and perhaps sensing their own culpability in the events, the response in San Francisco was immediate. Looking back years later, Bill Graham called Altamont "an event which was more costly to rock and roll than any single day in the history of entertainment". Despite his insistence on the Stones playing a free festival, Ralph J. Gleason immediately cited Altamont as "the end of rock's innocence". The pompous David Crosby, only a few months short of letting the world muse upon the wisdom of 'Almost Cut My Hair', opened with both barrels. He applauded the Angels' "absolutely definable code... they stick to it very carefully. They are in their own way, intensely moralistic..." Then finding fault with the Stones' "star trip, and who qualify in my book as snobs... ", he added, "I think [the Stones] have an exaggerated view of their own importance, especially the two leaders." Hubris courtesy of David Crosby was one thing. But worse was to come for the Stones.

When the full tragedy of Altamont became apparent, *Rolling Stone* co-founder Ralph Gleason excoriated Jann Wenner, railing that if theirs was a professional newspaper about rock'n'roll, the moment of truth was nigh: was Wenner a groupie or a fucking journalist? Gleason, whose columns played no small part in putting the Stones on the road to Altamont, fumed that the magazine should cover Altamont "like it was World War II". Gleason was backed up by the magazine's journalists Greil Marcus, Langdon Winner, Lester Bangs and John Burks, who had witnessed the tragedy unfold. To his credit, Wenner did just that – on January 30, 1970, they released their Altamont issue, a 17-page special that left little doubt as to who was to blame for the catastrophe.

Rolling Stone's coverage of the fatal rock concert elevated the two-year-old magazine to the grown-ups table. Under the front-page headline 'The Rolling Stones Disaster At Altamont: Let It Bleed', the magazine called the event a "product of diabolical egotism, high ineptitude, money manipulation and, at base, a fundamental lack of concern for humanity [...] all it lacked was mass rioting and the murder of one or more musicians". The writers then added a list of 10 ways in which Altamont's organisers had "worked out a blueprint for disaster", including "4) Make sure the grounds are barren, treeless, desolate [...] 6) Provide one-sixtieth the required toilet facilities [...] 8) Build the stage low enough to be easily hurdled. Don't secure a clear area between stage and audience."

Page after page levelled the finger at the Stones, the band coming under particularly fierce criticism. "As usual, the Stones trip included the best of everything. The best of hotels, limousines, cuisine. Maybe it was a free concert, but there was no good reason not to do it in style." The magazine blamed the band for hiring the Angels, who, the journalists insisted, "were in charge of the stage. They had taken it that morning. It was theirs, musicians or no musicians. What the fuck, wasn't nobody tough enough to take it from them... The Stones? Not likely. It had become, to a disturbing degree, a Hells Angels Festival."

Given that it was pieced together in a pre-fax, email, laptop and mobile world, within a matter of weeks over Christmas 1969, the *Rolling Stone* Altamont issue was an impressive piece of journalism. Moreover, given the scope and depth of the reporting, the magazine's coverage was particularly hurtful to the band it had so loyally supported. Co-founder Jann Wenner and Jagger had, of course, enjoyed a long friendship and a short-lived business partnership via the UK edition of *Rolling Stone*. Jagger was interviewed for the magazine's 40th anniversary in 1987. Gerri

Hirshey asked him what he felt back then about *Rolling Stone*'s Altamont coverage? "I didn't think it was justified, to be perfectly honest. Perhaps there was a feeling in the San Francisco community that that sort of thing shouldn't happen there... At the time it was such a traumatic event for the whole community. Of course we had to shoulder our share of the blame. Which we did. But we weren't the only people that were responsible."

So much symbolism has attached itself to Altamont over the years, but much later, talking to Jann Wenner, Jagger was dismissive of the stigma attached to the concert. "I didn't think of these things that you guys thought of, you in the press: this cathartic end of an era... It was more how awful... it was for someone to get killed and how sad it was for his family and how dreadfully the Hells Angels behaved."

The debate raged on into the early part of 1970, with the magazine's letters pages filled with both messages of support ("Don't blame the Stones. Mick Jagger isn't Jesus") and blame ("Thank you for the wonderful assassination of the Rolling Stones"). Astrologically too, apparently Altamont was doomed: "It was just a few days after the Winter Solstice when the forces of darkness are at their most powerful. The moon was in Scorpio, which is the time of the month when the Universal vibration is at its most unstable," wrote Lee Heflin from Los Angeles.

Altamont... Even today, and even after other events with far bigger crowds, with other tragedies and with far higher casualties, it is Altamont that still casts the longest shadow as the event that undermined the sixties.

It did not, however, end the festival frenzy. By August 1970, Canada's Strawberry Fields offered up Led Zeppelin (who never actually made an appearance on the day), Jethro Tull, Melanie, Sly & the Family Stone, and more, and promised "3 Days of Love Sun & Sound... with Chip Monck, the voice of Woodstock". Some of the other rock festivals that year alone were held in Atlanta, Bath, Winnipeg, Berlin, Ontario, Michigan and Washington state, while the Isle of Wight festival drew hundreds of thousands of hippie revellers to the tiny island.

Louisiana hosted the Celebration Of Life festival in June 1971. The organisers issued a detailed booklet about access and a ceiling on audience numbers, each of whom would be issued with "a special badge with a Polaroid photo". A *Melody Maker* report ran: "If all this sounds a little paranoid, one need only to remember the nightmare of Altamont."

Altamont did not end the rock festival, then. Rather it persevered and, if anything, grew in might and stature. There were big events held at the original Woodstock location to mark the 25th and 30th anniversaries and as we speak, archaeologists are digging up the site in anticipation of the 50th anniversary. And the all-time record for attendance goes to the Summer Jam at Watkins Glen, New York state, on July 28, 1973, at which a crowd of 600,000 gathered to see just three acts – The Band, the Grateful Dead and The Allman Brothers Band.

Hindsight of course is a wonderful thing, but coming as it did at the end of a golden decade, when the opportunity for youth, and youth culture, seemed limitless and the potential boundless, the fiasco of that one festival drew a line in the sand. What makes Altamont all the more heartbreaking is that the Rolling Stones had wanted to use it to give something back. It was as if all those cherished dreams and aspirations, all that buoyant optimism and fervent idealism, came to a bloody end in a desert, one dark December night, under a hail of knives.

CHAPTER 13

Gimme Shelter

'If' – one of the most tantalising words in the English language. If the Stones' 1969 US tour had ended in triumph in Boston on November 28, it would simply be a triumphant footnote in the annals of rock history. If they had lingered longer at Muscle Shoals… If they had agreed to a neighbourhood concert in San Francisco… If they had bitten the bullet and played Sears Point… All and any of these other scenarios may have prevented the bloody catastrophe that occurred at Altamont.

It might be worth considering whether or not the impact of Altamont would have been lessened were the whole event not captured on film, released the following year as *Gimme Shelter*. Altamont takes on a life of its own on video, DVD, Blu-ray and YouTube. The moment of death appears in a freeze-frame, the rock'n'roll equivalent of the shaky Zapruder film that captured the moment of President Kennedy's assassination in gruesome detail. Talking to *Rolling Stone* prior to the release of the *Gimme Shelter* documentary, producer Porter Bibb promised: "The film is not going to exploit the killing... We don't want to exploit the sensationalism of the thing."

Just prior to the film's release, a front-page headline in *Rolling Stone* read: 'Stones: The Money Is Superfluous To Them'. It is ironic to read further, knowing that the band were then locked in lengthy financial negotiations that would lead them into tax exile. "The Rolling Stones... will give it all away. Their profits will go to an as-yet-unspecified charity, or will be put back into the hip community through any number of good works," the article said.

David Dalton sat in on a mixing session for the live album of the '69 tour in London early in 1970. Mick, Keith and the Maysles were kicking around titles for the forthcoming movie – *Love In Vain... Naughty Ladies...* Al Maysles: "The slogan we could use might be: 'Peter Fonda went looking for America. The Stones found it'." Mick: "Call the film *Old Glory*. I don't know a thing about America. It's just the title of a song we wrote a year ago, so I'm suggesting it." When *Gimme Shelter* was finally premiered in New York on December 6, 1970 – exactly a year to the day since the tragedy – it was advertised with the strapline: "The music that thrilled the world... And the killing that stunned it!"

The studio was certainly keen to get *Gimme Shelter* in the cinemas. From a marketing standpoint, it was irresistible, and it was precisely the sort of movie that could lure elusive audiences back to theatres. 'Old Hollywood' had been all but bankrupted during the 1960s by bloated epics such as *Mutiny On The Bounty* (1962), *Fall Of The Roman Empire* (1964) and, particularly, *Cleopatra* (1963), which starred Elizabeth Taylor and was the most expensive film ever made up to that point due to monumental production issues and inflated budgets. Family entertainment such as *My Fair Lady* and *Mary Poppins* (both 1964) and *The Sound Of Music* (1965) had kept the studios in business. But by the end of the decade, even the star power of Julie Andrews and Rex Harrison couldn't save bombs like 1968's *Star!* and 1967's *Doctor Dolittle*.

Cinema attendance was steadily declining everywhere – in the UK during 1969, 28 million fewer people went to the flicks than in 1968. But it was the success of films like *The Graduate* (1967) and *Easy Rider* (1969) that made the studios salivate. Here, particularly in the case of Dennis Hopper's biker odyssey, were low-budget independent movies breaking box-office records. Long before the word was familiar, there was also 'synergy' between these films and their concomitant soundtracks (though *Melody Maker* chafed at the seven pounds, 10 shillings cover price on the three-LP soundtrack to *Woodstock*).

Gimme Shelter's distributors were assiduously courting the youth market, particularly in the light of Michael Wadleigh's 1970 documentary on the biggest festival of them all. Even coming in at over three hours, *Woodstock* racked up an estimated $20 million at the US box office alone during its first year of release. Other 'anti-establishment' films such as *M*A*S*H* (1970) were targeted squarely at the long-hairs ("*M*A*S*H* is what the new freedom of the screen is all about", stated the poster). Other movies released around the time – 1969's *Alice's Restaurant* ("Now you can see everything you want at Alice's Restaurant, where the heads of all nations meet"), 1970's *Getting Straight* ("*Getting Straight* lays it on the line") and *The Strawberry Statement* ("The film of now!") – were drawing in the peace and love crowd.

On its release, *Gimme Shelter* primarily provided an opportunity for fans to see their favourite rock'n'roll band in action, in colour and in stereo. Around the time of the release of *Gimme Shelter*, mainstream cinemas played host to innumerable rock films. The London Pavilion cinema had screened *Let It Be* in May ("An intimate bioscopic experience with The Beatles"). Several years later, the Rialto on Coventry Street would show *The Concert For*

Bangladesh ("The Greatest Concert of the Decade – Now You Can See It And Hear It As If You Were There!"), while the Warner, Leicester Square had shown the daddy of 'em all, the three-hour celebration of "Peace, Music & Love" that was *Woodstock*.

By the time the British premiere of *Woodstock* swung round in June 1970, not even a year after the event, Woodstock the festival had taken on a legendary patina. The film's marketing celebrated the festival's mythic status – "More than a gathering of tribes, it was a gathering of nations: This time it was more than a pow-wow, it was a holy invocation, a summit meeting of the world that was to come. This time the earth was strangely consecrated by the boys and girls who came... to find out what meaning life held and to find it here with each other."

At the Bath Festival of Blues and Progressive Music, held on June 27–29 that year, I remember they distributed free paper headbands to the audience as part of the marketing for *Woodstock* (we had all gone to the festival to feel a bit of that 'Woodstock magic'). On the film's release, the poster boasted: "No one who went there will ever be the same... be there."

That was precisely the sort of memorable gathering the Rolling Stones intended for Altamont. However, rewatching *Gimme Shelter* nearly half a century on makes for chilling viewing. Pre-Altamont, what is remarkable is the unimaginable access the Maysles got to the Stones. It's dislocating, too, to see the America the band traverses; just how *shabby* everything looks – the Holiday Inns, the tatty recording studios, the grungy backstage facilities. There is a derisory lack of security (Keith: "In 1969 there were no cops. All the cops were in Vietnam"), everyone smokes constantly, all are shunted from pillar to post... and Keith's English teeth are mesmerising.

But it is, of course, the road to Altamont that gives the film its force. The buildup is even more chaotic than you might imagine, the circus swirling around Mel Belli as he attempts to herd cats in the precious hours before dawn on December 6. Locked into the date, the lawyer is informed that the crowd is already making its way from far afield, "like lemmings to the sea". There is a chill foreboding as Woodstock mastermind Michael Lang blithely confirms that the switch from Sears Point to Altamont will be without incident. The chaos is tangible: Altamont's Dick Carter confidently expects to handle the oncoming vehicle logjam... the problems over the single-road access to Altamont are shrugged off... It is as if simply by being there, the Rolling Stones will make it all okay. So often are Yeats' lines from *The Second Coming* drawn to mind: "What rough beast, its hour come round at last/ Slouches towards Bethlehem to be born?"

As the filmmakers get to Altamont and the helicopter swoops over the event, the biblical parallels are more manifest. The tribes make their unsteady way beneath a cuticle moon across a desert-like landscape. Caped disciples huddle round campfires, awaiting their divinities. The sun rises over mile upon mile of abandoned cars, like a fossil-fuelled vision of the end of an automotive world.

On the ground, the film captures all the pre-concert sunshine and smiles: idiot dancing, dogs roaming, bum trips, nudity, soap bubbles, wizards, jugs passed convivially around. There's a collection for the Black Panthers. The Flying Burrito Brothers deliver a joyous 'Six Days On The Road'. Sam Cutler promises "the greatest party of 1969". You find yourself thinking, well, yes, maybe everything will be all right. Then 56 minutes in, there's the ominous roar of the choppers.

As the Hells Angels run riot there is a terrible, compelling fascination in watching the drama unfold. The believers of non-violence collide head-on with the bikers. It's like seeing a child play with a loaded .45. Ineffectual peace signs and proffered red roses are no match for the savagery that is returned. Even now, watching such real-life violence unleashed seemingly at random makes for uncomfortable viewing.

As the Stones take to the stage there is this overwhelming, obvious sense of… *helplessness.* Patently, no one is in control. The pathetic 3-foot-high stage offers no defence. You can almost taste the snarling venom emanating from the Angels, who stand guard on all sides. "This could be the most beautiful evening," a clearly stoned Mick offers, smiling as the band prepares to play.

But hippie-speak and pathetic pleas to "Keep it together" cannot stop the carnage. As the event descends into chaos, vainly Jagger turns to his guitarist: "Keith, will you cool it and I'll try and stop it." As if any one man – even a rock deity like Mick Jagger – can stop this juggernaut.

Then there it is… As the Stones meander through 'Under My Thumb', with Mick ad-libbing, riffing "I pray that it's all right…", a disturbance mere feet from the stage, a lime-green suit, a gun clearly visible against a white dress, a knife wielded and sunk into teenage flesh… And later, shaken and stirred, the Maysles' camera catches Jagger, as he watches the footage of the murder, before exiting the editing suite, dumbfounded by the scene. The shot freezes on one of the few occasions that Mick Jagger, supreme showman and control freak, had clearly lost control.

So yes, there was a gun, but what did Meredith Hunter intend to do with it? And yes, the Hells Angels might be said to have averted a wider tragedy by their brutal disarming. But watching *Gimme Shelter*, you are once again left with a sense of helplessness, not just towards the concert but to *all of it* visibly, manifestly falling apart at the seams.

Sonny Barger, founding member of the Hells Angels Oakland, California chapter, was interviewed on San Francisco's KSAN the day after the concert, when the full scale of events was becoming apparent locally: "I ain't no cop… I am not no 'peace' creep…"

Barger's justification for the level of violence attaching to the Angels? "Some cat throws something and dings my bike, or some cat kicks my bike over – he's got a fight."

Stefan Ponek was hosting KSAN's four-hour aftermath on Altamont. What comes across through the programme is the earnest dissection of just why Altamont wasn't Woodstock. Callers remarked on "so much tension", "the hostility", "a bum trip from the beginning". It was the betrayal of the brave new world, the children of the future had blown it!

Late in 1970, the distinguished film critic Pauline Kael wrote a corrosive review of *Gimme Shelter*. Her *New Yorker* essay took the Maysles to task, accusing them of "a cinéma vérité sham... when facts are manufactured for the camera". She also drew comparisons with Leni Riefenstahl's Nazi glorification film *Triumph Of The Will*.*

But, for all its faults, *Gimme Shelter* is as honest an account as you might expect from an authorised documentary. Few can match Bob Dylan's *Don't Look Back*, but *Gimme Shelter* comes close. It is a country mile ahead of *Cocksucker Blues*, Robert Frank's woeful account of the Stones' 1972 tour. In 1969, the Maysles got the access they needed, but they were also there when a real-life tragedy unfolded before their cameras. The Stones had always envisaged their free California concert as the highlight of their

---

* "The violence and murder weren't scheduled, but the Maysles brothers hit the cinéma vérité jackpot. If events are created to be photographed, is the movie that records them a documentary, or does it function in a twilight zone? [...] The Nazi rally at Nuremberg in 1934 was architecturally designed so that Leni Riefenstahl could get the great footage that resulted in *Triumph of the Will*." Pauline Kael, *The New Yorker* (December 19, 1970).

The Maysles' response to Pauline Kael's scathing review countered that, "In fact, the filmmakers were not consulted and had no control over the staging and lighting at Altamont. All the cameramen will verify that the lighting was very poor and totally unpredictable."

film. The murder of Meredith Hunter captured onscreen provided them with a climax that no one would ever forget.

★ ★ ★

Immediately following Altamont, Jagger flew to Switzerland, where he deposited the nearly $2 million of tour receipts far from the clutches of Allen Klein.

But poor old Sam Cutler was hung out to dry, terrified that the Hells Angels were out for his blood. He sat through tense meetings with the bikers, who demanded the film of the stabbing, and was "very frightened... after many blood curdling threats and MUCH hostility". Eventually, to his credit, and with any protection from the Rolling Stones long gone, Jerry Garcia sheltered Cutler from the storm, leading eventually to Cutler becoming the Dead's road manager.

In a letter to Ray Coleman, Sam wrote: "I was chased for the next five years by lawyers all over America trying to bring a damages suit against the band, and was eventually forced to give depositions to an ARMY of lawyers in Texas. I went into the deposition session determined to defend myself and the band, even though I felt (and still do!) that they behaved terribly in the aftermath of the concert and basically left ME to face the music."

In the welter of lawsuits that followed, Meredith Hunter was overlooked. We had entered the 21st century before the Altamont victim even got a headstone at the Skyview Memorial Lawn. To his credit, on learning that the Rolling Stones hadn't yet paid a cent to Meredith's family, Jann Wenner posted a cheque for $500 to his mother, Altha Mae Anderson. Talking to *Rolling Stone* early in 1970, she hoped Altamont might be turned into a public park: "My son's blood is on the land, and I would like to see the land serve a useful purpose for the youth of southern Alameda County. I cannot bring my son back, but by your action you may prevent any more wrongful deaths at Altamont." However, like so many aspects of the Altamont tragedy, the public park never happened.

On the evidence of witnesses and crucially the *Gimme Shelter* footage, Hells Angel Alan Passaro was charged with Hunter's murder, and stood trial in December 1970. He was found not guilty but returned to prison to serve other outstanding charges. Passaro died in 1985.

In retrospect, Altamont was spoken in the same breath as a Satanic convocation. Coming from that concert platform, there really was a great deal of sympathy for the Devil that chill December night. Rock'n'roll's infatuation with all things Satanic was well known. Aleister Crowley, "the wickedest man alive", was featured on the cover of *Sgt. Pepper's Lonely Hearts Club Band* – next to Mae West! David Bowie name-checked Crowley on his 1971 song 'Quicksand'. Led Zeppelin's Jimmy Page bought a former property of Crowley's and rumours of his Satanic fascination abound (he had Crowley's 'Do What Thou Wilt Shall Be The Whole Of The Law' etched onto early vinyl pressings of *Led Zeppelin III*). Black Sabbath's eponymous 1970 debut LP is steeped in black magic.

But it was the Rolling Stones who seemed closest to the 'dark side': after all, didn't the title of their 1967 LP *Their Satanic Majesties Request* say it all? In 1968, Mick Jagger was begging for some 'Sympathy For The Devil'. During the band's 1969 Madison Square Garden shows, you can clearly hear a voice from the audience shout "'Paint It Black', Paint It Black, Paint It Black, you Devils!"[*] Keith was known to have read Dennis Wheatley's *The Devil And All His Works* (1971). "In a sense, I believe the Stones have made a deal with the Devil," David Sinclair told me. "There is

---

[*] Impishly, the band sampled the soundbite for their 1991 album *Flashpoint*, where it appears between 'Ruby Tuesday' and 'You Can't Always Get What You Want'.

something daemonic about Keith, and you look at the casualties around them – Brian, Jimmy Miller, Bobby Keys, Gram Parsons, Andy Johns... There is something supernatural about their carrying on."

However, this was all by and large superficial self-indulgence from hedonists with too much time on their hands. Real evil was being carried out by self-serving shamen like Charles Manson. And for all the retrospective symbolism heaped upon the final Rolling Stones American concert of 1969, the tragedy of Altamont *did* amount to something more than a gig that went horribly wrong.

So, ultimately, where did the blame lie? In a sense, the Maysles' film exonerates the Stones. But nearer the time of the events, *Rolling Stone* magazine blamed the band. Elsewhere, Joel Selvin's forensic chronicle finds the Stones joined at the hip to the film, therein shouldering all the blame: "If Jagger had been willing to make a deal with Filmways to distribute the movie," he wrote, "the concert could have taken place at Sears Point... where the large crowd could have been accommodated, the Hells Angels wouldn't have been in control and the staging was already in place, but he wouldn't consider giving up movie profits from a distribution deal."

Unwittingly, Altamont was the end of an era. Peter Doggett, writing in his book *There's A Riot Going On* identified it as such: "After their 1969 US tour, nobody would ever mistake the Rolling Stones for political radicals. And in the wake of Manson and Altamont, it could no longer be assumed that the counterculture was a storehouse of moral virtue. If hippies could kill and watch others being killed in the name of rock and revolution, then maybe everything the movement accepted as true had to be rethought."*

---

* *There's A Riot Going On: Revolutionaries, Rock Stars, And The Rise And Fall Of '60s Counterculture* by Peter Doggett (Canongate Books, 2008).

Down the years, everything the sixties had represented seemed to come to a head at the Altamont Speedway on December 6, 1969. In the immediate aftermath, the Grateful Dead sing about the "darkness got to give" in 'New Speedway Boogie' on their first LP of 1970, *Workingman's Dead*. So often cited as a requiem for the end of the sixties, Don McLean left little doubt about the 'Jack Flash' figure in his all-conquering retrospective anthem of 1972, 'American Pie'. Ten years after the music had died, here was "Satan laughing with delight" at the chaos he had conjured up. The American music journalist Stanley Booth had been granted access to that epochal '69 tour, but was so scarred by the experience, he took 15 years to deliver *The True Adventures Of The Rolling Stones*. But, at the time, Booth was lucky to be there. He bonded with the band over music and gained undreamed-of closeness to the Stones. Of Altamont, he concluded: "There never seemed to be so much at stake… For one thing, we were never again in the desert, beyond all laws."

Looking back, in his rueful, head-shaking, sage way, Charlie Watts concluded: "It was like Woodstock in a way – it was the fashion of the moment, but it was the end of the fashion. If Woodstock started it, we stopped it."

Marianne Faithfull ruefully reflected that Altamont "is now seen as a rock & roll Black Mass… Mick may have sung his pantomime songs about the Devil and the Midnight Rambler, but he was in a total hippie mood when he went out there to do that concert. He wanted more than anything to be part of the counterculture utopia […] People imagine the Stones came to Altamont to incite murder, to summon up Beelzebub and his Satanic crew from the bowels of the earth. Not at all! It was meant to be a Hippie Love Fest. It's one of the saddest things that it turned into its opposite."

Ry Cooder put it more pithily. Already bitter at seeing his tunings ripped off for 'Honky Tonk Women', he was scornful of the dancing Devil: "He's stoned on himself. He's always in complete control and the whole thing is manipulation. It really bothers me that a twerp like Jagger can parade around and convince everyone he's Satan."

Above: Mick Jagger attends a meeting to set up *Rolling Stone* magazine in the UK before flying to Los Angeles later in the day, October 17, 1969 *[Mirrorpix]*; below: the Stones set off from Heathrow for their first US tour since 1966, October 17, 1969 *[Mirrorpix]*

(Opposite page) Mick Jagger pulls up his trousers mid-performance at Madison Square Garden, New York, November 27, 1969 *[Richard Busch/ Granger Historical Picture Archive/ Alamy]*; above: Mick Jagger, Mick Taylor and Charlie Watts impress the crowds at Madison Square Garden, November 28, 1969 *[Michael Ochs Archives/Getty]*; below: Chuck Berry and Mick Jagger with his Uncle Sam hat backstage at Madison Square Garden, November 28, 1969 *[Michael Ochs Archives/Getty]*

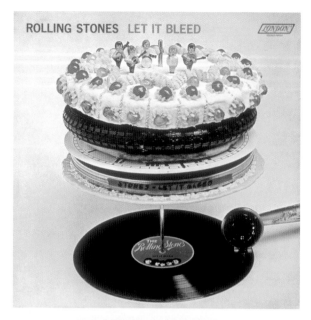

Above: the Stones release *Let It Bleed* on December 5, 1969, with an album cover featuring Delia Smith's cake *[Michael Ochs Archives/Getty]*; below: Mick Jagger and Keith Richards are distracted by the behaviour of the crowds at the Altamont Speedway, California, December 6, 1969 *[Robert Altman/Michael Ochs Archives/Getty]*; (opposite page) above: Hells Angels patrol the crowds before the Altamont concert *[William L. Rukeyser/Getty]*; below: the approximately 300,000-strong crowd at Altamont Speedway *[Bettmann/Contributor/Getty]*

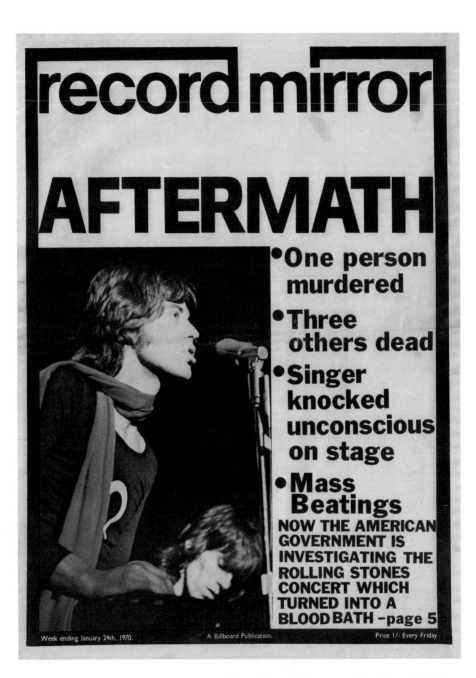

record mirror

AFTERMATH

- **One person murdered**
- **Three others dead**
- **Singer knocked unconscious on stage**
- **Mass Beatings**

NOW THE AMERICAN GOVERNMENT IS INVESTIGATING THE ROLLING STONES CONCERT WHICH TURNED INTO A BLOOD BATH –page 5

Week ending January 24th, 1970.   A Billboard Publication.   Price 1/- Every Friday

Above: *Record Mirror* covers the aftermath of the Altamont concert on its front page, January 24, 1970; (opposite page) *Gimme Shelter*, the film that captured the tragedy at Altamont, was released exactly a year later, December 6, 1970 *[GAB Archive/Redferns]*; (overleaf) the Stones rehearse at the Saville Theatre, London, December 14, 1969, (l-r) Mick Taylor, Mick Jagger, Keith Richards and Charlie Watts *[Press Association]*

THE MUSIC THAT THRILLED THE WORLD...
AND THE KILLING THAT STUNNED IT!

The Rolling Stones
Gimme Shelter

DIRECTED BY DAVID MAYSLES, ALBERT MAYSLES, CHARLOTTE ZWERIN · A MAYSLES FILMS, INC. PRODUCTION
DISTRIBUTED BY 20TH CENTURY-FOX FILM CORPORATION

CHAPTER 14

Let It Bleed

Talking to Lon Goddard in *Record Mirror* three weeks after the Hyde Park concert, Keith admitted that "There are only about three tracks with Mick Taylor on them recorded for the new album so far, but we have enough tracks down for an album and a half. We just have to choose which ones to use. It would be nice to use some photos from the concert on the cover. There are some good ones around."

The Rolling Stones had found a distinctive sound towards the end of the 1960s: building on the rock-solid rhythms produced by Bill and Charlie, it was a beguiling mesh, in which electric guitars shadowed acoustics. A foundation of acoustic licks would be laid. (Keith was enchanted by the compressed sound of the acoustic guitar when recorded on a cheap cassette: "You can get certain things out of acoustic guitars, a certain dryness and a ring that you'll never get on an electric guitar.") For much of February and March 1969, the Stones laid down the building blocks for *Let It Bleed*. 'You Can't Always Get What You Want' was in the can. Over two months, 'Love In Vain', 'You Got The Silver', 'Let It

Bleed' and the basic 'Gimme Shelter' were nailed. Also recorded was the single 'Honky Tonk Women'.

Unconsciously echoing St Matthew ("the last shall be first…"), the Stones' eighth UK LP begun with its end. Early versions of the closing track on *Let It Bleed*, 'You Can't Always Get What You Want', the song that drew a veil over the 1960s, commenced in late 1968, with Brian still a (barely) functioning member of the band.

A former drummer, the Stones' producer Jimmy Miller was demonstrating the song's percussive pattern to Charlie Watts, who just couldn't get behind the beat, so that is Jimmy you hear on the finished track (he also supplied the cowbell intro to 'Honky Tonk Women'). Charlie was always gracious in acknowledging the producer's percussive abilities: "Jimmy Miller was the person in the studio who helped me an awful lot," he told Max Weinberg. "He showed me how to do it… he showed me certain things that would work and things that wouldn't, like fills and things… He could hear songs better than I could. There's a whole period where Jimmy helped me out a lot without saying or doing anything. The result was that I began to realise I should work harder on my drumming."

The Stones were reinvigorated; they finally had a reliable producer. Pleased with the results Jimmy had achieved on *Beggars Banquet*, they quickly adhered to the twenty-seven-year-old New Yorker.

Jimmy Miller had cut his teeth working with Chris Blackwell at Island Records, overseeing production of LPs by Spooky Tooth and The Spencer Davis Group. That led Miller to a long relationship with Steve Winwood, through which he produced the early Traffic albums as well as the only record from the supergroup Blind Faith. Mick remembered being impressed by Miller's work with Traffic and also British band Nirvana ('Rainbow Chaser' rather than

'Smells Like Teen Spirit'), and that appealed to how he thought the Stones might be able to improve their sound.

"I was in Studio B in Olympic Studios and the Stones were in Studio A," Miller told Nina Antonia in *Record Collector* a few years before his death in 1994. "As luck would have it, Traffic and I had just finished working on a really basic smoking track, which sounded really good. Mick and Keith walked in just as we were having a very loud playback and the vibe was extremely positive. We visited their session later and nothing was happening, they were just sitting around. Mick told me how much he'd liked what I'd done with Spencer Davis and Traffic."

"People often say that I brought [the Stones] back from the *Satanic Majesties* album," Miller told *Record Mirror* in 1969. "But the Stones were responsible for that... I'm certainly no Phil Spector imposing my will on the artists [...] In the beginning of our relationship together they would come into the studio in March and ask how each other's Christmas had gone. They really hadn't seen each other for that time.

"Now they're back doing tours. It's required courage for them to do that. It used to take them three nights to get one song but now they're doing a song a night. They're playing as a group again."

Mick started writing 'You Can't Always Get What You Want' while on holiday with Marianne in Brazil. With its choir ushering in those pulsating rhythms, its beguiling Polaroid of London circa '69 and its swelling, orgasmic build, 'You Can't Always Get What You Want' may well be *the* Rolling Stones track. For once the band match The Beatles in studio magic – as the final statement on *Let It Bleed*, it magnifies and exceeds *Sgt. Pepper*'s 'A Day In The Life'. It concludes a decisive, divisive decade. Rarely one to blow his own horn, even Mick confirmed to Jann Wenner: "It's a good song, even if I say so myself. It's got a very sing-along chorus. And people can identify with it: No one gets what they always want. It's got a very good melody. It's got very good orchestral touches that Jack Nitzsche helped with. So it's got all the ingredients."

Brian Jones was evident at those early sessions, but clearly his card was marked. A visiting Jack Nitzsche remembers Brian asking Mick "What can I play?" only to be rebuffed with a withering: "I don't know. What *can* you play?" Bill Wyman recalled "Brian's contribution to 'You Can't Always Get What You Want' was to lie on his stomach most of the night, reading an article on botany."

A more welcome visitor was the multi-instrumentalist slash producer slash bandleader, the Zelig of rock'n'roll, Mr Al Kooper. It was Al who had inveigled his way into playing the distinctive organ that underpinned Dylan's groundbreaking 'Like A Rolling Stone'. It was Al who founded Blood, Sweat & Tears, before they disappeared under their own bombast. It was Al who jammed with Eric Clapton and who, in his downtime, found himself becoming the assistant stage manager at the Monterey Pop Festival. It was Al who engineered the concept of the 'Super Session' with Stephen Stills and Mike Bloomfield, and who also played on one of the most atmospheric live albums of the period, *The Live Adventures Of Mike Bloomfield And Al Kooper*. It was Al who helped out Jimi Hendrix on *Electric Ladyland*. And so it was Al who got the call from the Rolling Stones to help out on their new album.

To his own astonishment, Kooper initially declined; after working flat out for most of the decade, he was bushed. But it was bumping into Brian Jones one autumn evening on the King's Road that eventually got Al the gig. The two men had met at Monterey two years before. According to Brian's most sympathetic biographer, Paul Trynka, "Using the vestiges of that winning charm to persuade Kooper to attend and make the session a success was Brian's final contribution to the band he'd formed."

On a visit to London, Kooper arrived early at Olympic Studios. Charlie and Bill ("no-nonsense guys") arrived next, then Mick and Keith "exploding in through the door". Al contributed piano and organ to the album. Eight months later, Kooper was called upon by Mick Jagger to supply a substantial brass arrangement to 'You Can't Always Get What You Want'. But in the end, as the choir made its way back to Bach, it was Al's plaintive French horn that remained. But it was enough to begin the end.

Let It Bleed also marked the studio debut of Brian's replacement, Mick Taylor, the first 'new Stone' in seven years.

"I went along to do what I thought was some session work," Taylor told John Bungey. "We did 'Live With Me' and I overdubbed my part on 'Honky Tonk Women'. Then Mick asked me to join... I think I said 'I'll think about it'... My sister was a big Stones fan and I was a Beatles fan. She always reminds me of when she would put on 'Little Red Rooster' and I'd say, 'Turn that rubbish off and put *Revolver* on!'"

Mick Taylor had come from the 'John Mayall Academy of Lead Guitarists', with predecessors including Eric Clapton and Peter Green. Jagger recalled making the call: "We had this gig at Hyde Park coming up, so we just went with him. There wasn't a big audition process, because he seemed to fit in really well and there was pressure to do the gig. Maybe if we'd not had the gig coming up for six months, we'd have tried lots of others."

Keith recalls: "The last thing I wanted was a carbon copy of Brian, and after all Brian hadn't been playing guitar much recently, so I'd had to do all the parts. Mick Taylor turns up and plays like an angel, and I wasn't going to say no. I thought I'd let the guy develop, because by then I thought I was an old hand – I was all of twenty-five years old! That's what four years on the road would do to you."

In an issue of *Melody Maker* just prior to his Hyde Park debut, Mick Taylor told Royston Eldridge about his new band: "What they do is just a mixture of soul, folk and blues and I like playing all those things. I just don't like playing twelve bar blues all night." Later, when asked about the Stones' bad boy image, the twenty-year-old Taylor admitted, "I'm not really concerned about drugs at all... You should be able to feel good within yourself without drugs."

Poignantly, Mick Jagger was also asked about what Brian Jones would be doing next. "I can tell you very little – it's better you ask him yourself. I guess he just wanted to do something different and he has done for a long time. I hope whatever he does comes off." He also said that he and Keith "have written about 24 songs recently... In fact, we have done two albums and the first will be out in September. Two of the tracks will have Mick on guitar." An album, entitled *Sticky Fingers*, was provisionally scheduled for a September 1969 release. In his 2005 book *Rolling Stones And The Making Of Let It Bleed*, Sean Egan provided a track list for the album: 'Midnight Rambler'/'Love In Vain'/'Let It Bleed'/ 'Monkey Man'/'Gimme Shelter'/'You Got The Silver'/'Sister Morphine'/'Loving Cup'.

Talk of two albums emerging from the nearly-year-long sessions continued on into the year. In actual fact, only one album made it into the shops that Christmas, but it was enough. *Let It Bleed* was the first album the Stones recorded on eight-track. It was originally intended to run without breaks between tracks; the 2002 remaster painstakingly removed those pesky three-second gaps. Talking to *Rolling Stone* in 1987, producer Jimmy Miller said: "*Let It Bleed* is my favourite of the albums I did with [the Stones]. There was a unity to the band that peaked around then. Mick and Keith still lived down the street from each other. Got together every day and sat around with acoustic guitars, writing."

Early in February 1969, the Stones were back in Olympic Studios. The fire caused by Jean-Luc Godard's blazing lights had been repaired. Jimmy Miller was at the production helm. Glyn Johns was in charge of engineering duties. With the closing track now in the can, the band continued work on the rest of the new album in earnest.

I have tackled the tracks below in the order in which they were recorded, rather than as they appear on the record. (Even then the tracks listed on the back sleeve of *Let It Bleed* don't correspond with the playing order. But, hey, like the man was to mention more than once in passing over the years, it's only rock'n'roll...)

First up, 'Midnight Rambler'. The song was partly inspired by Albert DeSalvo, the 'Boston Strangler' who murdered 13 women in the Boston area between 1962 and 1964. A 1968 film loosely based on the case starred Tony Curtis as DeSalvo. Jagger certainly would have remembered the case, although in fact he does not sing "Boston Strangler" on the song, only mentioning the city. Talking to Jann Wenner in 1995, Mick recalled: "['Midnight Rambler'] is a song Keith and I really wrote together. We were on a holiday in Italy. In this very beautiful hilltown, Positano, for a few nights. Why we should write such a dark song in this beautiful, sunny place, I really don't know."

Lyrically, 'Midnight Rambler' exerts a powerful menace and chimes with the chilling times, through its references to crowing cocks, black panthers and "cold, fanged anger". Mick's harp playing lends a sinister edge, pushing the song along, skating over Keith's jagged guitar, until it diverts somewhere else entirely with the "don't do that" jam, inexorably building to a chilling finale. It was this song that became one of the highlights of the Stones' live concerts in 1969, Mick repeatedly thrashing the stage with his bejewelled belt.

Looking back, Keith's is no idle boast: "I don't think anyone could have written 'Midnight Rambler' but Mick and me."

Recorded on February 18, 1969, 'You Got The Silver' sees Keith making his solo vocal debut on a Stones album. Glyn Johns admitted it was his "total incompetence" that erased Mick's vocal, which had been cut a year earlier when the song was scheduled for *Beggars Banquet*, leading to the Stones using Keith's version. The track features Brian Jones on autoharp, one of his last contributions to a Rolling Stones record. "It's strange," Keith reflected in his autobiography, "we'd had to pull the plug on Brian in the studio… to be reminded that he was still playing on tracks early in 1969, the year of his death… Where did that come from? A last flare from the shipwreck."

Once again, it is Charlie's drums that elevate the song, crashing in, not destroying the intimacy, rather elevating it. There is a poignant nuance to the lyrics, an intensity of confession, weighing up of silver, gold and diamonds in the mine. Keith's frail vocal is matched by the peerless, jagged electric stabs of his guitar. Nicky Hopkins' piano finds a palimpsest in the organ that haunts the recording. The Italian film director Michelangelo Antonioni featured 'You Got The Silver' in his bludgeoning, unwatchable take on youth culture, 1970's *Zabriskie Point* (sample dialogue: "Want to share a joint?" "No. The people I'm running around with are on a reality trip… "). However, contractual problems led to the song's exclusion from the movie's soundtrack, which was mainly of interest for otherwise unavailable Pink Floyd material.

The joys of the iPod Shuffle allow 'You Got The Silver' to segue nicely into 'Love In Vain'.

Talking to author Victor Bockris, Keith remembered: "Around '68 comes this second Robert Johnson collection that included 'Love In Vain'… such a beautiful song. Mick and I both loved it, and at the time Gram [Parsons] and I started searching around for a different way to present it, because if we were going to record it there was no point in trying to copy the Robert Johnson style or version... We took it a little bit more country, a little bit more formalized, and Mick felt comfortable with that... It was just so beautiful: the title, the lyrics, the ideas, the rhymes, just everything about it."

It was Brian Jones' being unavailable for the recording of 'Love In Vain' that brought Ry Cooder into the mix, on mandolin. The shadow of Gram Parsons hovered. "We changed the arrangement quite a lot from Robert Johnson's," Mick told Jann Wenner. "Made it more country... Robert Johnson was a wonderful lyric writer, and his songs are quite often about love, but they're desolate."

Desolation came easy to Robert Johnson, whose death at twenty-seven (he was murdered by a jealous rival) came to haunt those who followed. Legend stalked the guitarist throughout his short life after rumours abounded that he had sold his soul to the Devil at the midnight crossroads in exchange for the ability to play guitar like no one else. The blues guitarist finally came to prominence with the release of *King Of The Delta Blues Singers* in 1961.

The mystery surrounding Johnson didn't end with the midnight crossroads tale. He only ever recorded a handful of songs, he faced the wall when he recorded, he was rumoured to have made electric recordings in New York, and only two photographs depicting him exist. Even his end was mysterious – there were three gravesites laying claim to his last resting place.

His death was equally controversial. The facts seem to state that Robert was poisoned. In a Mississippi juke joint, the jealous husband of a woman who had taken a shine to the guitarist took his poisonous revenge by slipping strychnine into Johnson's whiskey. His last moments were spent writhing on the floor and howling like a dog.

However, talking to Paul Trynka in 2000, Keith proudly showed him a copy of Robert Johnson's death certificate that refuted the claims: "Both sides! The back's never been seen…" A doctor's note on the back read: "It is my opinion he died of syphilis." Where on God's green earth did Keith Richards obtain such a document? "I can't tell you. My lips are sealed. Or I can never go back to Mississippi again…"

Upon signing to Columbia, Bob Dylan requested a copy of the Robert Johnson LP. In 1973, he went on to dedicate *Writings And Drawings*, the first volume of his lyrics, to both Hank Williams and Robert Johnson. Years later, Dylan wrote: "It felt like a ghost had come into the room, a fearsome apparition. I just couldn't imagine how Johnson's mind could go in and out of so many places. He seems to know about everything."

Three thousand miles away, Brian Jones played *King Of The Delta Blues Singers* to Keith Richards, for whom hearing it "was like a comet or a meteor that came along, and BOOM, suddenly he raised the ante… You can put the record on now and it's as fresh and interesting as the first day you heard it."

Next, to 'Love In Vain'. Early pressings of *Let It Bleed* credited the track to "Woody Payne", a Johnson pseudonym. His was a powerful presence that loomed large in the Stones' camp: the band had included a version of Johnson's 'Walkin' Blues' in between takes on the set of their *Rock And Roll Circus*. Their version of Robert Johnson's 'Stop Breaking Down' later appeared on *Exile On Main St.* And Mick was heard singing a Johnson blues number in *Performance*.

For all the criticisms of white boys ripping off black music over the years, it has to be said in mitigation that a wider appreciation of the blues came courtesy of acts like the Stones, and Eric Clapton, Led Zeppelin, Fleetwood Mac, John Mayall and Alexis Korner. Even today, visitors from Europe to the Mississippi Delta often know more about the music from that exotic location than many of its inhabitants. And that is largely down to ardent fans like the Rolling Stones.

Ironically, the Stones' decision to record 'Love In Vain' came from a source they despised – a bootleg. In the years since his death, it was believed that the only recordings Johnson cut were the 16 that formed the basis for the 1961 *King Of The Delta Blues Singers* LP. But rumours of more cuts became vinyl fact in the late sixties. A second volume of *King Of The Delta Blues Singers*, including 'Love In Vain', only appeared a year after the Stones' version on *Let It Bleed*, the sleeve notes mentioning the Stones' cover and concluding, "So if you dig contemporary music, especially the blues, give a listen to Robert Johnson, the original master".

In performance, 'Love In Vain' became a standout of the shows during the tour of '69. On disc, it retains its mesmeric power. Jagger's vocals hit the right note, balanced between poignancy and arrogance. His phrasing draws out the poetry of Johnson's lyrics. That sensitivity is underpinned by Keith's guitars and Cooder's mandolin. And once again, Charlie's drums shimmer in, like a ghost at the feast.

'Gimme Shelter', the song that began in Barnes in February and March 1969, was spellbindingly brought to life in Los Angeles in October and November the same year.

The ubiquitous Jack Nitzsche had first met the Stones in 1964 on their first visit to the States. Few other CVs could muster the diversity of Jack Nitzsche's, which included Bobby Darin, Tim Buckley, Doris Day, Phil Spector, Neil Young and, of course, the Rolling Stones. For *Let It Bleed*, he had initially been asked to arrange the choir on 'You Can't Always Get What You Want'. He was then asked to help with the arrangement on 'Gimme Shelter', for which a duet was envisaged. The Stones had been impressed by Delaney & Bonnie's debut LP earlier in 1969, so Bonnie Bramlett was invited to supply some Southern grits to the track. But it just wasn't happening, the chemistry wasn't there, and Bonnie's husband wasn't too happy with his wife singing alongside the notorious rockers. So session maestro Jack Nitzsche put in a call to Merry Clayton…

That last-minute request resulted in one of the most heart-rending vocal performances ever committed to disc. Merry's contribution to 'Gimme Shelter' stands as a shattering testament to the power of the human voice. For me, it is only rivalled by Lorraine Ellison's 'Stay With Me Baby'. But back to that phone call, and that night…

Merry was an in-demand session singer by the time the call came through. Starting with Ray Charles' Raelettes, she can later be heard *20 Feet From Stardom* (as the 2013 documentary of that name testifies) behind Neil Young, Carole King, Linda Ronstadt, Joe Cocker and dozens of others.

The fullest account of that tumultuous Stones session came in an interview that Merry gave to Rob Hughes in 2015 for *Record Collector*: "It was 11.30 at night, I had my hair in rollers… I was awful pregnant at the time. So I'm about to get into bed and the phone rings. It was maestro Jack Nitzsche. He goes [low whisper] 'Hi Merry, it's Jack, I know it's late, but listen. There's a group in town and they need somebody to sing with them'. I said 'Who are these children? Who is this group that you have to call me this late at night?'"

Merry's husband convinced her it might be worth making the effort: "Jack sent a limo, so I got in wearing my beautiful mink coat with pink slippers, my head draped in a Chanel scarf and with no makeup on… I see these guys coming round the corner. It's Mick and Keith. They play the track and I hear the lines 'It's just a shot away'… I said I could do that in my sleep, no problem.

There's Mick on my left and Keith on my right. Their hair is flying and they're just singing along with me.

"Then we go back into the booth and the producer says that Mick has given him these other lyrics. I'm reading them and saying 'Are y'all trying to do something strange here?' Why am I singing about rape and murder? I'd never sung words like that before in my life.

"So they go back into the studio and leave me in the booth by myself. I start singing the song and there were flashes in my head of all the things that were going on in the world at that time. You had the civil rights movement, the Vietnam War, bombings in the South and dogs being set on black people. There was all this ugliness going on. It was as if my soul was screaming out 'If you don't give us some kind of shelter, this is what's going to go on. It's going to be rape and it's going to be murder!' I'm screaming and wondering why my voice was cracking, but it was like my soul was crying up to Heaven.

"It was like my soul had gone to another place… I got a little dizzy and had to sit down for a minute as I listened to the playback. I could see the guys hootin' and hollerin' back in the booth. Mick and Keith were screaming and carrying on. I truly believe it was an out-of-body experience."

Tragically, Merry miscarried almost immediately after that epochal session ("I don't really want to talk about that. It's painful…"). She carried on a varied career, which saw her appear on the soundtracks to *Performance* and *Dirty Dancing*; sing – grudgingly – backing vocals on Lynyrd Skynyrd's redneck anthem 'Sweet Home Alabama' and appear as the 'Acid Queen' in the 1972 London stage production of *Tommy*.

The song itself had sprung from a Keith riff and a sense of the storm rising: "There was this incredible storm… all these people with their umbrellas being blown out of their grasp and running

231

like Hell," Keith recalled in *Life*. There was also the potential storm brewing with Keith's other half, Anita Pallenberg, who was off shooting *Performance* with Jagger at the time, rumours of sex scenes in the film being far from simulated...

Nobody had heard anything quite like 'Gimme Shelter', *Let It Bleed*'s eerie opening track. It churns and grinds, sounding like it comes from nowhere, but repeated plays reveal a sinister voodoo gris-gris, reminiscent of Dr John's sultry New Orleans R&B-infused 1968 debut. Mick and Marianne had been taken by the album, and The Night Tripper's hand could be discerned in the gumbo of 'Gimme Shelter'.

Long a live favourite, 'Gimme [or "Gimmie", as it's listed on the album sleeve] Shelter' took on a life of its own when it was used as the title track in the Altamont documentary. Its later use for an RAC television commercial raised the odd eyebrow. Many must have smiled though in 2018, when *Radio Times* did a gardening feature on arbours, gazebos and pergolas. Its headline? 'Gimme Shelter'!

Martin Scorsese was also fixated on the track. The song has featured on the soundtracks to crime dramas *Goodfellas* (1990) and *Casino* (1995), and is the opening track in *The Departed* (2006). In Marty's world, rock'n'roll runs parallel to his movie obsession. Scorsese was a cameraman on Michael Wadleigh's *Woodstock* film (fastidious as ever, he is credited as the only man to have worn cufflinks at Woodstock!), while his 1978 concert film of The Band's final performance, *The Last Waltz*, is routinely hailed as one of rock's best ever documentaries, even if it did open the door for Marty Di Bergi's *Spinal Tap*... But along with the films of Powell and Pressburger, and John Ford, for Scorsese it was "the Stones. Always, the Stones... Their music is part of my life." Eventually, in 2008, Scorsese would marry his two main passions through the concert film *Shine A Light*, which documented the Stones' Beacon

Theatre performance on their 2006 *A Bigger Bang* tour. Jagger joked that it was the only Scorsese film that *didn't* feature 'Gimme Shelter'...

'Gimme Shelter' remains the song on which newcomers continue to fixate. Half a century after its conception, it continues to cast its spell. Johnny Marr agrees: "I couldn't believe that something could be so perfect, with so much attitude and so funky. It really is tight but loose. It has a sense of impending something, but at the same time it felt very beautiful. The very idea of rock & roll is that it could be beautiful and dangerous at the same time."

Bobby Gillespie: "'Gimme Shelter' used to give me the creeps... it sounds like imminent evil, a real sense of dread. But it's also uplifting... There's something in the atmosphere of the record that the Stones never achieved before or after."

Jim Reid, of The Jesus and Mary Chain: "It's just got one of the best intros of a rock'n'roll song ever. Just fantastic the way the drums start, and that opening line... What a fucking brilliant line."

Mike Scott of The Waterboys: "Rock & roll dives headlong into the end of the sixties abyss and still feels great."

A 2002 *Uncut* magazine poll for the 'Greatest Ever Rolling Stones Song' put 'Gimme Shelter' at the top of the tree. Of that song and that riff Keith just shrugged: "You get lucky sometimes. It was a shitty day. I had nothing better to do... It just happened to hit the moment. Only later did I realise, this will have more meaning than I thought at the time."

'Monkey Man' was another song conjured up in Positano during that productive Italian vacation of March 1969 – indeed, it was originally titled 'Positano Grande'. Here, tongue in cheek, Mick can't resist the joyful rhyme of "messianic" and "Satanic". The louche "all my friends are junkies" reference only confirmed what most people thought about the Stones anyhow. It rocks along, but in truth even Keith's solo sounds half-hearted, and stacked alongside the rest of the tracks, it probably stands as the weakest on the album.

'Live With Me' marked the recording debut of Mick Taylor with the band. It's another of the album's weaker songs, and again the Jagger lyric places tongue firmly in cheek.* His "nasty habits" have him simply taking tea at 3 p.m., rather than the proscribed hour of 4 p.m. Helping Nicky Hopkins out on piano was Leon Russell, another recruit from the Delaney & Bonnie band, as was saxophonist Bobby Keys,** here on his first session with the Stones.

'Country Honk' was included on the album in this version as Keith originally envisaged it, recalling: "We put that other version of 'Honky Tonk Women' on because that's how the song was originally written, as a real Hank Williams/Jimmie Rodgers, thirties country song."

There's a lovely scene in the documentary *Olé Olé Olé!: A Trip Across Latin America*, which documents the band's 2016 tour of Latin America, where we see Keith and Mick backstage, running through an acoustic version of 'Honky Tonk Women' as it was originally planned. The Rolling Stones and their relationship with country music fully flowered when the Glitter Twins first met Gram Parsons while he was playing in London with The Byrds in 1968. The four-man lineup, led by Roger McGuinn, was struggling in the wake of the "jingle-jangle" success of their worldwide number one 'Mr Tambourine Man' from three years before. David Crosby had acrimoniously and petulantly quit the

---

* Legend has it that, on hearing the lascivious lyrics on this track (along with those on the risqué 'Midnight Rambler'), the London Bach Choir requested – unsuccessfully – that its name be removed from the LP sleeve.

** Keith and Keys had first met on an early Stones tour of the States, when Bobby Keys was blowing with Bobby Vee. He bonded with Keith on discovering they shared the same birthday – day, month and year! It was a relationship that would last until Keys' death in 2014.

band, The Byrds' main songwriter, Gene Clark, had also split and the 'American Beatles' had yet to find a new identity. When Gram came on board, The Byrds reinvented themselves as a country and western quartet.

It was Gram who steered The Byrds towards Nashville. Their 1968 album *Sweetheart Of The Rodeo* could lay claim to being the first 'country-rock' album. Initial sales were poor, the band's rock fans finding undiluted country hard to swallow, and diehard country fans unimpressed by a bunch of hippies. Over the years however, *Sweetheart* has gone on to feature on many of the 'most influential' lists. And for all the hyperbole poured on Gram's head following his untimely death in 1973 when he was just twenty-six, there was no denying his crucial role in steering The Byrds in a new direction.

The Byrds were due to play apartheid South Africa, when Keith persuaded Gram to jump ship. This began the guitarist's most significant musical alliance outside the Rolling Stones. "I think I probably learned more from Gram than anybody else," Keith told Perry Richardson.

The Stones took Gram under their wing during The Byrds' 1968 visit to the UK. No stranger to good living, this was where the country boy got a taste of the high life. Gram travelled to Stonehenge in Keith's Rolls-Royce, and was also particularly impressed with Mick's sang-froid in sending out a minion to buy new socks following a soggy trip round the Wiltshire countryside. Keith also invited Gram to Redlands, where they mined each other's musical history.

Following the initial meeting in the UK, the following year Keith reconnected with Gram while the Stones were in Los Angeles finishing *Let It Bleed*. The Stones took time out from mixing the album and rehearsing their 1969 US tour to see Gram and his new band, The Flying Burrito Brothers, in action at LA's tiny Corral Club. Gram became a regular visitor at the Los Angeles house the Stones rented prior to the tour.

Of all those gone before, Gram Parsons has become one of the most venerated posthumous casualties. His brand of "cosmic American music" became a direct musical influence on everyone from Elvis Costello to the Eagles. His championing of songwriters like Harlan Howard and Merle Haggard opened plugged-up ears.

However, critics say an early death has perhaps inflated his influence. They have him down as a dilettante, a rich boy indulging in music as a hobby. There was certainly bitterness from fellow members of The Flying Burrito Brothers, who Gram eventually quit so he could hang out with the Stones. Working musicians need to work; the Burritos didn't have Gram's trust fund, his substantial financial inheritance to fall back on. Gram didn't need to work. But when he did, he had an ear and an attitude and an impeccable musical pedigree.

And that was the bond he forged with the Stones that steered them away from Highway 61, the blues highway that runs from the Delta up to Chicago and Detroit. With Gram whispering in Keith's ear, the Stones detoured down to Music City USA, Nashville, Tennessee, and across the country to Bakersfield, California. It was Gram who added a little mint julep to the Stones' jambalaya.

It is worth recalling just how unpopular country and western was by the late 1960s. For many years, The Beatles' 1967 'Penny Lane'/'Strawberry Fields Forever' was routinely cited as the greatest pop single ever released. (As an aside, I do feel that 'Honky Tonk Women' plus 'You Can't Always Get What You Want', even in its truncated form, should be considered for that honour.) What was upsetting then, and still rankles today, is the fact that The Beatles were denied the UK number one by Engelbert Humperdinck's cover of the country standard 'Release Me'.

Country was what your parents liked. It was Tom Jones' 'Green, Green Grass Of Home' and Jim Reeves' 'He'll Have To Go'. It was all soppy lyrics espousing conservative values – President Nixon was a country fan. It was all glitter and rhinestone, with country stars like Porter Wagoner, George Jones and Dolly Parton antithetical to the revolutionary fervour that the Rolling Stones, The Doors and Bob Dylan engendered.

As ever, it was Dylan himself who changed all that. Bob needed a player who could bring an acoustic flamenco flourish to 1965's 'Desolation Row'. Producer Bob Johnston had run CBS's Nashville outpost and called in a favour from an old buddy, session musician Charlie McCoy. Dylan was impressed with his playing. "Hell," said Johnston, in response, "you should get your ass down to Nashville, they're all that good down there."

So in 1966 Bob decamped to the CBS Studios in the country music capital, the conservative town known as 'the buckle on the Bible Belt'. Each of Dylan's subsequent sixties albums – *Blonde On Blonde* (1966), *John Wesley Harding* (1967), *Nashville Skyline* (1969) and the bulk of *Self Portrait* (1970) – were recorded there. Charlie McCoy told me that there was a wariness when the skeletal weirdo who was Bob Dylan came to Nashville. The knives were out. But the fact that Dylan printed the names of the session men on the sleeve of *Blonde On Blonde* gave the players a legitimacy, a kudos and a career.

Thanks to Bob's benediction, then, country and western was bestowed with a new, hip cachet. Soon The Byrds, Joan Baez, Simon & Garfunkel, Leonard Cohen, Ringo Starr, Paul McCartney and many more took their cue from Dylan, recording in Music City. In hindsight, of course, country music should have been allowed space at the rock'n'roll table. There was more grit and integrity in Johnny Cash than the MC5. Willie Nelson, Johnny Cash and Harlan Howard wrote better songs than most of the 'new Dylans'. At its best, in the hands of the late, great Hank Williams, country music was white man's blues. But it took Dylan and, in his wake, the Rolling Stones to make the genre palatable to the audiences who flocked to the Fillmore in San Francisco or midnight courts at the Lyceum in London.

Once Gram Parsons had locked horns with the Rolling Stones, there was no going back. While the Stones were on their legendary 1969 US tour, Gram was almost a member of the band. Journalist Stanley Booth was also in the Stones' entourage, writing what would become his long – *long* – overdue account, *The True Adventures Of The Rolling Stones*. Like Gram, Booth was a good ol' boy from Waycross, Georgia, so that bond was further strengthened. However, there was resentment – Bernie Leadon, guitarist with the Burritos, told Ben Fong-Torres: "We had a working group. But... Gram was over at Keith's house all the goddam time and wouldn't show up for rehearsals. He just wanted to be with Keith. The music, the chicks, the drugs." Ex-Byrd and fellow Burrito Chris Hillman confirmed: "He was like a puppy dog around them."

While their record sales were negligible, The Flying Burrito Brothers were getting the right gigs and were picking up good notices in the underground press and music papers. But the band's future was in jeopardy as Gram's obsession grew: "The Rolling Stones got in the way tremendously," Chris Hillman remembered. "Gram was like a groupie: 'Oh, sorry guys, but I've got to go hang out with the Stones now'." Gram was even blowing out Burritos gigs to hang with the Stones, until – of all people – Mick Jagger took responsibility: "You've got a responsibility to Chris [Hillman]," he barked at Parsons, "to the other band members and the people who come to your show. You'd better go do your show now." Chastened, Gram honoured the engagement.

Gram's first and most overt influence on the Stones was recalled by Burritos road manager Jim Seiter to Ben Fong-Torres: "One night, Keith sang 'Honky Tonk Women' and Gram followed with a countrified version on the piano." Gram's version, he said, wound up as 'Country Honk' on *Let It Bleed*. When Jim told Gram he should have received credit, he replied: "It was an honor bestowed on me."

I remember upon the album's release, 'Country Honk' was seen as the joke track on *Let It Bleed*. Even by December 1969, country had yet to be fully embraced by rock audiences. But, for all his unreliability, Gram Parsons' knowledge of country music and its antecedents ran deep. It was Gram who demonstrated to Keith the difference between the softer, Jim Reeves sound of Nashville and the grittier Bakersfield sound,* exemplified by Merle Haggard.

It was obvious with the release of *Let It Bleed* that the Stones had expanded their musical palette. Gram was undeniably an influence at that time. It was Gram's closeness to Keith that saw the Burritos added to the Altamont lineup, and they also had them pencilled in as opening act on a future Stones tour. But it was a two-way street. "They wanted to get further into what I was doing," Gram told Bud Scoppa in 1970, "and I wanted to get into what they were doing." For all his heartfelt love of country, Gram wanted a slice of that good ol' rock'n'roll. For all his personal wealth and hedonistic lifestyle, Gram couldn't help but envy rock royalty, a life exemplified by the Rolling Stones. Hanging out with the Stones during that epochal US tour of '69 put Gram into an elite orbit.

---

* I was at an exhibition at Nashville's Country Music Hall Of Fame celebrating the 'Sound Of Bakersfield' some years back. A Dutch journalist was trying to recall the song about Bakersfield. "Dwight Yoakam's 'Streets Of Bakersfield'?" I ventured. Nope! "The Stones mention it on 'Faraway Eyes'!" Definitely not. "No, the song about Bakersfield – with the saxophone?" "Oh… 'Baker Street'!"

The Stones also got off on Gram's rebellious streak, like his getting The Flying Burrito Brothers to wear suits fashioned by Nudie, the country and western tailor, only Nudie's suits for the Burritos were emblazoned with marijuana leaf designs!

The Flying Burrito Brothers' version of 'Wild Horses' was in the shops a year before the Stones' version on 1971's *Sticky Fingers*. Talking to Bud Scoppa, Gram magnanimously called the song "a logical continuation between their music and our music. It's something that Mick Jagger can accept, and it's something I can accept."

Following 'Country Honk', the Rolling Stones further ploughed the country furrow. They had dabbled with country on 1968's 'Dear Doctor', and psychologists connected with Keith's boyhood identification with singing cowboy Roy Rogers. But the band's infatuation really manifested itself on 1971's 'Dead Flowers', 1972's 'Sweet Virginia' and 1978's completely, delightfully over-the-top contribution 'Faraway Eyes'. A lovely version of Hank Williams' 'You Win Again' was included as a track on the bonus disc of 2011's *Some Girls* reissue. In fact the old pedal steel was dusted down quite a bit for the original 1978 sessions, notably for the country riffs on 'So Young' and Mick's pronounced vocal on 'No Spare Parts'.

The night before Keith was due to go down following his Toronto drug bust in 1977, he spent the evening singing a selection of country songs culled from Gram Parsons' repertoire. Among the tunes that surfaced on the much-bootlegged *A Stone Alone* are Johnny Paycheck's 'Apartment No. 9' and Glenn Sutton's 'She Still Comes Around'. A particular highlight was Merle Haggard's poignant prison ballad 'Sing Me Back Home': a condemned man on Death Row asks to hear a few old gospel songs he remembers his Mama singing as he prepares to take that long and final 'dead man's walk'...

I remember years ago reading that the Rolling Stones did a version of Waylon Jennings' magnificent 'Bob Wills Is Still The King' (the original, incidentally, is one of the best live songs ever recorded – ever!). Idly, I typed 'Rolling Stones Bob Wills' into Google, and there it was... live From Texas, 2007, the first (and only) time the band ever attempted it. And what a treat it is. Bob Wills was 'the King of Western Swing', a phenomenally successful country and western act performing in the 1940s. His 'San Antonio Rose' and 'Take Me Back To Tulsa' are in many country acts' repertoires to this day.

Pursuing the Stones on a country and western jag threading through YouTube, I find another wonderful clip of Mick and Keith hamming it up on 'Faraway Eyes'. Then back to 1972 for a blistering live version of 'Dead Flowers'. But then that's the rest of the day gone...

Mick: "I used to love country music before I met Keith. I loved George Jones and really fast, shit-kicking country music, though I didn't really like the maudlin songs too much. And to me all those old rockers were really converted country singers; Jerry Lee Lewis is the most obvious version, but you could also hear it in Gene Vincent and Ricky Nelson."

Gram Parsons continued to grow ever closer to the Stones up to and following Altamont. He was convinced he would be an early signing to Rolling Stones Records. He and Keith bonded, over drugs and country music. And drugs. According to Keith, who knew whereof he spoke, Gram supplied "better coke than the Mafia".

Gram even hung out with the Stones during 1971 as they ploughed round Leeds, Coventry and Glasgow on their 'farewell' UK tour. The band were decamping to France and on into tax exile. For Gram, life in the south of France was undeniably more appealing than the grimy provinces of the UK.

So, independently wealthy, Gram followed the Stones to Villefranche. His footsteps echo round the villa's basement, where he was a ubiquitous presence during the recording of *Exile On Main St.*, and 'Sweet Virginia' certainly has Gram's stamp. Such was the druggy miasma surrounding the *Exile…* sessions though, no one can ever be 100 per cent certain if Gram isn't on background vocals somewhere.

However, by the time of *Exile*'s release in 1972, Gram was on a downward spiral. He died in 1973, having overdosed on morphine and alcohol at the Joshua Tree Inn in the southern California desert town of the same name. Even in death, Gram Parsons' legacy lives on: the location of his fiery immolation in the Cap Rock section of Joshua Tree National Park became a landmark (until park services removed a concrete slab commemorating the musician, transferring it to the Joshua Tree Inn). U2 also named their breakthrough 1987 album *The Joshua Tree* in homage to Gram's last resting place.

On record, 'Country Honk' came to life in Los Angeles. Gram Parsons knew Byron Berline and recommended him to the Stones – the track needed a fiddler, not a violinist, and Byron had country flowing through his Appalachian veins. When Byron got the call, he remembered: "Oh yeah, my roommate in college played all that Rolling Stones. I'd say 'Man, would you turn that off?'" The fiddler was met at LAX and driven direct to Sunset Sound. Glyn Johns and Mick thought it would be cool to record Berline playing out on Sunset Boulevard, with added background traffic noise for atmosphere. The actual 'honk' was a car horn supplied by (memories are vague) either Phil Kaufman or Sam Cutler… or Mick Jagger.

Today, with country a more familiar, rock-friendly experience, 'Country Honk' stands on its own two, albeit wobbly, feet. The song has a gritty, downhome feel, and a first verse that relocates the location of the story from Memphis to Jackson, Mississippi.

Honky-tonks had played a key role in country music. These were venues, in the words of the song, of 'Dim Lights, Thick Smoke (And Loud, Loud Music)'.* Floozies hung around the bars and drank rotgut whiskey. Punters let their hair down and let rip on a Saturday night. Come Sunday morning, they may have still been hung over, but they were still sober enough to totter along to church. The honky-tonk bars inspired artists from all genres. Hank Williams had hit pay dirt decades earlier with 'Honky Tonk Blues' and 'Honky Tonkin''. Hank Thompson's 'Wild Side Of Life' blamed the "honky tonk angels" for his journeys to the dark side. Kitty Wells was quick off the mark with one of the first 'answer songs' in rebuttal, 1952's 'It Wasn't God Who Made Honky Tonk Angels'. In 1974, a Flying Burrito Brothers compilation, *Close Up The Honky Tonks*, was released posthumously to commemorate Gram Parsons.

Like the bar owner said in *The Blues Brothers*, "We got both kinds of music here, country *and* western!" In keeping with the country vein, Keith contributed a delightfully ragged version of 'You Win Again' to a 2001 Hank Williams tribute album. Mick eventually delivered a heartfelt version of 'Long Black Veil' to a Chieftains album in 1995. And shame the Stones never found room to record or perform Jimmie Rodgers' plaintive 'Waiting On A Train' – you can imagine the mileage Mick could wring out of an empty pocket book, a pain-filled heart and a thousand-mile journey home while "Waiting on a train…"

The final track on Side One, 'Let It Bleed', just *lurches* into life. Opening with a request, a plea, delivered in oak-soaked bourbon, there is something sinuous, eerie, a sulphrous menace about the

---

* Written by Joe Maphis, Rose Lee Maphis and Max Fidler in the early fifties.

song. A scintilla of unidentifiable wickedness infuses 'Let It Bleed' – the parking lot referenced was Marianne Faithfull's nickname for her vagina. The Stones continue their subverting... In 1953, Robert Anderson's play *Tea And Sympathy* was premiered, and the phrase soon entered public parlance as "a caring attitude, especially towards someone in trouble". By 1969, what the notorious rock'n'roll band require is some cocaine and sympathy. The song drips blood – knives flash – and all the while, the loose melody gets looser and no one sounds capable of bringing it to an end.

Paul McCartney's hymnal, near contemporaneous 'Let It Be' offered balming, calming words of wisdom. The Beatle proffers answers and light in the darkness. But as ever, the Stones flip, taking you over to the dark side. The stale musk of a Ladbroke Grove basement permeates the song. 'Let It Bleed' comes dripping in spunk, junk and jasmine tea...

Finally, 'You Can't Always Get What You Want' was the Stones at their majestic best, imperial and imperious, no questions asked. A simple fact: the best ever last song on a rock band's album.

While *Let It Bleed* has its flaws, it has long ranked among best ever Rolling Stones albums. And what better way to climax an album of the sixties with the song that somehow encapsulates that decade?

'You Can't Always Get What You Want' has a confused narrative: a stroll through London streets; a demonstration (Grosvenor Square?); a connection (a drug dealer?); a reception (thrown by a record company?). There's no confusing the stop-off at the Chelsea Drugstore – along with Biba and Carnaby Street, the drugstore on King's Road was a focal point of Swinging London. You get a flavour of the place in *A Clockwork Orange*, as Malcolm McDowell roams around there, before settling on the record department. While there, the song's narrator encounters "Mr Jimmy" (Hendrix? Miller?)... Amid the bacchanalia of *Let It Bleed*, the scene on this particular track is restrained – there are cherry-red sodas, a glass of wine, a desperate sense of needing.

Neil Croally, Stones fan and Head of Scholarship and Liberal Studies at Dulwich College, kindly agreed to share with me his thoughts about this most intriguing and enigmatic of songs.

"The Rolling Stones are good at having their cake and eating it. By their look, their demeanour, their sound, they seemed to be the embodiment of the sixties: rebellious, dirty, sexy. Like 'Street Fighting Man', 'You Can't Always Get What You Want' – the last song on the band's last album of the sixties – is similarly ambivalent. Its anthemic qualities, often exploited in live performance, seem to chime with the collective strain of sixties counterculture. But the sixties was also the decade of rampant individualism, advocating the satisfaction of desire above all. In this context, the chorus seems resigned and conservative. And the exhortation that effort leads to need(s) being met sounds like a parent addressing a child or, alternatively, a perversely naive Marxism.

"Amid the song's intimations of drug (ab)use – connections, prescriptions, the wretched-looking Mr Jimmy – that same Mr Jimmy responds to the singer's song by announcing some sort of death. Of the sixties perhaps? The unusually specific quality of some of the lyrics (it doesn't matter exactly who Mr Jimmy is, but he is met at the Chelsea Drugstore), allied with some obscure but suggestive lines (e.g. a man who is footloose) do not really prepare the listener for the repeated generalisations of the chorus. But the doubleness is finally most apparent in the sound. Harmonically simple, the song is relatively complex rhythmically, and even funky in that peculiar Stones way. This is in sharp contrast to the mellow tones of the French horn, and the sweet warblings of the treble choir (who sound particularly out of place when the rhythm changes to a 2/4 stomp near the end).

"The song has no single tone or view, and is permeated by abuse and death. Perhaps, as the cover of *Let It Bleed* shows, the Rolling Stones like to have their cake and break it."

By the time the London Bach Choir trooped into Olympic, the song's original gospel roots had been abandoned. Engineer George Chkiantz told Sean Egan of the night the choir were called in: "The hard rockers at one end, swathed in billowing smoke in the control room, and then fifty feet of no man's land with the choir at the other... Every time something needed changing, a lone brave person was detailed to go across no man's land and talk to the arranger. It really was like they almost needed white flags!"

As well as hearing a classical choir on a Rolling Stones album, I was always baffled by the name-check of actress Nanette Newman on backing vocals. How did the actress wife of film mogul Bryan Forbes and onetime co-star of Peter Sellers and Tony Hancock end up on a Stones album? Doris Troy and Madeline Bell, also listed in the album's credits, were familiar backing vocalist names. But what of Nanette Newman? Thanks to the wonders of the internet, it turns out that the American singer Nanette Workman had moved to the UK, and a contact at Olympic Studios put her name forward. Nanette didn't have a work permit, so she simply 'borrowed' the actress's name for the sessions! She ended up on 'Country Honk' and 'Honky Tonk Women', as well as here.

If 'You Can't Always Get What You Want' was designed as a riposte to the Beatles' marathon 'Hey Jude', it succeeded better than either side could have imagined. Ebbing and flowing, rising and falling, it is titanic in its ambition and magnificent in its achievement. Without doubt, it is the summation of the Stones' greatness, the track on which to end the decade that bred them.

In the same way that the threnody 'Flowers O' The Forest' was written to mourn the fallen at the Battle of Flodden in 1513, but down the centuries has come to represent a wider lament, 'You

Can't Always Get What You Want' has come to mean more than its original intention as the culmination of a Rolling Stones album. It stands and acts as more than a disjointed commentary of a time and place. It has come to represent nothing more than the end of an entire era.

★★★

So it was that the LP bled over nine tracks, spread over two sides and 42-odd minutes. And like many of the Stones' albums, outtakes are few and far between. I interviewed Bill Wyman once, around the time The Beatles began their *Anthology* releases, and asked him if there was ever a likelihood of the Stones mounting a similar project? "Not really," shrugged Bill, "there's a lot of instrumental, unfinished things, because that's the way we worked. Most of the stuff is instrumental, Mick's not interested in having any of them released 'cos he's not even on them."

In Julian Dawson's biography of session man Nicky Hopkins,* his colleague Jon Mark tells the story: "I was booked on all the sessions with Glyn Johns and so was Nicky. We would turn up there at six o'clock and Glyn would say, 'They're not here yet, why don't you guys go over to the pub.' We would have a few pints of beer and come back at eight; they still weren't there. Nip back to the pub and come back at nine, still not there. We'd hang in and then perhaps one of them would turn up, sometimes three, but it would be twelve or one o'clock in the morning."

For all the patina of glory that surrounded the Rolling Stones, *Let It Bleed* wasn't a particularly generous gig for the session musicians. Reluctant to share songwriting credits, the band were equally stingy with session fees. Mick Taylor to Julian Dawson:

---

* Author of *And On Piano... Nicky Hopkins: The Extraordinary Life Of Rock's Greatest Session Man* (Backstage Press, 2011).

"Nicky was trying to renegotiate his session fee, which probably wasn't very much, because they used to pay their musicians minimal wages... Much as they admire the musician they've hired, they cannot seem to get out of the session musician mentality when it comes to paying them; it's almost as if they think 'These guys should feel honoured to be playing with me.'"

Playing with the Stones did require a great deal of patience, and a decent amount of 'hanging-around time' was built into the session. If the band were on 'Keith time', it was wise to bring a good book. Nicky Hopkins' mum, Freda, was furious: "They used to phone him in the middle of the night and he'd hire a taxi and go up to London. I used to get so cross. It was nothing to them was it? But he'd come home exhausted."

Bill Wyman confirmed: "There was always a complete lack of regard for the inconvenience to other people... You'd arrive and it would be cancelled, but no one would have phoned to say. You'd find Mick had gone off to dinner with some celebrities or Keith never made it... There was that lack of consideration for other members, it might have been a power thing, I don't know."

But it wasn't always wasted time. A flavour of the jams ('Blow Blues', 'Hillside Blues') cut while 'hanging around' came with the release in 1972 of *Jamming With Edward*, often credited as a Nicky Hopkins solo effort. The sleeve also credits Ry Cooder, Mick Jagger, Bill Wyman and Charlie Watts. Songs culled from the *Let It Bleed* sessions that made it onto the Hopkins album include 'It Hurts Me Too' and 'Boudoir Stomp'. "We were right in the middle of doing a track," Hopkins recalled, "and Keith had to go back to the house because Anita was sick. So I thought, 'Fuck it, let's play for a while until Keith gets back', which is just what we did."

Let It Bleed did produce some outtakes for the Stones, too – 'I'm Going Down', 'Jiving Sister Fanny' and Bill Wyman's 'Downtown

Suzie' appeared on the Stones' 1975 compilation, *Metamorphosis*. It was one of the few collections Decca released, with a little help from Wyman, that wasn't a disgrace. 'Get A Line On You' was reworked as 'Shine A Light' for *Exile On Main St.* three years later, as was 'Give Me A Drink' (or 'Loving Cup' as it was later retitled). In his comprehensive look at the Stones on record, Martin Elliott also cites 'The Jimmy Miller Show' and 'I'm A Country Boy' (aka 'And I Was a Country Boy'; 'I Was Just A Country Boy') as rejects from the *Let It Bleed* sessions.

'Aladdin Story', aka 'Aladdin Stomp', was reworked and appeared as the bonus track 'So Divine' on the 2010 rerelease of *Exile On Main St.* This was one of the instrumental tracks for which Jagger wrote lyrics, dubbing on contemporaneous 21st-century vocals, a trick that was criticised upon release. Also from the 1969 sessions, Little Walter's 'Hate To See You Go' had to wait half a century before it was rerecorded for 2016's *Blue & Lonesome*.

Unlike The Beatles, whose 200–track-plus career could be largely contained within the walls of Abbey Road, London, NW8, a thorough chronology of the Stones recordings is nigh on impossible. Far from EMI's civil service bureaucracy, as free agents, the Stones roamed far and wide, from London to Los Angeles, from the Caribbean to the south of France. And of course the binning of the Decca archive further muddies the waters.

CHAPTER 15

You Got The Gold

Sessions for *Let It Bleed* had begun in Barnes in late 1968 but they wrapped in Los Angeles. On October 21, 1969, the band adjourned to Sunset Sound Studios to finish the record.* By December, the Rolling Stones were ready to unleash their new album on the world.

First they needed a suitable album cover. American designer Robert Brownjohn** was commissioned to design the sleeve for *Let It Bleed*. Brownjohn had relocated to London in the early sixties, where he was approached by Harry Saltzman to create the electrifying opening credits for the second and third James Bond films, *From Russia With Love* (1963) and *Goldfinger* (1964).

However, for all the greatness in its grooves, *Let It Bleed* suffers with one of the worst ever covers on a classic album. Maybe it was

---

* Engineer Bruce Botnick is convinced that the Stones finished *Let It Bleed* at Elektra's studios, where he recorded The Doors. But as with much to do with that band, details get a little… hazy.

** *Let It Bleed* proved to be one of Brownjohn's last commissions, as he sadly died from a heart attack in August 1970 at the age of forty-four.

the enthusiasm Keith exuded when Brownjohn showed him his original designs while the album was still called *Automatic Changer*. At least that goes some way to explaining the sloppy sleeve imagery with its record arm and vinyl disc. "Only the cover lets the album down," wrote Jonathon Green in his *Friends* review. "In almost unparalleled ugliness it serves to keep the album clean and dry, it certainly doesn't enhance the package." Greil Marcus concurred: "the crummiest cover art... with a credit sheet that looks like it was designed by the United States Government Printing Office."

It isn't often that a cake merits its own place in the history of rock'n'roll. "I was working then as a jobbing home economist with a food photographer who shot for commercials and magazines," recalled the baker. Delia Smith, OBE, CBE went on to become one of the best-loved and best-known television chefs. Her cookery books dominated bestseller charts for decades and were a compulsory purchase for every newlywed couple. 'The Delia Effect' was a phenomenon that saw supermarket shelves empty out after she had used an ingredient on her cookery shows – as a case in point, sales of cinnamon sticks shot up 200 per cent at Sainsbury's after Delia's Christmas 2009 series aired!

"I'd cook anything they needed," Delia said of starting out in the industry. "One day they said they wanted a cake for a Rolling Stones record cover – it was just another job at the time. They wanted it to be very over-the-top and as gaudy as I could make it." Job done! Many years later, Delia revealed her recipe, noting that you needed to "find a tyre for that all-important presentation". She remembered that when the Stones heard she was the creator of the famous cake, Mick sent her an autographed LP sleeve "with fondest memories", adding "it tasted delicious". Ironically, to commemorate his eightieth birthday in 2012, Sir Peter Blake recreated his *Sgt. Pepper* LP cover, this time with figures he admired – one of whom was Delia Smith. So the creator of one of the world's worst LP sleeves was featured on a reproduction of probably the best loved!

It could have been so much better. In the early seventies, posters of the work of Dutch graphic artist M.C. Escher covered the walls of student flats and bedsits up and down the country. Escher's pieces were quite literally mind-bending. How did that waterfall work? Where did those stairs go?

In 1970, *Rolling Stone* alerted its underground constituency to the artist: "At the age of 71, the great Dutch graphic master has finally arrived." Around the same time, another Rolling Stone was getting interested, enough to contact Escher to commission him for the LP. "Dear Maurits," Mick wrote, "I think your work is quite incredible and it would make me very happy for a lot more people to see and know and to understand what you are doing."

However, even Mick Jagger must have been taken aback by the artist's courteous, but withering rejection:

Dear Sir,

Some days ago I received a letter from Mr Jagger asking me to design a picture or to place at his disposal unpublished work to reproduce on the cover-sleeve for an LP record.

My answer to both questions must be no, as I want to devote all my time and attention to the many commitments I made; I cannot possibly accept any further assignments or spend any time on publicity.

By the way, please tell Mr Jagger I am not Maurits to him, but

Very sincerely,

M.C. Escher

Elsewhere, anticipation for the new Stones album was now running high. The US trade paper *Record World* reported its arrival in typically staccato style: "The Rolling Stones, touring and tearing up America with their raunchy rock, have a nitty gritty new album platter called *Let It Bleed*."*

Let It Bleed was finally released on December 5, 1969, just in time for Christmas. It was the last Rolling Stones studio LP (over which the band exercised any control) for the Decca label. "This record should be played loud", the sleeve insisted.

Other landmark LPs released around the same time included debuts from The Allman Brothers Band, Yes, Humble Pie and King Crimson, Pink Floyd's *Ummagumma*, Frank Zappa's *Hot Rats*, Jefferson Airplane's *Volunteers*, Fleetwood Mac's *Then Play On* and The Byrds' *Ballad Of Easy Rider*.

The band needed *Let It Bleed* to succeed. At the time of the album's release, bands relied on record sales for their prime income. They'd release a single, such as 'Honky Tonk Women', as a teaser for the new direction they'd be taking on the upcoming album. The success of that single then guaranteed airplay and, hopefully, a chart placing. This would set the ball rolling for the expensive LP release and purchase. After the LP would come the tour – more promotion for the current album, which would by that point be stocked in branches of WH Smith, Harlequin, Woolworths and HMV. Teased by unfamiliar live material, loyal audiences would flock to the stores to purchase the studio recordings.

---

* The album's title was seen by some as a riposte to The Beatles. Although *Let It Be* (both LP and single) would not be in the shops until the early part of 1970, throughout 1969, rumours abounded of the mixed-media Beatles project. As well as *Get Back*, one of the titles in circulation was *Let It Be*. In other origin stories, Sam Cutler once joked that *Let It Bleed* came from Allen Klein bleeding everyone dry on the 1969 tour! True or not, there is something nasty, offhand, about the Stones' album title, something vicious that once again tied in with the public's appreciation of the band.

The most popular release date for albums fell in the lead-up to Christmas and accounted for a high percentage of all UK record sales. A pre-Christmas release also allowed for a post-Christmas spend, when festive record tokens could be splurged along the high street. The idea that the majority of an act's income would come from tour merchandise rather than record releases would have been laughed out of court in 1969.

If you were short of inspiration, a greatest hits collection would suffice, an opportunity to gather up all those 45s onto one LP. This would replace those singles that had been scratched, flaked in fag ash or soaked by Watneys Party Sevens at parties. Failing that, a 'live' album might act as a reminder of a band you had enjoyed in performance, a souvenir allowing you to replicate the concert experience at home.

Come release day, and with Christmas on the horizon, the British record buyers of 1969 were spoilt for choice when it came to deciding which album to lavish their one pound, 17 shillings and six pennies (£1.87, give or take a halfpenny) on.* That year alone saw the following in store: Bob Dylan's *Nashville Skyline*; The Band's eponymous follow-up to *Music From Big Pink*; a brace each from The Beatles (*Yellow Submarine* and *Abbey Road*), Led Zeppelin (*I* and *II*), The Byrds (*Dr Byrds & Mr Hyde* and *Ballad Of Easy Rider*) and Pink Floyd (the soundtrack to *More* and the double *Ummagumma*); *Goodbye Cream*; The Who's all-conquering rock opera *Tommy* (an expensive double-LP purchase); *The Soft Parade* from The Doors; King Crimson's debut *In The Court Of The Crimson King*; The Nice's third album, simply titled *Nice*; Jeff Beck's second solo album *Beck-Ola*; *Ssssh* by Ten Tears After; *Ahead Rings Out* by Blodwyn Pig; The Moody Blues' *On The Threshold Of A Dream*;

---

*   This was the time, remember, when hit singles – which the record-buying public had already purchased, sending them flying up the charts – were not included on subsequent UK albums. Even the surly Stones thought that bad form.

Crosby, Stills & Nash from the newly formed California-infused supergroup of the same name; *Blind Faith* from the English rock supergroup comprising Clapton, Winwood, Ginger Baker and Ric Grech; Leonard Cohen's *Songs From A Room*; Fairport Convention's folk-rock-founding *Liege & Lief*; the Velvet Underground's self-titled third album; Procol Harum's *A Salty Dog*… the list goes on.

The Stones had already essayed the excellent greatest hits compilation, *Big Hits (High Tide And Green Grass)*, which was a souvenir of their 'pop' years, in 1966. Then in September 1969 *Through The Past Darkly, (Big Hits Vol. 2)* had hit the shops. This latest compilation gathered favourite EP tracks ('You Better Move On'), key album cuts ('Mother's Little Helper'; '2000 Light Years From Home') and recent hit singles ('We Love You'; 'Honky Tonk Women'). Two months after his death, Brian was remembered on the sleeve, and the album title aptly paraphrased Corinthians: "When I was a child, I spake as a child, I understood as a child, I thought as a child: but when I became a man, I put away childish things. For now we see through a glass darkly; but then face to face." *Record Mirror* called the sleeve "An octagonal slap [sic] of pop history".

Through The Past Darkly was denied the UK number one LP slot by a triple whammy of Jethro Tull's *Stand Up*, Blind Faith's debut (indeed, only) LP and The Beatles' all-conquering *Abbey Road*. But with the summer number one of 'Honky Tonk Women', and ears still ringing from Hyde Park, the compilation had been enough to convince the band that their fans had not forgotten them.

Around the same time, Decca had been advertising new albums by Ronnie Aldrich & His Two Pianos, The Bachelors, The Satin Bells, Donald Peers and Genesis ("a very talented and inventive group [who] don't have to resort to gimmicks to get their music across").

But it was *Let It Bleed* that became the UK's number one album over the Christmas of 1969, going on to spend 29 weeks on the album charts. It was only the Stones' fourth number one album in their homeland. In the USA, it reached number three on the *Billboard* Top LP chart; mind you, it was kept off the top by *Abbey Road* and *Led Zeppelin II*, and eventually went two times platinum.

Upon release, *Let It Bleed* attracted acclaimed reviews from the all-important music weeklies. "What a great album!" enthused *NME*'s Richard Green. "The Stones have obviously put a lot of thought and hard work into it, and I have no hesitation in naming it one of the Top Five LPs of 1969 – people are going to have to go a long way to beat it. There's so much variety that each track makes you want to hear it again and again."

Melody Maker's Chris Welch: "It's tremendous! The Stones have suffered many wounds during their careers, but *Let It Bleed* is probably the best album they have produced for consistency in both material and performance. After much sidetracking into different influences since their early days, the Stones have found themselves again."

In *Friends*, after dismissing the cover Jonathon Green added: "What's inside is the thing that really counts, and what is inside adds up to the best Stones album yet... They are the anarchist band, they do things that no-one else would dare."

Lon Goddard went into overdrive in *Record Mirror*: "'You Can't Always Get What You Want' is the daddy of all and everybody's daddy is on it, twice... Unlike other groups who bring in the National Guard and half the IRA, this huge production is an absolute jewel from start to finish.

"The choir brings the depth to twenty thousand leagues under the sea and the myriad bangs and thumps rotate the rhythm with great creativity. Rises to a religious experience and leaves you with the satisfaction of a good you-know-what. The Stones have guts like nobody else and this LP is a real slap in the solar plexus."

Even the stuffy *Gramophone* magazine enthused: "The Rolling Stones create more interest than normal for me with *Let It Bleed*, partly by recruiting some additional instrumental talent, to say nothing of the London Bach Choir, which participates effectively in the long closing track 'You Can't Always Get What You Want'. The album is a reasonable exercise in rock blues, happily devoid of the grotesque excesses of previous LPs by this group. Youthful recipients will find an extra bonus inside the sleeve in the shape of a full colour poster of the Stones."

In the States, enthusiasm was equally unanimous. For *Rolling Stone*, Greil Marcus picked up on the album's bookends: "It's a long way from 'Get Off My Cloud' to 'Gimme Shelter', a long way from 'I Can't Get No Satisfaction' to 'You Can't Always Get What You Want'… In *Let It Bleed* we can find every role the Stones have ever played for us – swaggering studs, evil demons, harem keepers and fast life riders – what the Stones meant in the sixties, what they know very well they've meant to us. But at the beginning and the end you'll find an opening into the seventies – harder to take, and stronger wine."

Time magazine was enthusiastic, if wary: "*Let It Bleed* has plenty of the Stones' old power and ominous tension. But despite its professionalism and preoccupation with sex and violence, the LP has a retrospective quality. The Stones, in fact, seem to have become the last thing they ever wanted – an institution."

But the plaudits kept on coming. The 1969 *Rolling Stone* Annual Poll named the band as 'The Best Rock and Roll band of All Time', and 'Gimme Shelter' as Track of the Year, while *Let it Bleed* tied with *Nashville Skyline* as Album of the Year.

The long haul through the sixties was nearly over, the end was in sight and, to everyone's amazement, the survivors were still standing, and at liberty. At the end of the decade, the Stones spoke to a generation, a generation dissatisfied with the pressures their elders had placed upon them, raging against a war nobody wanted. And in that despair and disillusionment came the troubadours to mirror their anger and frustration. New LPs by Dylan, The Beatles and the Stones were greeted with awe and wonder, like Moses bringing the tablets down from the mountain. All were subject to forensic lyrical analysis.

Lyrically, the Stones lagged behind: no one could match Dylan for his vivid imagination and wordplay, while The Beatles had two writers whose lyrics encompassed their experiences. The Kinks were blessed with Ray Davies (nobody has written a more quintessentially English song than 'The Village Green Preservation Society'). But at their best, Jagger's lyrics are certainly up there, alongside those of Pete Townshend and Robert Plant.

Even today, though, Stones lyrics remain inscrutable. From *Sgt. Pepper* on, it became de rigueur to include the lyrics on the album sleeve. Of the giants, only Bob Dylan and the Stones bucked the tradition. Of course now you can Google to your heart's content and the secrets are stripped away. But there is a mysterious murk and swirl to 'Gimme Shelter', or 'Salt Of The Earth', or 'Tumbling Dice' – to this day, I still have no idea what Mick is really singing about on these magnificent tracks. "Mick always wrote good lyrics," Bill Wyman stated, emphatically.

And for all the kudos and critical marvelling, all the prurience, one of the elements that plays such a key role in the Stones' legend are those lyrics, courtesy of Michael Philip Jagger.

Talking to Richard Buskin in 1990, producer Jimmy Miller remembered asking: "'Mick, why are you always asking for less voice [on the mix]? Aren't you confident about how your vocals sound?' He said the reason was when he was growing up with what he described as Negro blues songs, it was always a contest to be able to decipher the words. Kids were always trying to be the first one in the neighbourhood to know all the words to a record, and they couldn't do this by hearing it now and then on the radio. They'd have to go out and buy it and play the record over and over. So in his practical way he believed that as a result of mixing down his vocals, people... would now actually be more prone to buy the Stones record in order to be able to get all the words!"

Often in the studio, the band would work around a riff, with Mick humming or improvising lyrics on the spot. Inspiration came from all sources. While Mick was in a relationship with Marianne Faithfull, the pair would swap ideas, discuss books they'd read, turn each other on to different cultural values and mores. "I mean," Marianne said when we met, with a laugh, "it wasn't drug-fuelled orgies every night..."

★★★

With *Let It Bleed* dominating the charts, and to counter the flood of bootlegs emanating from the US dates, the band was scheduled to deliver a live album that would effectively end their relationship with Decca. Even then, the battles continued to the bitter end. A triple live LP was unheard of – that monster would have to wait until a few years later, with the pomp majesty of Yes and Emerson, Lake & Palmer. But a double live album could work, and the Stones were determined to give fans the full concert experience using recordings from the US tour. Thus, Disc One would feature opening acts Ike & Tina Turner and B.B. King. However, Decca was equally determined that a live Rolling Stones LP would feature *only* the Rolling Stones. And so the double-album idea was aborted.*

---

* An acetate of the aborted live double-album souvenir '*Get Yer Ya-Yas Out!*' was auctioned for £650 in 1988.

However, the official album release of '*Get Yer Ya-Yas Out!*', which features live recordings of the band – and no one else – from their US tour stops in New York City, Baltimore and Maryland, is a joy. And for all the problems facing the *Beggars Banquet* sleeve and the critical hostility *Let It Bleed*'s cake cover aroused, '*Ya-Yas!*' sleeve was a triumph. Taking its cue from Dylan's 'Visions Of Johanna', in particular the "jewels and binoculars" that hung from a mule's head, for the Stones it is drums and guitars, and a rare smiling Charlie, bounding towards David Bailey's camera, wearing a white T-shirt featuring a black-and-white photo of a woman's breasts.*

However, with the contractual live album now fulfilled, the Stones still owed the label one more track, resulting in the (purposefully) unreleasable 'Cocksucker Blues'. Marshall Chess, who had worked on his father's record label Chess Records for 16 years and was hired as president of the new Rolling Stone Records, gleefully recounted playing the song to Decca's venerable chief, Sir Edward Lewis, on July 31, 1970. One can only imagine Lewis's reaction to the plaintive blues, with its catchy chorus concerning fellatio and anal sex. It's unlikely that Jagger's suggestion for the novel use of a police truncheon raised a smile...

This was the final face-to-face confrontation between the Stones and their stuffy label boss. Now approaching seventy, Sir Edward had clearly fallen out of touch with the burgeoning switch from pop to rock.

In the tsunami that was Beatlemania, Decca had always been seen as the poor relation to its main rival. EMI's subsidiary Parlophone label had landed the goose that laid the golden eggs – two Beatle LPs and two non-album singles a year – while Decca's

---

* The cover image was shot in either Hendon, or New York, as suggested by footage from the opening segment of the *Gimme Shelter* documentary.

A&R executive Dick Rowe has famously gone down in history as 'the man who turned down The Beatles'. Although, as Mark Lewisohn once and forever explained in *Tune In*, the first volume of his monumental Beatles trilogy,* it wasn't quite that simple...

It was actually Rowe's young assistant, Mike Smith, who oversaw The Beatles' Decca audition of January 1, 1962. He had previously seen them live, in action at the Cavern. He'd come away impressed and was keen to hear how the band sounded in a studio.

While Smith oversaw the session, he had to defer to Dick Rowe for the final decision. He had also auditioned Brian Poole & the Tremeloes around the same time, and Rowe authorised him to sign only one of the two groups. Geography played a part in that decision: Essex was demonstrably nearer to London's Decca Studios than Liverpool. We all know which way the decision went.

In fairness, by the time the bleary-eyed Beatles dragged themselves into Decca's studios in Broadhurst Gardens on New Year's Day 1962, they already had a long history of rejection – Columbia, HMV, Pye, Philips and Oriole had all turned them down. So, while Decca's decision to decline the UK entertainment phenomenon of the 20th century is legendary, it is at least consistent! Plus, I remember finding myself agreeing with Dick Rowe when the Decca audition tape was finally released as a bootleg in the 1980s. There is, understandably, palpable nervousness emanating from The Beatles; the performances are muted; the choice of material is undistinguished – the band's versions of the jokey 'Three Cool Cats', 'The Sheik Of Araby' and 'Searchin'' sound more suited to someone like Bernard Cribbins. There is

---

* *The Beatles – All These Years: Volume 1: Tune In* by Mark Lewisohn (Little Brown, 2013).

little – actually, *nothing* – to suggest their future greatness. Even Mark Lewisohn politely calls the Decca audition "a lacklustre performance, restrained, subdued, the handbrake on".

However, until his death in 1986, Dick Rowe was damned by his choice. It was a decision made all the more ironic when, on May 5, 1963, the Decca executive found himself in Liverpool. He was judging a talent contest at the Philharmonic Hall just as Beatlemania was breaking out big. One of his fellow judges, looking for the 'next big thing', was George Harrison. Talking to Louis Barfe, Decca executive Hugh Mendl recalled the circumstances: "Dick was a very nice bloke and said to George, 'I'm sorry. I feel so embarrassed.' George said, 'We were terrible weren't we?... We hadn't had any sleep... we'd driven down overnight. We were awful. I don't blame you.' Then he leant over and said, 'I'm sorry you had all this trouble in the press about it. Do you want to do yourself a bit of good? There's a band called the Rolling Stones and they appear at the Station Hotel, Richmond'."

As esteemed Beatle historian Bill Harry later wrote: "Frankly, instead of being known as the man who turned down The Beatles, which is inaccurate, [Dick Rowe] should have been lauded as the man who signed up the Rolling Stones."

The Stones' relationship with Decca really began when Dick Rowe and his wife travelled down to Richmond: "From the bright sunshine into the dark room I couldn't see anything...," he later recalled of that first sighting. "I said to my wife, 'What do they look like?' and she said, 'The lead singer's very good'!"

The roots of the label that would release those classic Stones records for the remainder of the decade are mundane. Decca goes back to the company Barnett Samuel & Sons, which started out producing doorknobs, combs and knife handles. By the time of the Great War, it had switched to manufacturing a portable gramophone, which proved popular with officers serving on the Western Front. That gramophone was called the Decca Dulcephone. According to label historians Dick Weindling and Marianne Colloms, the label name came from a 1930s Sunday radio show, which used five notes as its call sign: D–E–C–C–A Barnett Samuel also wanted an easily pronounceable alliterative name for their Dulcephone.

The company was then sold to former stockbroker Edward Lewis in 1929, who transformed Decca into one of the most successful record labels in the world at the time. The label's early hits included discs from bandleaders Jack Hylton, Billy Cotton and Ted Heath. On Lewis's watch, Lonnie Donegan cut that quick version of Lead Belly's 'Rock Island Line' in 1954, launching the skiffle boom. Lewis had also encouraged Decca to actively pursue new technology in the shape of stereophonic recordings and the development of the long-playing record.

But later years were unkind to the label and, prior to signing the Rolling Stones, Decca had begun trailing in the wake of its rival. EMI ruled the roost from its futuristic Manchester Square offices. If anything, Decca had an even more imposing HQ on Albert Embankment, overlooking the Thames. The label had enjoyed phenomenal success in licensing the American recordings of Bing Crosby's 'White Christmas' and releases by Bill Haley, Buddy Holly and Johnny Burnette. But as the 1950s progressed, Decca suffered. Its biggest-selling acts of the 1950s were those with cosy 'Mum and Dad' appeal, such as Vera Lynn, Winifred Atwell, David Whitfield and Mantovani & His Orchestra.

Until Dick Rowe signed the Rolling Stones, the label could claim Tommy Steele and Billy Fury among its homegrown talent. After the Stones, Decca got luckier – Van Morrison, Rod Stewart, David Bowie, Marc Bolan, Al Stewart and Joe Cocker all had early releases on Decca, before moving on to greater success. Following the Stones, the Small Faces, Tom Jones, Engelbert Humperdinck, Marianne Faithfull and John Mayall (with Eric Clapton) all enjoyed sustained success for the label. In 1966, Decca launched its 'progressive' Deram offshoot, which gave houseroom to Cat Stevens, The Moody Blues and, fortuitously, the debut single from Procol Harum, the timeless 'A Whiter Shade Of Pale'.

It also has to be said that for all the tension that developed between the Rolling Stones and Decca, the glory years between 1963 and 1969 laid the foundation for the band's future greatness. Just think of the much-loved and much-celebrated material the Rolling Stones recorded for Decca, and which still lives on into the 21st century on film soundtracks, innumerable greatest hits compilations and in live performances.

In 1980, Decca was taken over by PolyGram. Insiders were convinced that consumers were mainly interested in the label's classical repertoire rather than its rock'n'roll – it was the back catalogues of Benjamin Britten, Kathleen Ferrier and Herbert von Karajan that got them salivating. Shell-shocked staff members recall the label's historic correspondence, including Hugh Mendl's work diaries, being binned into huge skips. Shame, as it might have given a fascinating insight into the company's history, and its fractious relationship with its top rock act.

However, for all its run-ins with the Stones, Decca recognised that the band was still their only cash cow. After all, the Rolling Stones had outlasted The Applejacks, Brian Poole & the Tremeloes, Unit 4 + 2, The Fortunes, Pinkerton's Assorted Colours, Amen Corner, the Pete Best Four, Hedgehoppers Anonymous and Davie Jones & the King Bees.

But that relationship was not at an end. After six long years of pitiful royalties and banging their heads against a brick wall, the Stones were ready for freedom. Keith was particularly scathing about their old label. On learning that the company also made radar hardware designed to steer US bombers over Vietnam, he sneered, "I'd rather the Mafia than Decca." The two-finger, fuck-you delivery of 'Cocksucker Blues' was the final severing from the label they'd been with since 1963.

The Stones were buoyant following their American tour, and negotiations were underway to extricate the band from both Decca and Allen Klein's grip, and escape the punishing UK income tax. Whichever label got them – and Ahmet Ertegun's months of courting looked like paying dividends – the tracks cut at Muscle Shoals in December 1969 suggested that whatever followed could comfortably compete with *Beggars Banquet* and *Let It Bleed*.

However, Decca was reluctant to let the band go without a struggle. In August 1971, once the Stones were off Decca, the label released a compilation album shockingly entitled *Gimme Shelter*, with a live shot of the band on the cover, implying that the image came from the recent documentary film. Featuring previously released recordings from 1968 and 1969, it was an LP deliberately designed to cash in on the documentary's recent release. Completists were enticed by Side Two's six tracks, "previously unavailable in the UK". In fact, they were each culled from the band's American releases on London Records.

The Decca compilation *Gimme Shelter* only reached number 19 on the UK charts, however another Decca release, 1971's *Stone Age*, reached number four on the UK charts. The Stones reacted angrily: "It is, in our opinion, below the standard we try to keep up, both in choice of content and cover design," their statement to the music press read. The following year's Decca releases, *Milestones* (number 14) and *Rock 'N' Rolling Stones* (number 41) came either side of *Exile On Main St.*, both testament to the old label's tenacious adherence to their troublesome protégés. It had been a fractious seven years. Initially, like all young acts, the Rolling Stones were enamoured with the power Decca exhibited. By 1968, though, they were in open dispute with the label and the power was erring on their side. Once The Beatles launched Apple and appeared to have gained independence from EMI, Jagger seized the opportunity to try and gain the Stones their independence.

★★★

Polls never mattered much to the Rolling Stones, though they always did well in them. From 1964 to 1968, *NME* readers voted the Stones 'Best UK Blues & R&B Group', until Fleetwood Mac stole their thunder in 1969. In its first R&B poll, in 1964, *Record Mirror* placed the Stones third, behind The Miracles and The Coasters, in the 'Best Male Group' category. In 1968, the *NME* poll placed the Stones behind The Beach Boys in the 'World Vocal Group' category, and below The Beatles and The Hollies in 'British Vocal Group'. When it came to *NME*'s 'Best Single' that same year, 'Jumpin' Jack Flash' came in third, behind Mary Hopkin's 'Those Were The Days' and The Beatles' 'Hey Jude' in the top spot. For five consecutive years, from 1963 to 1967, the Stones came second only to The Beatles for 'Best Band' in the *Melody Maker* Poll Awards, although by 1969 Jethro Tull had hijacked their second place position. They were also eclipsed in the 'Best International Group' by The Beach Boys. 'Honky Tonk Women' did not feature in *Disc* magazine's 1969 'Best Single' category; however, based on chart longevity, *Record Mirror* had 'Honky Tonk Women' as the year's best, four points ahead of the Stones' old nemesis Dean Martin, with 'Gentle On My Mind'.

More wounding was the prestigious *Melody Maker* poll in its September 19, 1970 issue, on which the front page screamed 'Pop Poll Rocked'. The 'shock horror sensation', was that, after seven years, The Beatles had been beaten in the 'Best Group' category by... Led Zeppelin. The Stones came in at number six. while 'Honky Tonk Women' was only sixth best single (number one was the eerily Stones-sounding 'All Right Now' by Free). *Let It Bleed* didn't even make the 'Top 10 Best Of Year' album list.

The times were clearly changing. The Beatles were soon to be no more, and young-buck rockers were moving in from the wings to take their position on rock's biggest stages. And so it was that culmination of the sixties involved a deep inhalation. Already the writers, philosophers, hacks and social commentators were sifting through the entrails to try and make some sense of it all; to try and sew together the staggering changes in politics, fashion, culture and society the decade had witnessed. Even as the sixties breathed its last, there was a sense that something extraordinary had occurred during the preceding 10 years.

Private Eye founder Christopher Booker was first off the mark with 1969's *The Neophiliacs: Revolution In English Life In The Fifties And Sixties*. A few months later, Bernard Levin's *The Pendulum Years: Britain In The Sixties* hit the stands. The author proclaimed of the previous decade: "It was a credulous age, perhaps the most credulous ever... Never was it easier to gain a reputation as a seer... Teachers, prophets, sibyls, oracles, mystagogues, avatars, haruspices and mullahs roamed the land, gathering flocks about them as easily as holy men in nineteenth-century Russia."

Just nipping in before Big Ben rang the midnight hour on the decade was David Bailey's *Goodbye Baby & Amen*, a photo book starring the decade's most luminous faces. In it, fashion designer Douglas Hayward lamented, "Everyone is so insecure... what can a Rolling Stone do at forty?" Bailey, too, was his usual iconoclastic self: "I've done a superficial book about a superficial period."

That Altamont occurred in December 1969 surely counts for its attached significance to the end of the sixties dream. It *was* an idealistic time, the music really *did* seem capable of shaking the walls of the city. It and *Let It Bleed*, however, represent the *fin de siècle*, the end of an era. It is demonstrated on many discs, in innumerable memoirs, autobiographies and histories. It is celebrated in documentaries. One I particularly treasure is a scene from the Tom-Hanks-produced 10-part documentary *The Sixties*. In one scene, Mancunians Graham Nash and Peter Noone are shown locking horns backstage somewhere. Nash is filled with the passionate intensity of the acid advocate, the believer that, post-Woodstock, music can change the world, that he and his fellow knights of the road are the harbingers of a golden dawn. Peter Noone (Herman) is not so convinced: he argues that his job, and that of his fellow Hermits, is to entertain, pure and simple. The scene very much captures the spirit of the time: Noone happy to keep on delivering singalong favourites, such as 'I'm Henry VIII, I Am' and 'Mrs Brown You've Got A Lovely Daughter'; Nash exulting the joys of the 'Marrakesh Express' and the hazy freedom its journey implies.

But for all the naivety and easily mocked idealism, the after-effects are largely positive and enduring. We think today of racial tolerance, the ecology movement, anti-war demonstrations, women's rights, the dismantling of class barriers, gay liberation... These were only some of the movements whose foundations were laid during that pioneering decade.

And you know, you just know, that every time a documentary chronicling that tumultuous period is aired, the soundtrack will groan with music from one of the two bands who came to epitomise the period. What songs they were. What songs they *are...*

CHAPTER 16

Salt Of The Earth

Critics have the Rolling Stones fleeing Altamont, hunkering down and not breaking cover until they fled into tax exile in the south of France in January 1971. In fact, as a thank you, and to apologise for no other UK dates since Hyde Park, the band played four London shows, which are often overlooked in the aftermath of 1969. December 14 and December 21 found the band holding court at the Lyceum and the Saville Theatre for two shows a night. My recollection of that time is that the full tragedy of Altamont had yet to become apparent – in the UK, at least, we were probably aware that a fan had died at the festival, but Woodstock had not been free from fatality either.

Still, with Altamont's failures still fresh in the memory, the Stones' camp wasn't taking any risks. The press reported 10 bobbies outside both venues, 32 security men inside and 15 members of the St John's Ambulance. They were in attendance, according to one top cop, "to see that no one is born improperly or dies illegally". Unlikely, surely, on either Wellington Street or Shaftesbury Avenue?

The music press picked up on the fact that the Stones' show at the Saville Theatre would coincide with The Who playing the Coliseum. Peter Rudge, The Who's tour manager, commented on the story: "It's a great shame that the two greatest LIVE bands in the country are appearing in the same city on the same night. It would seem we are cutting each other's throats – but that's not the case because we are very friendly with the Stones."

Nineteen-sixty-nine. I was there and, true to form, I do not remember it. It wasn't the drugs – at seventeen, Double Diamond ale was my drug of choice. But I was there when the Rolling Stones played one of their least-known gigs. Somehow, bless her, my mum had managed to get her precious only child a ticket to the Saville Theatre show – I think, through a friend, she knew someone in the box office. As a diehard rock'n'roll fan – someone who religiously bought not only the four weekly music papers, *NME, Melody Maker, Disc, Record Mirror*, but also, on trips into the West End, *Rolling Stone* – I actually got to see with my own eyes Satan laughing with delight.

So, for something to confirm my sixties credibility, yes, I saw the Rolling Stones in 1969, although my abiding memories of that gig have little to do with the band onstage... Instead, I was transfixed by my companions further along the row – director Tony Richardson (who had probably come to atone for *Ned Kelly*) and Sir John Gielgud.

I was disappointed that I missed the best opening act of the two dates – my favourite band of the period, Procol Harum, who opened for the Stones at their Lyceum show on December 21 – and instead I was entertained by rock'n'roll revivalists Shakin' Stevens & the Sunsets.

The opening act wasn't the only disappointment. Years later, Bill Wyman told me: "We finished the American tour... then Christmas came and we did a few gigs at the Lyceum, the Saville, which were a bit disappointing compared with what had had happened in America. You come back in all your glory to England, and you find the audience… I mean, we hadn't played England for years, not since '67, except for one *NME* Poll Winners' concert, and we expected the same kind of adulation… It was just a bit of a disappointment, we thought, oh, English audiences are so boring!"

Certainly, the reviews of the Saville show confirm Wyman's memory. *Variety*'s review was headlined 'Stones London Bash Leaves Youths Cold'. In *Disc*, under the headline 'Wild Satanic Mick Gets No Satisfaction', Mike Ledgerwood reported Jagger telling the crowd, "You'd better get out of your seats or I'll crown you", as he "'camped it up' outrageously, wiggling his bottom and walking hand on hip".*

NME's John Wells was more encouraging, if flippant: "There were no births or deaths… no one tried to kill Mick Jagger… in fact there was very little except some extremely good music at the first of the four London concerts, their first paid-for British concert since October 1966." Delightfully, Wells found room to complain that the show was late starting – by 20 whole minutes!

In *Record Mirror*, Lon Goddard went into familiar overdrive, noting, "it took numbers like 'Satisfaction' and 'Sympathy For The Devil' to get the masses moving… 'Street Fighting Man' stirred the troops into spasms of foot stomping rain dances and praises to Watuka, god of fertility… The aisles were jammed with twisters, boppers and contortionists, jiving to the beat."

Friends magazine's January 1970 review was scathing, and symptomatic of the era's sexism: "The PA seemed to be having a

---

* It seems fitting that 1969 was the Year of the Earth Rooster in the Chinese zodiac – "Earth is a balance of both yin and yang, the feminine and masculine together."

monthly... [Jagger] retained a constant smile of the ten year old chick wearing her first little bra before she really needed it."

Of the Stones themselves, I remember Keith standing stock-still, stage right. Mick was prancing about in his Satanic stage outfit, trying to gee the crowd up. And... uh, that's about it...! I lost my Saville ticket; I have to rely on memory. I *want* to remember more. I want it to have been one of the pivotal events of my otherwise uneventful teenage years. In the cosy glow of the computer screen, I can now see the set list, which accords with that of the band's recent US dates.

Is memory like a computer? As I reach the age my father was when he died, do memories fall by the wayside as the hard disk becomes full? Is there a sifting and a sorting, where only the truly key events are recalled, those events that are worth recalling? Has a gig by a rock band half a century ago been deleted? Or maybe the Stones just weren't that good. It didn't help that I had little or nothing to compare it with; my mum wouldn't let me go and see The Beatles – all those riots. But I did get to see the second best band to come out of Liverpool, The Searchers. Illness prevented me venturing out for a couple of years during 1967 and 1968, so I missed a lot of gigs. But, even so, you'd have thought the Rolling Stones would have left more of an impact...!*

The intervening years saw me see the band at various periods of our lives, at locations that made me wish I could recall more about the intimacy of the Saville Theatre show. Bigger halls, more fireworks, more expense. With my end nearer than my beginning,

---

* Thinking back, my mum loved Mick Jagger and the Stones, so much so that I took her to see the band at Earl's Court in May 1976, when she was sixty-eight. My mum, who won the MBE for her work evacuating wounded soldiers under enemy fire in Normandy in 1944, taking in the Rolling Stones... It's another of those 'did it really happen?' moments. It did – it's one ticket I do still have!

I've made sure to pay homage one last time – Dylan at the London Palladium; Paul Simon in Hyde Park; Paul McCartney at the O2…

Then for me, a south-east London boy, I ventured to the Far East for what will be The Last Time…

★★★

What do the stalwart Stones see as they search all their strange, faceless crowds…? They can't look real.

Event: Rolling Stones *No Filter* tour
Venue: Queen Elizabeth Olympic Park
Date: May 22, 2018

Black-coated staff swarm the stage just before 8 p.m., an army of worker ants seething over a surprisingly sparse set. Just the noise from the crowd's chatter makes conversation difficult, even before a note is struck. At 8.25 p.m., only 25 minutes late, the Rolling Stones emerge to a thunderous response.

The band hits the ground running. Mick covers the stage, sprinting across it like the recently deceased Roger Bannister. He rules it. It is his territory. Jagger's spry athleticism belies his age. If he had persisted in a career outside music, and concentrated solely on economics, he would be a good 10 years past his official retirement. His confidence exudes from the platform he commands.

Keith moves… less. His gambolling is more reminiscent of the sauntering style of British actor George Sanders. But from somewhere, those riffs come like a blitzkrieg. All Keith has to do is rise from his semi-recumbent posture, and hurl himself into one of those riffs, and 160,000 hands are united in delight.

When it premiered in 1974, 'It's Only Rock 'N Roll (But I Like It)' saw the Stones threatened by the likes of Freddie Mercury,

Bolan and Bowie. But in 2018, they have outlasted and outlived them all. Tonight, the song sounds spritely and timeless.

Then the band launches into 'Tumbling Dice', a song that emerged from a basement murk few thought the band would themselves emerge from. This is a career-spanning set, yet you could put ready money on which songs from which era would get the biggest cheers. I mean, really, what's *not* to like? We had two hours in the presence of rock'n'roll greatness, with hit after hit from every era, punched out by a band who only sound like they're just hitting their stride.

Mick conducts the crowd during the seven-word symphony of 'You Can't Always Get What You Want'. If you could bottle the sheer sense of joy that 'Honky Tonk Women' ignites in the crowd, move over Paco Rabanne and tell Joop! Homme the news. Then the football terrace companionship swells the chorus. The crowd is wilfully united by a song about the demon drink and a debauched divorcee. Upon its release, 'Honky Tonk Women' was testament to the swaggering sinfulness of the band – tonight, it sounds about as threatening as Dame Vera Lynn.

As Keith's face fills the monitors, you can't help but smile at the broadly beaming visage. The teeth are unnaturally white. He obviously relishes the approval – it's like 70 years before, and a London Palladium crowd greeting Max Miller. Except now the notoriety and the crowd are magnified. When playing, Keith crouches, like he's about to make a quick bolt. The guitar is held at a threatening angle. He remains static but still somehow threatening.

The unflappable Charlie Watts sits behind a surprisingly tiny kit. Daryl Jones solos on 'Miss You'. Poor old Bill Wyman never got to play a bass solo. But the Rolling Stones have become your dreams. Quite unwittingly, they hold sway over you and your past. 'Sympathy For The Devil' retains its sinister samba charm, with

Keith's amp turned up to 11 for added menace. The guitar scythes through the "woo woo" chorus. The Rolling Stones live, in the 21st century? Immortal!

As the sky darkens, the searchlights sweep the stadium, like those from a Lancaster looking for the right dam to bomb.

Dismissive flicks of the guitarists' wrists usher in another familiar riff from a back catalogue, which finds few equals. It is only when it ends that you find yourself reflecting on what has been missed.

As is right and proper in the short-fuse industry that is rock'n'roll, the Rolling Stones are accorded a reverence neither Kasabian or Coldplay will live to relish. It is not simply that the Stones have been doing this for so long; rather, it is the quality, the breadth and depth of their music. There's the bayou grit of 'Midnight Rambler'... the steamrollering 'Sympathy For The Devil'... the barroom mystery of 'Tumbling Dice'... the majesty of 'You Can't Always Get What You Want', the song which is the rock'n'roll equivalent of 'Land Of Hope And Glory' at the Last Night of the Proms.

Charlie cracks a rare smile during 'Midnight Rambler', no doubt knowing he's on the home straight. The visual incongruity is delightful; the drummer now looks like the sort of mid-European diplomat sold down the river at Munich.

You take a back seat and ally yourself to all those who know all the words to 'Brown Sugar', instinctively more memorable than the Chaucer they were studying the year of the single's release, a band of brothers whose only real appreciation of Shelley came from Mick's dive into the canon in Hyde Park.

'Gimme Shelter' is the first apocalyptic encore, Mick parading in a piece of headwear of the style favoured by the late V.I. Lenin. For many of the younger element in the audience, it is a 'Jeremy Corbyn cap'.

The appreciation is not, as lazy critics would have it, redolent of a Nuremberg Rally. It is rather a party political conference, where every target reached and promise made is greeted with rapturous applause and standing ovations. Gone are the Zippos and Swan Vestas that used to flare up to encourage an encore; the 21st-century equivalent see tens of thousands of mobile phone LEDs light up in the darkness.

The final encore, the last song of the evening, is that half-remembered riff that Keith hummed into a cassette recorder in 1965. 'Satisfaction' is still the encore that elevates and unites both snowflakes and pensioners, bringing them all to their feet to sing satisfactorily in unison.

(I find myself as captivated by the audience as the band's activities onstage. Sharing the lift with a posse of breathless teenage girls on the way in, I remark, "Bit old for you, this lot, aren't they?" A general consensus disagreed: "Oh my God... They were the Rolling *Stones*!" Earlier, I had been fascinated by a character who looked like the sort of crusty High Court judge C. Aubrey Smith often portrayed. Was this someone who had shuffled an efficient shoe at the Crawdaddy back in the day?)

Then, finally, the performers come to take their bows. Backing singers and bass players do the wraparound shoulder thing. But it is when the fab four take their own bows, two hours and 10 minutes after they began, that it registers. There is something poignant and oddly touching about seeing Mick, Keith and Charlie (and, I suppose, arriviste Ron Wood) together again. You cannot help but marvel at the battles they have fought, and survived. And the paths that you have trod with them. The survivors, alive and, in some cases, kicking... The quality of the music that night transcends nostalgia – these are legends made mortal. Nowadays, everyone and everything goes on 'a journey'. But seeing the Stones that night, I really do get the feeling that I have accompanied them – not that

I can claim a Marquee moment, or a particularly close encounter, but rather a shared experience of turmoil and tumbling times. Of mixed emotions, highlighted and united by the music made by the grizzled, grinning veterans now bowing before us. This really is rock'n'roll royalty deferring to their loyal subjects. For them, for me, for us, it has really been quite a journey...

★★★

No one there that night could ever have imagined it thus. There was surely a consensus that, come the end of the decade that bred them, the Stones would cease rolling.

Less than a week after Altamont, the band was at the BBC, recording a performance of 'Honky Tonk Women' to be aired on the Christmas Day edition of *Top Of The Pops*. That same day, December 12, 1969, the band recorded a version of 'Let It Bleed' for a BBC2 special, *Ten Years Of What?* The programme was to be a celebration of the decade that had just ended. Uncertain of what lay ahead, and baffled by what had been left behind, the Beeb were covering their options as they looked back on the sixties.

Looking at the list of names appearing on the programme makes for a perfect Polaroid of the period – Macmillan, Kennedy, Jagger, Gagarin, Luther King, the World Cup, Concorde... They never got the recognition from their government or monarch that The Beatles did, but what was obvious at decade's end was that, for better or worse, the Rolling Stones were cemented into the nation's psyche.

In another century, Keith was in reflective mode, asking author Rich Cohen: "What's it like to live in a world where the Stones were always there? For you, there's always been the sun and the moon and the Rolling Stones."

The Rolling Stones' story did not end in a Californian desert. It did not end with the expiry of their Decca contract. You could, however, argue that the true greatness did end with the decade they came to embody. For all the compilations, reissues and retrospective wisdom, I would argue that the real, lasting supremacy of the Stones concluded with their final contribution to the 1960s, 'You Can't Always Get What You Want'. Anything beyond that is a bonus. For all the sporadic resurgences and odd brilliant album tracks, their legacy began in 1963, bringing R&B to a pop audience. A line in the sand is drawn with the decadent sprawl, the all-encompassing sweep, of *Let It Bleed*.

PART 3

Aftermath

CHAPTER 17

The Glimmer Twins

Bruce Robinson's cult 1987 film *Withnail & I* is firmly located at the squalid end of the sixties, its grubby 1969 bedsit setting far removed from any dewy-eyed appreciation of the glittering decade. It is Danny the drug dealer (inventor of the notorious 'Camberwell carrot') who passes judgement: "They're selling hippie wigs in Woolworths, man. The greatest decade in the history of mankind is over. And… we have failed to paint it black."

As the new decade dawned, chill realisation came in the wake of the Summer of Love. The Rolling Stones, the embodiment of anti-establishment values, were preparing to flee into tax exile, their place at the helm of the revolution filled, in early 1970, by that other radical rock'n'roll outfit… Chicago! To promote the jazz-rock band's second album, signed full-page ads appeared in the press, promising that "With this album, we dedicate ourselves, our futures and our energies to the people of the revolution: And the revolution in all of its forms". Well I never. If you leave me now indeed…

Nineteen-seventy was the year that marked, in Tom Wolfe's immortal phrase, the emergence of 'radical chic'. This was the era during which Liberal America played host to the revolution, when the composer and conductor Leonard Bernstein feted the Black Panthers at his Park Avenue apartment – "What does one wear to these parties for Panthers?" Tom Wolfe marvels. "Wonder what the Black Panthers eat… Do [they] like little Roquefort cheese morsels wrapped in crushed nuts…?"

Elsewhere, Bob Dylan wrote a tribute to the imprisoned Black Panther leader George Jackson, while John and Yoko, radical chic ringleaders, celebrated black feminist and activist Angela Davis* on their limp, knee-jerk revolution album *Some Time In New York City*.

As the Stones swanned off to the south of France, it really did seem to mark the end of an era. Under *Melody Maker*'s all-too-familiar headline 'This could be the last time', Michael Watts covered the band's "possibly final tour of Britain" in March 1971. As if to rub salt in the Stones' wounds, Led Zeppelin were about to begin their 'back to the clubs' series of gigs, a breathless Chris Welch reporting from Belfast as "the world's top rock band hits the road".

Yet, it definitely wasn't the last time. In fact, on and on the Rolling Stones swaggered, rambled, reeled and rolled. From the "grand celebration of jet-set debauchery and chic demonic postures"** that was *Sticky Fingers*, to the subterranean murk of *Exile On Main St.*, to the Jamaican gumbo of *Goats Head Soup*, to the departure of Mick Taylor and the testing of guitarists on *Black And Blue*, the band took care of the mischief and basked in the glare of their legend as the seventies lurched on. Keith got his plasmatic MOT at mysterious Swiss clinics… There were exalted backstage guests (the wife of the Canadian prime minister! Jackie Kennedy's sister!)… Mick celebrated his wedding to Bianca… the

---

* The Stones also paid tribute to Angela Davis on 1972's 'Sweet Black Angel'.

** *The Illustrated New Musical Express Encyclopedia Of Rock* (Salamander Books, 1977).

walking ghost that was Keith Richards endured ("You only hear about me when the warrants are out..."). It was the seventies-model Stones that epitomised junkie chic ("Sunshine bores the daylights outta me...").

Fast forward to a London sweltering in the summer of 1976, and the first generation of bands to have grown up in the wake of the Rolling Stones had emerged, kids too young to have known the excitement of the sixties, now with fashionably cropped hair, snarling their way through three chords and vilifying all that had gone before. Punk was year zero, acknowledging nothing pre-New York Dolls and The Stooges. On '1977', The Clash decreed the end of Elvis, The Beatles and the Rolling Stones. And this, despite the manifest example of the band's guitarist, Mick Jones, striving as hard as humanly possible to look, act and behave as irresponsibly as Keith Richards.

Keith was always the 'cool' Stone, the man who defined the description "elegantly wasted", from whom a sense of menace had always exuded. Journalist David Sinclair has witnessed Keith at close quarters over the decades: "There *is* something sinister about him, those dark, obsidian eyes. He is very accommodating and jovial, but he can be intimidating. On at least a couple of occasions he pulled out his huge Jamaican knife, a working Yardie knife, cleaned his nails, jammed it into the table on another occasion... frightening." No wonder Keith's luxury item on *Desert Island Discs* was a machete.

Despite the casualties, falling like ducks in a shooting gallery, Keith endured. From afar, there was something magnetic, magnificent about that junkie insouciance. But that was Keith. Few had his inner strength or resilience. Phil Kaufman, Stones minder and the man who took Gram Parsons' body to Joshua Tree for cremation, reflected: "Gram thought he could do what

Keith Richards did. He thought he had Keith's metabolism. He was wrong."

Junkie chic is not appealing. I genuinely believe, though, that at least initially the drug 'heroes' of the sixties, pioneers like The Beatles, the Stones and Pink Floyd, began that dance with the Devil in search of enlightenment. Keith always said his initial journey into drugs in the sixties was more Thomas De Quincey[*] than a desire to get fucked up.

Some of the drugs were necessary, just to keep up the momentum – Wardour Street to Bradford to Aberdeen to Truro to the back of beyond, squashed into a Bedford A30 van, was enough to send anyone to the edge of exhaustion. Later, the narcotics provided a shortcut to nirvana, a chance to venture through the white light at the end of the tunnel. Once the addiction bites and the needles sink in, though, nirvana is replaced by Valhalla, and it's a junkie's solitary, seeping death, bleeding in a dingy basement.

It is the nature of society to admire the survivor, and you do have to admire Richards' tenacity. Like when Mick would challenge Keith to a game of tennis – Keith would go off to shoot up between sets, and would still win. And for all Mick's adolescent keep-fit programmes and well-publicised fitness routines, "Remember," Keith once said, "I learned to ski on heroin!"

If you're lucky enough to gain access to bask in the band's presence, it's Keith's wheezing rasp you want to preserve forever on cassette. You want that laugh, like a punctured pantechnicon sliding across a skid patch. It's Keith's winning way with words you hope to witness firsthand (which other rock legend could slip the phrase "warp and weft" into an interview?), not Mick's class-switching tones, or the blithe indifference of a yawning "Are we done yet?"

---

[*] Thomas De Quincey (1785–1859) was the author of hundreds of essays, including, most famously, 1821's *Confessions Of An English Opium-Eater*.

Jagger. But as someone once wrote, if the Stones were Keith's band, they'd be lucky to keep a residency at the Bulls Head in Barnes. Not for Keith the motivation to secure sponsorship for the tours, or the endless negotiations as, once again, the band switches record labels.

Lisa Robinson accompanied the Rolling Stones on their 1975 tour of America as 'rock-press liaison'. She recalled the tour in a 2000 feature for *Vanity Fair*, which also included the only full interview Ian Stewart ever gave. "The thing is, Keith basically cares 90 per cent about the music," Stu observed, "and he can't be bothered to go to any of those business meetings. If we're not recording or on tour, the phone in the office will go all day, every day, with accountants and lawyers who have to speak to Mick immediately. The others care, but they have neither the ability nor the desire to be as involved. Mick never stops."

It is Mick's motivating persistence that keeps the Stones rolling on through the centuries. It's Mick that has the tenacity to engineer the deals, to sift through the small print. That determination is as much a part of the Jagger makeup as, well, the Jagger makeup! In 1965, the *NME* gave astrologer Ernest Page birthdates, times and sexes of a dozen pop stars, and "after compiling a mass of charts and diagrams", Page profiled Mick Jagger as someone who "can be enthusiastic, yet at the same time 'couldn't care less'... This person might not believe in the conventions of life, but he will largely keep to them so as not to lose the good opinion of others. Is capable of originating schemes and ventures to catch the public imagination. 1972 will be a most important year, bringing true many dreams."

Following Altamont, and after a further three-year delay, the Rolling Stones finally returned to the American battleground in the summer of 1972, for the legendary 48-show US tour supporting the release of *Exile On Main St*. Altamont was now a memory and the band emerged onto a different landscape. In 1972, Vietnam was still sucking in American troops, but hopes were riding high on George McGovern's ability to depose Nixon in that year's election. Chicago's commitment to the revolution had waned, the band now starting to settle into a softer sound. Jimi and Janis were long gone, Jim Morrison had died in a Paris bathtub, and the rebels of 1968 were looking for careers away from hurling paving stones.

This time round, the Stones' tour party numbered 30, double the size of the crew that had accompanied the band in '69. Laminated backstage passes restricted access. Radio DJ Wolfman Jack, just shy of his *American Graffiti* immortality, growled: "If Jesus Christ came to town he couldn't sell more tickets."

Even Bill Graham, who had numerous run-ins with the band over the years, conceded that "the biggest difference between 1969 and 1972 [...] was Mick Jagger's ability to control an audience [...] As far as I was concerned, the previous tour had left a lot to be desired. On this one, they came as professionals. In 1969, it had been just pure anarchy. Nobody was in control anywhere. It was just this huge, bewildering moving of tribes."

It was largely through Mick's tenacity that the seventies saw the Stones outlast and, on occasion, outclass the competition.* A series of flabby mid-seventies albums were soon overtaken by a revved-up *Some Girls* (1978). Punk may have ridiculed, gobbed and sneered at the Stones, but it gave them a much-needed kick up the arse.

Then, for the first time since Brian's death, it looked like the end really was in sight. In February 1977, the Stones were in Toronto to record *Love You Live* at the El Mocambo club. Upon landing in Canada, Keith was arrested and charged with possession

---

* "The pleasing quality which is now emerging", Mick's headmaster had presciently written in a recommendation in 1960, "is that of persistence when he makes up his mind to tackle something."

of heroin, a charge that carried a minimum of seven years upon conviction.

Keith finally faced the music at the University Avenue County Court in Toronto on October 23, 1978. However, a sympathetic judge and a stint in rehab found the guitarist avoiding a prison sentence.

One good thing that emerged from the Canadian experience was the 1977 double live LP *Love You Live*.

With their extensive seventies tours and improving technology, I often wondered why there was a seven-year gap between '*Get Yer Ya-Yas Out!*' and *Love You Live*. Fred Goodman, in his definitive biography of Allen Klein, supplied the answer: during the endless court battles between the band and Klein, "Jagger and Richards dropped the challenge to ABKCO's publishing rights, and the band pledged not to record any songs they'd cut for Decca for at least five years, essentially a ban on live albums, so as not to dilute the value of the Stones albums ABKCO manufactured."

All the while, business matters took place under the watchful eye of the Stones' longtime financial manager, Prince Rupert Loewenstein, whose financial acumen was of a higher quality than his prose. His leaden contribution to the official *According To The Rolling Stones* reads like the sort of school report Joe Jagger was used to reading of Michael Philip: "The ten years that followed 1978 definitely marked a transitional point for the Stones, and the fact that they overcame their youthful problems and matured into a highly professional, but still enthusiastic, group that they are today, is a noteworthy fact."

Enshrined and ennobled, 'twas not ever thus. In the vicious post-punk music industry of the early eighties, the Stones were largely ridiculed. A series of tawdry albums did nothing to enhance their standing. Is 1980's *Emotional Rescue* ever given preference over

1971's *Sticky Fingers?* Does anyone stream, play or even remember 1986's *Dirty Work?*

In terms of impact and influence, however, the Rolling Stones were still venerated, even if their new stuff barely passed muster. When the band did tour on the back of a strong new album, they usually regained pole position – in both 1978 and 1981, they became *Rolling Stone*'s 'Band of the Year' once again, off the back of tours for *Some Girls* and *Tattoo You* respectively.

From 1978 onwards, news of a new Rolling Stones album did little to animate interest. As a live attraction, however, it was a different matter. Even when teetering on the brink, they could always pull it back. The Stones would return to the States many times over after 1969, but Bill Graham singled out one particular tour as a landmark: "By 1981, the country was fairly smoothed out... It was also a much bigger deal by 1981. The money. Things like the corporate sponsorship were coming to it." Indeed, *The Rolling Stones' American Tour 1981* enters the record books as the very first rock'n'roll tour to be sponsored: Jovan perfume paid $4 million for the privilege.

I remember while on the staff at *Melody Maker* in 1982, my dear colleague, the late Carol Clerk, was dispatched to "give the Stones a good kicking" at a warmup gig at London's 100 Club. Over bottles of warm Guinness and packets of Player's No. 6 at the Rock & Roll Table at the Oporto Tavern (the *Melody Maker* staff local), Carol had stridently laid out her musical penchant – she loved punk, but had a worrying fondness for all those ghastly post-punk bands like The Exploited, UK Subs and Vice Squad. So, expectations were predictably high on the sort of dismissive dispatch that would run after the Stones' set. I remember Carol coming back from that gig, everyone anticipating a career-ending critique from the wee girl. 'They were a-*mazing*...', she breathed in her Belfast brogue. 'Keith's arse was only inches away...'

The remainder of the eighties saw the band sweeping from innumerable sessions cobbled into a series of even more ramshackle albums, the post-Decca back catalogue once again available in the marketplace. This time around, Columbia got lucky, not so much with *Undercover* (1983) or *Dirty Work* (1986), but with the widespread availability of compact discs. For the first time, Stones fans could get their hands on shiny, indestructible copies of *Sticky Fingers*, *Exile On Main St.* and *Some Girls*.

This was also the decade of the solo albums, open petulance, Bill Wyman's increasing disinterest, and Mick and Keith not speaking. Keith was furious when news of Mick's solo deal with CBS leaked (leading to 1985's *She's The Boss*); the guitarist's ire increased when the singer announced that he'd be including Stones material at his solo concerts. The fact that Keith's splinter group, the New Barbarians,* had earlier crossed the Rubicon had obviously slipped his mind.

Even the implacable Charlie lost his rag. According to Keith: "Charlie is very strong physically, and you don't want to be on the end of a drummer's right hand... Mick got pissed, and when Mick gets pissed he gets sloppy." Inadvisably, the singer put in a phone call, asking: "Where's my drummer?" Keith: "There's Charlie Watts dressed in a Savile Row suit, hair done, shaved, cologne. He walks across to Mick, grabs him and says, 'Never call me *your* drummer again' – bang!"**

---

* The New Barbarians were formed by Ronnie Wood, the lineup also including Keith, bassist Stanley Clarke, keyboardist Ian McLagan (former Faces), saxophonist Bobby Keys and drummer Joseph Zigaboo. The band played 20 shows across North America in 1979 and supported the Rolling Stones at two charity gigs.

** It fell to Charlie to make one of the best-remembered quotes on the Rolling Stones. In 1989, when asked what it was like celebrating the band's 25th anniversary, the drummer reflected: "Well it's not really work is it? It's five years' work and twenty years' hanging around!"

However, one thing that did unite the band during this period was the death of Ian Stewart.

Upon becoming manager of the band, Andrew Loog Oldham, living up to his image of the 'teenage tycoon shit', had immediately sacked the curmudgeonly Stewart because he "didn't look right". But he was invited to stay on as road manager and play piano on recordings.

Stu took it on his prominent chin, and for the next 22 years he hung with the Stones, refusing to marvel at their superhuman status. He observed them on Olympus with a scathing eye, and when he consented to accompany them, it was strictly on his terms. According to Glyn Johns, Stu "refused to play anything that he considered to have 'Chinese', or minor, chords in it. That is, anything that was not the traditional rhythm and blues or boogie-woogie format... He still played at every gig. He just played the songs that he wanted to."

Ian Stewart occupied an extraordinary place in the history of the Rolling Stones. During the time he was a member of the band proper, he was also their agent, booking gigs because he was the only one with access to a telephone (VICtoria 4444). He was also the only one who held down a proper job, with ICI at their Millbank offices, just opposite Decca's HQ on the other side of the Thames (he would share his luncheon vouchers with the rookie group). Stu is the link to those long-ago Alec Douglas-Home, fish and chips, Woodbine cigarette, refunded beer bottle, Edith Grove days. In later years, he was equally at home trundling around the stadiums of the world.

While on tour, the band were always baffled by how far they had to travel from their hotels to the venues. Legend has it that it was all down to Ian Stewart; a keen golfer, he'd make sure to arrange accommodation close to the greens! Keith: "It took us years to realise why we were living in these places. We thought all hotels had golf courses. We'd say, 'What are we doing here, Stu?' 'We get better rates… and to keep you lot out of trouble'; that was his usual reply. And in the morning you'd wake up and see Stu heading out on to the golf course to practice his swing!"

Charlie: "Stu was deemed not good looking enough and certainly not hip enough to look at. He never changed that look he had. He wore those golf shirts – and the week he died, he looked exactly like the first time I saw him!"

Stu loved the minutiae of life with the Stones. He loved tinkering with the equipment, marshalling the band into shape, hustling them onto the stage. When the single van was replaced by three jumbo jets, Stu hunkered down with his own little group, Rocket 88, playing the sort of music he loved in the type of venues he used to play when he *was* a Rolling Stone.*

Keith Altham happened to be drinking buddies with Stu at the Green Man in Ewell, Surrey. He underlined Stu's importance to the Stones: "Him and Charlie, men of few words, but when they spoke, or if they were upset, then all the others would listen." As the Rolling Stones progressed on their upward spiral, each with their separate managers and the spider's web of financial threads spread far and wide, Ian Stewart provided them with a link to their beginnings, to their roots. To normality.

Regular Stones pianist Chuck Leavell shared some lovely memories of Stu in his engaging memoir – of the permanent golf shirt, of the sandwich and camera he'd take onstage with him. Of how, after a powerhouse performance before 80,000 fervent fans, he would remark "Well, that was lovely."

To Keith, the Stones were always "Stu's band". Testament to this was the fact that all five Stones attended Ian's funeral after he

---

* Stu had apparently walked out of the *Some Girls* sessions, as, according to him, the band "Sounded like bloody Status Quo!"

suffered a heart attack on December 12, 1985. I do believe the guitarist, when hearing of Ian's death, asked: "Who's gonna tell us off now when we misbehave?" When the Rolling Stones were inducted into the Rock and Roll Hall of Fame four years later, they made sure that Stu's name was included.

While Ian Stewart's death had brought the band together personally, later came the chill realisation to the two principals that neither Mick's *Primitive Cool* (1987) nor Keith's *Talk Is Cheap* (1988) would ever come close to matching any title with the imprimatur 'Rolling Stones'. To survive and carry on in the style to which they had become accustomed, Jagger and Richards *had* to compromise. The reconciliation came not in a dingy Earl's Court flat or a sprawling Berkshire mansion – in January 1989, Mick and Keith chose Barbados to bury the sword. Fortuitously, it was not in each other.

With relations now patched up, the Rolling Stones were ready for a comeback. And by general consensus, 1989's *Steel Wheels* was the strongest Stones album in a decade. There was a tautness, a renewed vigour on new material like 'Mixed Emotions', 'Rock And A Hard Place' and Keith's poignant 'Slipping Away'. In a touching recognition of their founder, 'Continental Drift' included a contribution from the Moroccan musicians that Brian Jones had taped 20 years before.

Jagger knew the album was important, and he wanted the world to know it. CBS supreme Walter Yetnikoff recalled a conversation with the singer about the label's marketing budget: "I want you so excited," Mick enthused. "I want that giant CBS cock up the arse of every radio station and record chain in every major market around the world."

Once the public spats had been settled, the reconciled nineties saw the Rolling Stones return to the road and the tours grow into bigger and bigger bangs for your bucks. The first time my wife saw the band was at one of those thankless Wembley Stadium shows of 1990. I have an enduring image of Mick waving a long pole, and poking the testicles of some huge inflatable dogs as they floated over the stage. Or hovering over the crowd from a hydraulic lift. (Keith: "And Charlie is a short bus ride away... If Mick has disappeared somewhere it's a question of we ain't stopping this riff until we see him again!") Or Mick announcing: "We're gonna do a song from the new album..." to the disappearing backs of 20,000 punters making their way to queue at the bar or toilet.

By the middle of the decade, the tours had become lean and honed. In exchange for a substantial leap in ticket prices, fans were being treated to a 150-minute-long show. On occasion, a new song might edge its way into the set, but it was the fusillade of hits and tasty, rarely heard LP tracks that sent the faithful home, battered, shattered and delighted. But, hey, that is the changing face of rock'n'roll: when the Stones began touring, they and Ian Stewart fit into the back of a Bedford Transit. The 1993 *Voodoo Lounge* tour involved 50 articulated trucks, three jumbo jets (plus a 747 for the band and crew) and a £2.6 million stage. As it goes up in Stockholm, another set is erected in Helsinki, while another makes its way to Copenhagen. D-day was thrown together quicker than the 2002–2003 *Licks* tour, which lasted 14 months, spanned four continents and played to audiences of 1,625,496. Journalists hoping for a glimpse of backstage bacchanalia were greeted with a ping-pong table and Keith with his bottles of HP sauce and his own, his very own, shepherd's pie. (Tony King, tour manager: "There's always one shepherd's pie for the tour, and one for Keith – no one must break the crust on Keith's before he breaks the crust!")

Since then, each Stones tour has run like a well-oiled machine, each date planned like a military invasion. Paul Dugdale's 2016 *Olé! Olé! Olé!* documentary is a compelling account of the Rolling

Stones' plans to conquer South America. It chronicles the jaw-dropping mechanics of keeping a band of this stature on the road. Just getting the Rolling Stones to play Cuba involved high-level diplomacy – as the band hits the stage in Havana, the sense of accomplishment, of keeping both presidents and popes satisfied, is quite something. And these days, of course, it's all done under the umbrella of a sponsor so that the costs of mounting such huge invasions are shouldered. But the Stones are not alone in their sybaritic demands: I heard that for a recent world tour, Deep Purple took their own chiropodist. Today, it is bunions and ingrowing toenails and rock'n'roll…

Johnny Rogan took a look at the Stones' finances for a feature in *Vox* magazine in 1994, and it makes for a fascinating read. On July 30, 1965, for example, Mick and Keith had less than £1,000 each in their Bradford & Bingley accounts. In 1971, the Rolling Stones Ltd bank balance was a paltry £1,728. Rolling Stones Promotions, Mobile Studios, Mirage Music and Porthdyke were some of the other companies Rogan tracked down. But as he queried of that sixties income: "So where are the millions? You can trudge through other Stones companies… but they provide few clues. The fact is that most of the Stones' income during the sixties remained abroad."

Compare that with the companies listed alongside the cherry-red 'tongue and lip' logo on the back of CDs today and try to imagine the eye-watering amounts of cash that flow into Rolling Stones plc. A snaking thread of financial companies are, or have been, linked to the band over the years, enough to make Mick's former professors at the London School of Economics swell with pride. They include Promotone B.V., Promotour, Promopub, Musidor B.V. and Bravado B.V. It is the last that holds the trademark for 'Rolling Stones and tongue and lip design'. In October 2018, a poll announced that the famous Stones logo had beaten Che

Guevara's visage, the Hard Rock Café logo and Nike's *Just Do It* 'swoosh' to be named "the most iconic T-shirt design of all time".

In 2018, it was also announced that the band would extend their decade-long partnership with Universal Music. You can imagine Mick gleefully eyeing the minutiae of the contract, seeking out royalties 'for some new technology yet to be invented'. Then some novelty format will underpin another greatest hits compilation so that, once again, like some blousy honky-tonk woman, that famous back catalogue will be hauled out, dusted down and tarted up.

The band will occasionally tantalise with talk of a 'new studio album', but it is news of the Rolling Stones back on the road that sends subeditors into overdrive – combined ages are compiled, the amount of income generated is speculated upon and, once again, we are asked, 'Is this the last time?'

Occasionally, if required to shift tickets, Mick will break cover, grit his teeth and go through the painful and, for him, tedious interview process.

Dutifully trawling through teetering piles of newspaper features and biographies, TV documentaries and magazine profiles, you come away amazed at just how incredibly *little* Mick has given away over the past half-century. When you consider that whole books of quotes from Dylan, Lennon, Springsteen, Bono, Keith have been assembled, Mick's reticence sticks out like a sore thumb. He emulates Bob, who once sang "nothing is revealed". In fact, Jagger never breaks cover, unless there is product to promote. The eyes will roll, the groans will start, but, as he has done for the bulk of his working life, Mick will offer face time to an interviewer. Every Jagger encounter, usually at the end of a phone, ends with a "Have you got enough?", "That do you?" or "Almost finished now?" But every seasoned journalist, celebrity profiler or wide-eyed fan hopes that theirs will be the one, theirs will be the close encounter in which Mick Jagger actually makes a revealing and once-in-a-lifetime revelation.

It hasn't happened yet. Mick patently loathes looking back. He would rather stick needles in his eyes than remember...

Paul Sexton has been granted regular access to the Rolling Stones for many years. Initially, he would prepare the audio press kits to coincide with a new album release. As a seasoned journalist and broadcaster, the Stones' people appreciated that time granted to Sexton would likely result in a Radio 2 documentary, a national newspaper feature and a trade magazine profile, so three out of one ain't bad.

As Paul told me, the irony is that when he first began interviewing the band, the past was *verboten*. Subsequently, with the archive reissues of *Sticky Fingers*, *Some Girls* and *Exile On Main St.*, the past is a foreign country that is now perforce regularly revisited.

"Mick and Paul McCartney are the supreme media manipulators," Keith Altham said. "It always struck me that Mick was interested in money, birds and fame... then music. As a fan and journalist, I loved the Stones in the sixties; they were pilloried by the establishment, they were on our side. They were anti the bubbly pop stars of the period. From the beginning, though, Mick hung out with that aristo crowd, delighted to be in a room with Princess Margaret. Mick *always* wanted to be Sir Mick Jagger."

Stephen Schiff profiled the frontman for *Vanity Fair* in 1992 ("half the fun of being with him is watching him change colors"). But, like so many before, and the many who came after, the writer found that, when pressed to go back to the sixties, "or anything else that might appear under the heading of Sex, Drugs and Rock & Roll", all you get is "a symphony of sighs and groans, a cartoon display of rolling eyes and flailing rubber arms. 'I'm not interested in all 'at shit', he growls, reverting to deep Cockney, 'an all 'at history; 'at's not history to me. History is, well...'" Then the switch, to Mick the bibliophile, as recent biographies of Dickens, Bernard Shaw, Stalin and Hitler are duly weighed and merited.

In 1980, to promote the release of *Emotional Rescue*, Jagger told Chet Flippo: "Rock'n'roll is a funny thing. There are two different attitudes, right? One is the English attitude, like when Pete Townshend talks about rock'n'roll like a religion. And then there are others, like me, who think it's really a lot of overblown nonsense. Why bother? I mean, it's not worth bothering about. As a form of art or music."

The acclaimed documentary maker Molly Dineen ("a lifelong Rolling Stones fan") was approached and initially granted access to the band. But, as she told Ben Lawrence in 2018, "It was like the British Empire. You saw the hierarchy of the tour. There was the rock'n'roll culture at roadie level, but then at the high end you had Keith Richards drinking PG Tips watching *Hobson's Choice...* I thought this was a bloody interesting film. But Mick Jagger, who is over PR-savvy, almost to the point of self-destruction, did not trust someone else's vision of him. He was very clear, saying, 'You will have access when we choose and if we don't like it, it will never come out.'" Dineen walked.

But then eyes are what you pull the wool over, especially if there's a journalist in your orbit. Seasoned Stones-watcher Nick Kent hung around with the band on tour. "Anyone who's ever known him will tell you what an interesting bunch of guys Mick Jagger can be... I'd seen him turn into a leering hedonist, the would-be aristocrat, the working-class 'oik' with a social edge, the concerned family man, the life and soul of the party, the 'don't approach me' prima-donna, the narcissistic old queen, the ruthless businessman, the loving husband, the rapacious adulterer. There was really no limit to the masks he'd don, but in his ceaseless quest to always stay one step ahead of everyone else he somehow lost contact with his own humanity."

Many dwelt on the Jagger ability to suck blood and manipulate. In his autobiography, after years fighting drug and alcohol abuse, Eric Clapton felt he'd found a real "life teacher", the model Carla Bruni. Learning she was a Stones fan, "we went to the show, and afterwards I took her backstage to meet the guys. I remember saying to Jagger 'Please Mick, not this one. I think I'm in love' ..." Well, you can guess the rest...

Melody Maker's Chris Welch: "[Mick] was always charming, very bright, articulate. He used to enjoy travelling on the Tube, unrecognised. I saw him once at the Cromwellian, just sitting on his own at the bar. I was never sure just how seriously he took it all; I mean, he did say to me, and he can only have been about twenty-two, 'I can't see myself doing this when I'm thirty!'"

Sam Cutler was as close to Jagger as anyone during the turbulence of 1969: "Mick was absolutely insufferable. He used to come on like a camper version of Cecil Beaton... and be kind to people one minute and then 'verbally cruel' the next."

Keith Altham was the band's PR man for three years from 1980. "Congratulations on getting a job as Mick's butler," Ian Stewart commiserated. With a chuckle, Altham fondly remembers Mick's tongue-in-cheek set-piece routine before meeting the press: "Let's check: got me long hair, got me sardonic smile and me couldn't-care-less attitudes – let's go." Like everyone in his orbit, Altham was both impressed and repelled, but came away convinced that "it is impossible to believe he is anyone other than his greatest invention – Mick Jagger".

And it... *he* is an incredible invention. Timeless and immortal. By the time Marlene Dietrich was in her seventies she had suffered broken toes, broken feet and broken shoulders. A shattered thighbone broke through her skin. She really did let it bleed... "I survived two world wars," she growled. "It'll take more than falling off a stage to make me cancel a performance."

I found echoes of that same indomitability in Jagger in the following from Dietrich's biographer, Steven Bach: "Survival was her last great theme. Her long-term endurance acquired a moral dimension for its stamina, grace… and courage – what Remarque called "the fleeing forward". Some of it was manifest in her songs, some in her history; most of it in sheer presence, in the dignity she displayed and granted her audience. She endured, and burdened us with no compromise, with no confessional pleas for sympathy or indulgence. She never embarrassed us by embarrassing herself. She never asked for our approval; she won it."

Indeed, it is Jagger's own 'greatest invention', the man who *is* the Rolling Stones… It is the Jagger visage that dominates album sleeves. It is Jagger who decides if the band tours or lingers in limbo. It is Jagger who painstakingly ponders over contracts. It is Jagger's triumph of the will that decides the future, or lack thereof, of the Rolling Stones.

Lifelong Stones fan David Sinclair first interviewed Jagger for *The Times* with the release of his debut solo album, 1985's *She's The Boss*. "Nervous? Yes! It was at the Stones office, I think in Cheyne Walk, which was just like a student let. He was incredibly confident… And dominant, no way I didn't know my place. Combatative, confrontational, but also, casual…"

Which is why 1995's massive *Rolling Stone* retrospective by Jann Wenner, with a little help from Rich Cohen, was so informative. Because Wenner wasn't thwarted by Mick's "I can't fuckin' remember" schtick. "Being interviewed is one of Mick Jagger's least favourite pastimes," Wenner began. Over 12 hours and two continents, Wenner did his best to pin down the elusive butterfly on a wheel. He persisted in making Mick remember which album 'Salt Of The Earth' was on, insisted he could remember key events and albums, talked him into discussing his songwriting process.

In fairness, Jagger has never succumbed to the ideas that 'the Stones defined the sixties' or 'the sixties ended at Altamont'. A singer with a working band, a songwriter when inspired. a businessman when demanded, a well-read bon viveur, a sated satyr – Jagger lives for the now; the 'then' is for everyone else to relish and replay.

Jagger may find the fans' obsession with the Stones and their interest in the band's activities of half a century ago rather risible. His ambitions always exceeded simply being a singer in a rock'n'roll band. But he appreciates the cash that the devoted pour into the coffers of the organisation he has so successfully run these past decades. "I'm not a historian. I have no idea about our history. I don't even know which songs appear on which albums... We all have different memories of what happened 40 years ago. People distil their stories over time and they polish them up. And after a while you don't know whether they're true or not."

Paul Sexton again: "The thing with Mick is, he is so good at self-editing. He has been doing this for so long, he knows how everything will be spun. Rather weirdly, he talks of himself and the Rolling Stones in the third person, but latterly, he speaks of the Stones with a sense of ownership, and pride. It was Mick who drove *Exhibitionism*. He was the one sorting through the boxes. He took it seriously, that sense of a Stones... legacy. Funnily enough, one of the best interviews I did with Mick was for a James Brown documentary I was doing for Radio 2 in 2006. He was really animated. And I remember him being flattered when Maroon 5 did 'Moves Like Jagger'.

"I remember when we were talking about the *Exile...* reissue, and this is typical, I got him to agree to a Radio 2 programme – *Mick Jagger's Jukebox* – but he would only talk about tracks from the *Exile...* era, that is what he was focusing on. I remember saying to him about the criticism of re-recording new vocals over the original Nellecote tracks and he rather proudly said, 'My voice is still the same'. [...] But yes, the most regular question you will hear from Mick is 'Are we done yet?'"

Occasionally Mick would let the mask slip. When Nigel Williamson asked him in 1998 if he felt a prisoner of his own past, he responded: "Well, it is very odd. The more I think about it the more awful it is. It is like being onstage in *The Mousetrap*, not just for a year but forever. No one is forcing me to sing [the back catalogue] but it is like being trapped in a soap opera really."

Some things never change: for all the energy Mick expends (he is still estimated to run 5 miles a night onstage), all Keith has to do is run a hand through that densely populated hair and slur "I dunno where I am, but it's great to be here", and the place goes mad. Whenever the drummer is introduced, a mighty roar is evoked. Charlie smiles at some private joke, and still looks as though he'd really rather be at Ronnie Scott's.

"I would love to have been born in the era when jazz was the thing," Charlie told E Street Band drummer Max Weinberg. "I wish I could have been around when it was a struggle to get in the door, when jazz musicians were the stars... I always wanted to be a black New Yorker. You know, the sharpest one on the street."

With his background as a jazz drummer, Chris Welch forged a bond with Charlie: "I remember interviewing him very early on, and Charlie saying, 'I'm not really bored, I've just got a boring face'... We did talk drummers, and bonded over 'Big' Sid Catlett, who Charlie said was his favourite. He died when he was only forty-seven, came out of the Swing era, played with Louis Armstrong and Charlie Parker, so he spanned the gap between New Orleans and Bebop. I remember Charlie telling me he really admired Sid's syncopation."

David Sinclair: "You never get Mick and Keith together in the same room... Charlie fits the role well, they all respect Charlie;

none of the band has a bad word to say about Charlie – he's the peacemaker, the Nelson Mandela of the band!"

Mick and Keith and Charlie and... the Rolling Stones. The world's enduring fascination with them continues at every level, from tabloid journalism to university campus; from scandalous kiss'n'tell memoirs to academic theses; from tribute band to auction house.

Since Sotheby's launched the world's first rock'n'roll auction in 1981, the Rolling Stones have been well represented. There are autographs, grabbed on the run during those furious, nonstop touring years. There are concert posters, and rather sweet letters to fans: "I am glad you enjoyed the show at Rochester. No you didn't hurt me, love..." (Keith, £350). Mick's original lyrics to 'The Spider And The Fly' came under the hammer in 1996, with Sotheby's noting "Examples of manuscript Stones' lyrics are extremely scarce."

Mick & Keith... Jagger & Richards... the Glimmer Twins... inseparable and unsupportable. They recognised that, for the Rolling Stones to function, it needed them both. For the band to have a future, it could manage without Wyman, or Taylor. But to shift industrial quantities of those tickets, to land those salivating record deals, the Stones needed the dynamic duo.

Conversely, that was why Jagger was so desperate for a solo career. An acting career, anything to prove there was life outside the Stones. Anything to prove that he could act alone, unsupported by his wayward guitarist. Acting had been an option for Mick, but the roles soon turned into lacklustre cameos. As an actor, his choices were not wise, though had he been able to persevere with Herzog's *Fitzcarraldo*, critics might have been kinder.*

---

* Lon Goddard asked Keith in July 1969 if he envied Jagger's switch to cinema. "Acting is for Mick, not me... ! I wouldn't like to do movies. I couldn't do what Mick does. He likes it... When anyone mentions movies, I disappear, I couldn't

As a producer, Jagger was luckier: Jagged Films began well with the World War II thriller *Enigma*, but a remake of George Cukor's *The Women* (from 1939) did little to trouble multiplexes. The 2016 American period drama *Vinyl*, set in the New York music scene of the 1970s and created by Mick and Martin Scorsese, however, showed promise, though it never made it to a second series.

So, after decades in each other's pockets, there is still the mutual need. But however much they recognise it, the enmity also remains: "They're like a bitter married couple," Rich Cohen wrote, "who stay together for the kids. Only the kids are grown. Or maybe the money is the kids."

Over the years, rumours of tensions and animosity have filtered through: Keith nixing a Stones book because he was told there were more pictures of Mick… Mick and Keith having a blazing row as the band were setting up *Exhibitionism* at the Saatchi Gallery – did the electric fire at the Edith Grove flat have two or three bars? They're like snipers taking potshots across no-man's land. Keith is happier with the two-finger response, threatening to slit Mick's throat when he toured solo, performing Stones songs, famously citing "the only way anyone leaves this band is in a coffin". He questions the size of Mick's manhood, queries his parenting abilities in his seventies.

To his credit, Mick has always been very diplomatic, dummying up when asked about Keith and his drug habits, or just letting his Glimmer Twin hoist himself with his own petard. "The media

---

do it, because I can't work when I'm being told what to do." Ironic, really, that when Keith did make the switch, some 40 years later, it was to appear in the most expensive film ever made! Johnny Depp freely admitted the fact – though only a pirate with an eye patch over both eyes could have missed it – that he based Captain Jack Sparrow on Keith Richards. But it was nonetheless a treat to watch 2011's *Pirates Of The Caribbean: On Stranger Tides* (budget $378 million) and see Keith pop up as Depp's dad. Worth it, too, to hear him deliver the line, straight-faced: "Does this face look like it's been to the fountain of youth?"

portrayal of Mick versus Keith is very one-sided," David Sinclair told me. "Keith says the most outrageous things about Mick. He's got a small willy, he should stop having children, etc. And Mick never retaliates or responds in kind. You will search in vain for virtually any quote from Mick that is even mildly critical of Keith. In fact, he often praises Keith for his talent and defends him as someone who has had to go through a lot of rough times. The media buys into Keith's side of the story willy-nilly about 95 per cent of the time." Keith just can't let it go though – "When is this bitching going to stop between you and Mick?" he was once asked. "Better ask the Bitch!"

But then Keith always gave good quote (he famously likened Mick's 1985 solo debut *She's The Boss* to *Mein Kampf* ("everybody had a copy, but nobody listened to it"), whereas trying to find anything original, interesting or revealing falling from those famous Jagger lips is a hard trawl. Critics find it hard to reconcile the astute businessman with the rock'n'roll legend.

Friends of Jagger bridle at the sniping and criticism. "Mick is infectious in his love of life," testified a colleague who has known the singer since 1989. "He has a thirst for knowledge. On tour, he's the one who seeks out the local musicians, he's the one out there visiting the galleries and exhibitions. His love of cricket is not an affectation – he loves the game. He loves his music. It is the arrogant, lazy journalists who have been told to dig the dirt. They have been told by their editors not to come back until they have an original quote about... oh, you know, old girlfriends, drugs, the Stones in the sixties. But Mick Jagger is a man who has 'Don't Look Back' emblazoned on his T-shirt! He's forward-looking, he's erudite, funny, sharp, inquisitive. He is great company."

And of Keith, the inspirer of all those disciples – is there anything to be said anew of this enigmatic wastrel? Those who have attended close by say it's all a mask. A journalist colleague of mine was at an awards event with Keith, chatting amicably: "He was remarkably clear-minded and decisive at the table... But his acceptance speech, delivered in a halting, wheezing drawl was a monumentally scatterbrained monologue that was almost a caricature of himself." In other words, he became 'Keith' once he took to the stage, the shambling, slurring rebel, aware of his legend but carrying it lightly. "Keith plays up to his reputation a bit," Charlie told Will Lawrence, "He exaggerates a few things."

Miraculously, a man for whom the term 'survivor' was penned does endure. Watching the Scorsese/Stones concert film *Shine A Light* at the BFI IMAX on the South Bank, the sight of Keith's ravaged and raddled head on the huge screen was terrifying ("like watching Godzilla lumbering out of a primeval murk to wreak havoc on the world," Allan Jones wrote of him at a 2013 show).

Keith reeled through the years and, never a slave to political correctness, you were willing to overlook his rather... antediluvian attitudes. When asked why the Stones didn't play the Concert for Diana, a benefit concert held at the newly built Wembley Stadium on July 1, 2007, the guitarist shrugged: "Never met the chick."

When the bad times really hit in the 1980s and the duo weren't on speaking terms, the likelihood of the Stones getting back together was as remote as a Middle East peace settlement. Bands splitting and reforming still exercises an undue fascination. I once interviewed David Byrne and asked him if he would ever reform Talking Heads. "God, no," he retorted, laughing, "it would be like moving back with your parents."

On tour, musicians were salaried, and while other band members came and went, the departures were attributed to the usual "musical differences". Actually, most departures were down to Mick and Keith's parsimonious attitude to sharing songwriting credits. Everything new emanating from the Rolling Stones had to come courtesy of the Glimmer Twins.

While Mick punched his pocket calculator and made the deals, he appreciated that his partner in crime was a necessary evil. Mick & Keith: they were the ones who decided when to go to the mattresses.

When it began, it looked like their own record label might allow more lassitude. But Rolling Stones Records never amounted to a hill of beans. As early as 1968, Mick had spoken of his plans for 'Mother Earth Records', but by the time the label – renamed Rolling Stones Records – came into being, it was simply used as an umbrella under which to release records by... the Rolling Stones. There were occasional solo releases, and the odd, *very* odd, signing. (Peter Tosh? Kracker? Me neither.)

Of course if anyone could have been arsed, Rolling Stones Records could have left its mark: potential releases from Gram Parsons never materialised. Keith was also keen to sign Rory Gallagher. Neither did a Bill Wyman protégé, Eddy Grant, make it to the label. Rolling Stones Records also passed on Robin Trower.

But for sustained success, to maintain the lavish lifestyles they have grown used to, the Stones need each other. They need that familiar platform. Solo work postpones boredom but attracts a mere modicum of interest – first week UK sales for Mick's 2001 album *Wandering Spirit* amounted to a meagre 950 copies. Compare that, in the era of streaming, with the 31,287 first week sales for the reissued and expanded *Exile On Main St.*, which even beat Faithless' *The Dance* to become the UK's number one album in May 2010.

However many features are written, and however dismissive critics are of the Rolling Stones today, the band's 21st-century pulling power is something to witness – and this from a band that hasn't had a Top 10 US hit single since George Bush Sr. was president ('Start Me Up', 1981)! Their last UK Top 20 hit was when Stones fan John Major was prime minister ('Like A Rolling

Stone', 1995). It is, of course, the lucrative back catalogue that fuels the engine, which lubricates the machinery. Over the years, Rolling Stones albums have been hauled around Atlantic, CBS, Virgin, Polydor and Universal. Astute as ever, Prince Rupert Loewenstein appreciated, in his schoolmasterly, ponderous but prosperous way: "It will also be realised that many attractive songs could provide potent advertising slogans and catchy tunes, which could help the great corporations in selling their wares."

First came the television commercials. In 1995, Microsoft paid an estimated $3 million to use 'Start Me Up' to launch Windows 95. Keith's 2008 fee for promoting Louis Vuitton ("some journeys cannot be put into words") remains unknown.

Then, it was the *Steel Wheels* tour of 1989/1990 that really set the offstage revenues rolling; while ticket sales fuelled the receipts, the tour finances leapt into the black via lucrative sponsorships. Next came the spinoffs, with concert DVDs, simultaneous cinema screenings and paid online viewing. Then the merchandising, with 50-plus items sporting the Stones logo available to buy on every sortie into the urban jungle. In fact, the merchandising has taken on a life of its own: a press release accompanying 1998's *Bridges To Babylon* tour announced: "In keeping with the musical diversification of the Stones new album, we have introduced a comprehensive array of clothing, accessories and collectibles. Perfect for all ages and seasons." The 2018 *No Filter* tour saw the Stones sponsor a pop-up shop at Selfridge's. As well as the £40 tour T-shirt, the iconic tongue and lip logo could be found licking £25 tote bags, a pool table for £8,200 and a Rolling Stones armchair for £10,000 – just right for one of the Stones to relax in (reviews of the shows kept reminding its readers that the band had a combined age of 294!).

It is the jaw-dropping revenue generated by a Rolling Stones tour that truly leaves you reeling – *Voodoo Lounge*, $320 million...

40 Licks, $311 million… *A Bigger Bang*, $558 million. In August 2018, *Billboard* announced figures for the *No Filter* tour – a gross of $117,844,618 paid by 750,000 punters. The venerable, venerated Stones quantifiably outgross Taylor Swift, Beyoncé and Jay-Z.

"Ever since those far-off days in Richmond, when we'd have to drive through crowds to play in a club that only held 200, there's never been a shortage of audiences when the Stones play live," Keith told Roy Carr. "All we've ever done is to announce that we are to tour, and then it's up to the public if they want to come and see us or stay away."

But what of the music? Over the years (the decades, the *centuries*!), the set lists have been nipped, tucked and tweaked. Certain songs have to be included, others are dropped along the way. "As long as we're not bored with a song, that's the worst thing," Keith told David McGee. "That's why 'Midnight Rambler' had to go (laughs). I mean, it was a great song for years and years, but after a while you start saying, 'Oh no, now he's gonna get the whip out.' And you hear Mick going (groans softly). You get to that point and you know it's time to drop it."

However, while rumours of a new album are periodically dropped, with the reimagining of classic albums – *Some Girls* (2011), *Sticky Fingers* (2015) – the band did finally begin to look back. Not as exhaustive as Dylan's *Bootleg Series*, or as thorough as The Beatles' *Anthology*, they nonetheless gave fans a welcome opportunity to hear superior versions of crackly bootlegs. Not everyone was happy, though; the 2010 tinkering with the original masters of *Exile On Main St.* came in for harsh criticism.

Revisionist wisdom has *Exile On Main St.* down as the 'best' Stones album. The original reviews, though, were pretty withering – in his *Rolling Stone* review of *Exile* upon its release, Lenny Kaye found it left him "vaguely unsatisfied, not quite brought to the peaks that this band of bands has always held out as a special prize in the past... Hopefully *Exile On Main St.* will give them the solid footing they need to open up, and with a little horizon-expanding... they might even deliver it to us the next time around."

In *Melody Maker*, Richard Williams was less damning ("the best album they've made"), but even he found that, "Oddly, despite its length, *Exile* doesn't have the musical scope of *Sticky Fingers*."

Even Mick was wary of all the praise heaped on *Exile*. "I wouldn't consider it the finest of the Rolling Stones' work. I think that *Beggars Banquet* and *Let It Bleed* were better records. They're more compressed." And later, "It's a bit overrated, to be honest. Compared to *Let It Bleed* and *Beggars Banquet*, which I think are more of a piece."

Talking to Steve Grant in 1989, and on being told *Let It Bleed* was his favourite album, Mick responds with the old "Wotsonnit?" 'Gimme Shelter'... 'You Can't Always Get What You Want'... "Oh yeah, that's good as well. No, seriously, we were recording so much at that time that everything just bleeds into everything else."

Sheryl Crow became obsessed with *Let It Bleed* when she first heard it as a teenager growing up in Missouri: "*Let It Bleed* was the first record I'd heard that incorporated the country music I'd grown up listening to with rock'n'roll," she told Sylvie Simmons. "That album transformed the way I perceived myself, which set me apart from my school friends... *Let It Bleed*... was very influential on the sound and tone of my first album – right down to the sonics and the loose feel and the really bad seventies country clothes we were wearing at the end of those sessions!"

As a crucial part of the jigsaw (puzzle), *Exile* is certainly up there, and brings to an end that remarkable sequence of four albums. You would certainly nod your bandana to concur with the E Street Band's Steve Van Zandt as he looked at the Stones' "second great era: *Beggars Banquet*, *Let It Bleed*, *Sticky Fingers* and *Exile On Main St*. They make up the greatest run of albums in history – and all done in three and a half years."

And it is that quartet that keeps fans coming back. No revisionism. No benefit of hindsight; simply the four greatest albums by the band who defined, then redefined, rock'n'roll. With the CD revolution, Keith Richards allowed himself the luxury of nostalgia and concurred: "The ones that impressed me were the ones I always thought were superior – *Beggars Banquet*, *Let It Bleed*, *Sticky Fingers* and *Exile On Main St*." For Keith, they shine because they were "a burst of energy done under fire and on the run". For Mick, *Let It Bleed* is "a good record. I'd put it as one of my favourites."

(Personally, I would make a modest suggestion that room might be found for at least half of *Goats Head Soup*.)

No doubt the fans are drawn to hearing the rich back catalogue, and the Stones' stage shows hold major sway, rivalling those of any other act working today. Along with Charlie, it's Mick who dictates the space the Stones traverse. "No one seems to be doing anything very innovative in stadium shows," Jagger told Kurt Loder in 1983. "Keith thinks that rock'n'roll shows should just be a few lights and a good sound system and a square stage... I like to do more than that. I want to have more lights, a better stage. I want to be able to see 360 degrees. I want to give the people in the back something to look at, and I want it to look right."

It is as a touring attraction, a *real* rock'n'roll circus, that the Rolling Stones continue to entice.

★★★

Even today, the title of *Sir* Mick Jagger still remains unlikely. Mind you, Jerry Hall as Mrs Rupert Murdoch still reads like fake news to me. But there he is, the spritely seventy-six-year-old, careering onstage at an age when a bath chair on the Bexhill seafront would be more appropriate for his contemporaries.

Jagger refuses to kowtow to the passing years, he is still hard at it, strutting that inimitable turkey strut, capering across the stage, that grounded grammar school education seeping out as he greets audiences around the globe in the style of Tony Hancock opening the East Cheam Drama Festival: "Bonjour... Guten Tag... Buongiorno... Buenas días... Or, to use my native tongue... Wotcher!"

And Keith, still going, still outliving the obituaries, still furthering the legend. Tom Waits recalled an encounter: "He came in... On the clock he stands with his head at three and his arm at 10. I said how can a man stand like that without falling over unless he has a 200lb test fishing line suspending him from the ceiling? It was like something out of *Arthur*."

It is this very longevity that gives cause for caustic observations. As Philip Norman wrote so witheringly of Keith and Ronnie at Live Aid in 1985: "Unsteady on old-fashioned boot-heels, faces blurrily confused, skinny forearms cluelessly pumping scrub-board guitars, they seemed less like Rock immortals than a pair of disreputable charwomen, half-heartedly washing out some socks."

Yet that very immortality is what so many of their disciples find so inspiring... Fill in the name for the latest 'new Rolling Stones' – out they come onstage, skeletal figures, weaving and tottering, cheekbones as hollow as famine survivors, scarecrow wardrobes and crow's nest hair. They eff and blind, they stagger and teeter, at times looking like the only thing keeping them upright is the wire connecting their electric guitar to its speaker. The new breed try just a mite too hard, they struggle to be debauched. In interviews, they boast of drugs taken, of titanic orgies. On they stumble at awards ceremonies, swigging from bottles of bourbon, swearing like squaddies on a 48-hour pass.*

The Stones have done all that before. They have copyrighted rock'n'roll decadence.

But you can hardly blame them; which boy wouldn't want to emulate the Stones in a rock'n'roll band? As David Hepworth later reflected: "The more the majority of the people who had grown up with rock'n'roll spent their days tethered to a work cubicle... the company's badge on a lanyard round their necks... the more they looked to rock stars to be the people they were no longer permitted to be."

Admired by boys, adored by girls, all for a few months' slog mastering an instrument, then a gruelling succession of tours before entering the bright, sunlit uplands of fame and fortune. Along the way, getting to pick and choose from those adoring girls, unwinding in their company after two hours spent being idolised. All surely better than a daily commute to a job you at best tolerate and at worst detest, in an office populated by colleagues with whom you have nothing in common. No, I think I may prefer the louche lifestyle of a rock legend, savouring the wealth and taste such legend brings, capering across continents, relishing the finest wine known to humanity, dining at five-star restaurants, never having to obey orders. Never having to go bending your knee to The Man. Sure there's a downside – take Hunter S. Thompson on the industry: "The music business is a cruel and shallow money trench, a long plastic hallway where thieves and pimps run free and good men die like dogs. There's also a negative side..."

---

* Ironically, the most rock'n'roll moment I've ever encountered at an awards ceremony was when staunch Republican Johnny Ramone was inducted into the Rock and Roll Hall of Fame in 2002: "God bless President Bush and God bless America!"

The problem with the wannabe bands that arrived in droves in the Stones' wake, of course, is their inability to appreciate that you had to write half a dozen classic hit singles, match that with four timeless albums, face off the establishment in a court of law, take a lot of drugs and *then* spend decades in an elegantly wasted style. And then, only then, do they start writing songs about *you*!

Even as early as 1968, Peter Sarstedt commemorated the Rolling Stones in his worldwide number one 'Where Do You Go To (My Lovely)?' In 1970, Kris Kristofferson appeared at the Isle of Wight festival and performed 'Blame It On The Stones'.* At the height of his influence, David Bowie name-checked the Stones on 'All The Young Dudes', while singling out the singer for 1973's 'Drive-In Saturday'. On his 1975 debut solo album, Nils Lofgren pleaded 'Keith Don't Go (Ode To The Glimmer Twin)'. On 1985's driving 'Stainsby Girls', Chris Rea remembered the girls he lusted after who "loved the Rolling Stones". House of Love had a minor hit in 1990 with their single 'Beatles And Stones', while on their 1999 album *13*, Blur sang of the Stones on 'Trailer Park'. The Stones could also be found on releases by Harry Chapin, Captain Beefheart, Kid Rock, The Fratellis and Yo La Tengo.

If anyone needed reminding, or the fact needed underlining, when they start writing songs about you, you can take pride in the fact that you have arrived. And survived.

And, unimaginably, the Rolling Stones have been surviving for *so* long... In 2015, Chris Welch remembered interviewing the band half a decade earlier: "Nobody in 1965 would have predicted the Stones would be rocking 50 years later. In 1965, 50 years earlier was 1915, when the second battle of Ypres was raging and

---

* The crowd of 600,000 thought he was pillorying the band, when in fact the song was about the hypocrisy of 'Mr Marvin Middle Class' and his fondness for Martini while castigating the Stones for their perceived decadence.

the hits included 'A Little Bit Of What You Fancy' by Marie Lloyd…!"

So long taken for granted, it is worth considering that the week the band's debut single, 'Come On', was released, in June 1963, it was six months before President Kennedy was assassinated on Dealey Plaza, while benevolent Edwardian relic Harold Macmillan occupies 10 Downing Street.

The capital city the band members knew like the backs of their hands has now changed beyond all recognition – not just the cycle and bus lanes or the gender-friendly traffic lights, but landmarks like the Chelsea Drugstore have been turned into a McDonald's franchise. They have seen Decca HQ demolished. They have witnessed the Magistrates Court where Mick, Marianne and Brian were all tried turned into a luxury boutique hotel.

They have outlasted the venues they once played – the Ealing Club, the Marquee (Oxford Street, Wardour Street *and* Charing Cross Road branches), Eel Pie Island, Studio 51, the Crawdaddy, the Ricky Tick, the Flamingo… They have outlasted the high-street chains their parents took them shopping in – Woolworth's, Kennedy's, British Home Stores, David Greig's… They have outlasted the tax discs on the cars they used to drive. They have lived to bid adieu to Mansize Kleenex. They have outlasted the boutiques that clothed them during those heady, colourful days – Mr Fish, Hung On You, I Was Lord Kitchener's Valet, Granny Takes A Trip… They have outlasted the clubs they used to cavort in – the Cromwellian, Tiles, the Scotch of St James, Blaises, the Speakeasy, Bag O'Nails… all gone.

They have effectively outlasted the Common Market, the EEC and all manner of other familiar acronyms – LCC, GLC, BOAC, NFT, ATV, EMI…

They have outlasted the weekly music press that coruscated and praised them in equal measure. All those yellowing copies of

Melody Maker, NME, Disc And Music Echo, Record Mirror, Sounds that tracked the trajectory of the Rolling Stones… They are in danger of outlasting the print medium itself.

They have outlasted dictatorships in Cuba, Czechoslovakia and the USSR. Unlike The Beatles, they got to play those countries in which rock'n'roll was once seen as the music of rebellion.

They have been going since the Berlin Wall went up and Nelson Mandela was jailed; they were touring *Steel Wheels* when the wall came tumbling down and Mandela walked free. They have remained above the fluctuating musical trends that have washed over these Isles since they began bashing out their unfamiliar brand of R&B in a Thameside pub, which would, by law, have closed between 2 p.m. and 7 p.m. every Sunday. Theirs was a world of smoking on trains and boats and planes, but they have outlasted the brands they used to smoke – Senior Service, Kensitas, Craven 'A', Piccadilly, Woodbine…

They have outdistanced the acts that influenced them and, in many cases, they have outlasted the bands that came in their wake.

For all the faults biographers and fans find with Mick's elusiveness or Keith's ramshackle pirating, at the end of the day they are Mick Jagger and Keith Richards. They are the Rolling Stones, and we mere mortals are not… Never have been and never will be.

CHAPTER 18

The Wild Bunch

What will likely bring the Stones to a grinding halt? Not, hopefully, a wild drug orgy or a desert apocalypse, but probably something as mundane as a Jagger hip replacement, a Charlie Watts torn ligament or Keith's worsening arthritis.

Incredibly, the guitarist endures. Paul Sexton marvelled at what Keith regarded as a 'healthy' drink: "It was vodka, and some disgusting sugar-heavy orange drink like Sunkist!" Marianne Faithfull told me in 1994: "I was in Jamaica last year for my birthday. Keith was there, and something happened that was like a metaphor for everything. We went swimming, and I was very good going out, but coming back in, I started to tire. Keith got back to the bank ages before me and called out, 'See Marianne, as far as you go out, you have to swim back again'!"

Leaving the mythical drug and blood transfusions aside, what has laid Keith low over the decades is, strangely, small beer – cut fingers, a slip in his Connecticut library resulting in three broken ribs and a punctured lung, caused by a tumble from a palm tree.

The arthritis is a condition he shares with his audience. These days if you follow the Stones on tour, and steer yourself towards a bar near the venue, you'll like as not find it filled with tour veterans. Most sport a head full of grey hair – if they're lucky – and proudly display that familiar emblem on T-shirts, badges, leather jackets, fleeces… all reminiscent of veterans' campaign medals from earlier conflicts. They huddle together, sinking the beers or, if they're feeling reckless and feeling like paying tribute to Keith, necking the Jack.

Off the marital leash, the memories pour out: of 'first times'; of favourite LPs; of changing playlists. They speak of unbelievable close encounters in a pub near Redlands, or unimaginably turning round at a barbecue and bumping into Mick. And of gigs they grow misty-eyed, like survivors of long-forgotten wars, moving the condiments around the dinner table over a bottle of port and reliving long-gone and impossible-to-access gigs: the *Rock and Roll Circus*, 1968… the Marquee, 1971… The 100 Club, 1982… Shepherd's Bush Empire, 1999… The Astoria, 2003… Or, if feeling particularly flush, after a gig they retire with their compadres to a basement room with a bottle of Crystal Head, "the official vodka of the Rolling Stones 50th anniversary".

And still they come in their droves, from all walks of life, to worship at the feet of the greatest rock'n'roll band in the world, to relive those classic songs and hopefully draw new meaning and experience from them.

Since its release in 1969, 'You Can't Always Get What You Want' has taken on a life of its own. In 1983, it featured as the haunting church organ accompaniment to the funeral of (the never actually seen) Kevin Costner that opens Lawrence Kasdan's moist-eyed sixties memoir *The Big Chill.*[*] In the 2000 film adaptation of Nick

---

* Astutely, Allen Klein allowed the song to be used in the film but not, as Fred Goodman pointed out, "on the soundtrack album. If someone wanted a copy of the song for his record collection, he would have to buy *Let It Bleed*."

Hornby's *High Fidelity*, Jack Black's blustering Barry insists 'You Can't Always Get What You Want' be played at his funeral – only for the quiet Nick to impose "immediate disqualification because of its involvement with *The Big Chill*". When the Stones celebrated their 50th anniversary, one of the many show highlights was the inclusion of local ensembles the London Youth Choir, the Choir of Trinity Wall Street and the Emory University Concert Choir delivering a magnificent choral underpinning to the track.

In June 2015, the most unlikely candidate – ever! – for the US presidency announced that he was running. Critics scorned the chances of a bloated egotist, Wall Street opportunist and TV celebrity. But Donald Trump was serious. And the song he chose to set him on the road to the White House, and beyond? The Rolling Stones' 'You Can't Always Get What You Want'…

On the eve of the Stones' 2018 *No Filter* tour, Mick was asked about Trump's choice of victory song. "It's a funny song for a play-out song – a drowsy ballad about drugs in Chelsea! It's kind of weird he couldn't be persuaded to use something else." But then, aged twenty-three when he first heard it, the song would have likely meant something to the future president. Like so many, he would have invested something of himself in the band's myth and legend.

Maybe what the fans want from the Stones is that which the band can't give them – their lost youth. They will never, ever again feel the thrill of hearing 'Gimme Shelter' or 'Sympathy For The Devil' for the first time. Never again will they be able to splash out a few bob and tell their mates at work: "I saw this amazing group at the Station Hotel in Richmond last night."

What you get from seeing the Stones in concert in the 21st century is a fragment; a moment that recalls the past, that captures a fleeting, long-gone sensation that says you are young, alive and well. It recalls a moment in time where you felt comfortable, your hand stretched out to grasp the future, and even if it eluded you first time around, you were young – you had time to try again. And again…

Maybe you can grasp it, maybe you can't. "You can't repeat the past," says Nick Carraway, admonishing Jay Gatsby. "Can't repeat the past?" Gatsby gasps incredulously. "Why of course you can!" F. Scott Fitzgerald's Gatsby is, like Mick Jagger, the blank canvas on which dreams are painted. Is Gatsby a German spy? A bootlegger? A killer on the run? An Oxford graduate? A scion of European royalty? So, to Jagger, is he the urbane diplomat? The cockney wide boy? The erudite historian? The foul-mouthed sybarite? The astute businessman? The scurrilous predator? The cricket-loving gentleman?… For the rock knight, he repeats the past as and when it suits him.

In the end, and at the end, though, the dream eludes Gatsby. For all the looking forward, it is left to his penniless friend to reflect that, like the Rolling Stones, "we beat on, boats against the current, borne back ceaselessly into the past".

★★★

Sam Peckinpah's *The Wild Bunch* (1969) is a watershed movie, a landmark in just how far one could go with depicting violence onscreen. Although set on the Tex-Mex border in the years leading up to World War I, Peckinpah always saw the film as an allegory for Vietnam, and how endemic and corrosive violence was in everyday American society. The film remains a bloody line in the sand – *Bonnie & Clyde* had pushed the envelope two years before, but *The Wild Bunch* soaked the envelope in gore. It was even estimated that more blank cartridges were shot during filming for *The Wild Bunch* than bullets fired during the actual Mexican Revolution!

The film boasts fine performances from perfectly cast Old Hollywood veterans William Holden, Edmond O'Brien and Robert Ryan. They play a group of men who have outlived their time; the world they once knew has moved on. New technology holds no interest for them – theirs is a world of horses and six shooters, not automobiles and machine guns. They know they are dinosaurs, but cannot – will not – move with the changing times. These are men who have to start "living beyond our guns, those days are closing fast".

Barry Norman selected *The Wild Bunch* as one of his '100 Best Films of the [20th] Century'. Martin Scorsese said it was "obviously a masterpiece. It was real film-making." While rewatching the film myself, I keep finding echoes in the dialogue of that other band of brothers, the Rolling Stones:

"We started together, we'll end it together."

"What are your plans?"

"Drift around down here; try and stay out of jail."

"Well, me and the boys we got some work to do. Ain't like it used to be, but it'll do."

"When you side with a man, you stick by him to the end, or you're nothing better than an animal."

Ironically, *The Wild Bunch* was funded by Warner Bros., the same studio still dithering over the release of *Performance* around the same time. Both projects were dogged by controversy from the very outset. At the first screening of Peckinpah's western, the director counted 32 people walking out in the first 10 minutes! As the discord raged, the film's star, William Holden, defended it in sentiments that mirrored Mick Jagger's on the same year's 'Gimme Shelter': "Are people surprised that violence really exists in the world?" he queried. "Just turn on your TV set any night. The viewer sees the Vietnam War, cities burning, campus riots; he sees plenty of violence."

If any one film epitomises Yeats' line about "a terrible beauty", it is *The Wild Bunch*. The violence is orchestrated; the butchery, balletic; the slow-motion killings are visceral. It pulls no punches, and, like the group, which – to my mind – it parallels, it packs a helluva punch.

And so it was that *The Wild Bunch* struck a deeper chord in me as I was writing this book, and I turned to the eminent film historian David Thomson for his take: "Throughout Peckinpah's work there is the theme of violently talented men hired for a job that is loaded with compromise, corruption and double-cross. They strive to perform with honour, before recognising the inevitable logic of self-destruction." Remind you of anyone?

The point is… at the film's climax, 'Pike Bishop' (the Wild Bunch's leader, played by Holden) enters a seedy Mexican bordello after a bloody shootout, where the gang's survivors are carousing. Bitter and twisted, he knows he has forsaken what little honour he had in sacrificing one of his gang as a plaything for the sadistic Mexican dictator. Inside the shabby whorehouse, the scarred survivors of his gang lie sprawled, soused in tequila, whores draped like scarves around their necks. They bitch with each other, they haggle with the harridans. All the while, they know their end is nigh. They know their horses have no place in a world of flying machines. They are redundant, spent forces. They know that what time remains to them is worthless.

Holden appreciates that, for him, for them, to salvage any dignity, he has to try and rouse them. He has to get them on one last mission, to rescue their captured comrade. You are braced for a lengthy "a man's gotta do what a man's gotta do…" speech. You are anticipating: "Look, Angel is our buddy, our comrade-in-arms, and we cannot abandon him. So even though it means our certain death, to maintain our integrity and bruised honour, we have to be prepared to rescue him, to sacrifice ourselves."

That speech never comes. Instead, a grizzled Holden casts a jaundiced eye over his gnarled compadres and simply grunts: "Let's go." They know that death lies in that decision. A bitter anticipation, a sense of impending fatality is etched in every line of their weather-beaten faces. The quartet's final walk down the street to certain death reminded me of the Stones taking their final bow as the curtain falls.

For all the books, documentaries and biographies, for all the websites and magazine articles groaning under speculation over influence, motivation and historical context, it all comes down to one thing – getting the old gang together, and one of those grizzled survivors just saying it out loud: "Let's go."

I believe there are more parallels between *The Wild Bunch* and the Rolling Stones, especially when you compare the violence in the movie to the turbulence that enveloped the band, and indeed the world, in 1969. Maybe Meredith Hunter had been looking for some sort of warped infamy… for all the chaos that ensued, maybe the Stones were just a shot away…

But this band is a band of survivors, and they have proceeded with a degree of dignity in their elevated status, not just in the pantheon of rock, but in society, in culture. These men in the eye of the hurricane, who cross continents, brave contempt and face up to real menace, continue to endure. In time, ennoblement and unimagined riches came their way, along with domesticity and old age. But also a kind of serenity, unimagined and unimaginable.

For them, for us, as ever… ahead lies the unknown.

But as the anniversaries roll by and the coffers overflow, as the stadiums fill up with fans, eager for one – last? – look at the legends, the Rolling Stones are testament to the fact that, perhaps, maybe, You *Can* Always Get What You Want.

Bibliography

Steve Appleford, *The Rolling Stones, It's Only Rock & Roll, The Stories Behind Every Song* (Carlton, 1997)

Saul Austerlitz, *Just A Shot Away, Peace, Love, And Tragedy With The Rolling Stones At Altamont* (Thomas Dunne, 2018)

Steven Bach, *Marlene Dietrich, Life And Legend* (HarperCollins, 1993)

Rob Baker, *Beautiful Idiots And Brilliant Lunatics: A Sideways Look At Twentieth-Century London* (Amberley, 2015)

Louis Barfe, *Where Have All The Good Times Gone? The Rise And Fall Of The Record Industry* (Atlantic, 2004)

Victor Bockris, *Keith Richards, The Unauthorised Biography* (Omnibus Press, 2002)

Stanley Booth, *The True Adventures Of The Rolling Stones* (Canongate, 2012)

Rich Cohen, *The Sun & The Moon & The Rolling Stones* (Headline, 2017)

Julian Dawson, *And On Piano... Nicky Hopkins: The Extraordinary Life Of Rock's Greatest Session Man* (Backstage Press, 2011)

Peter Doggett, *There's A Riot Going On: Revolutionaries, Rock Stars, And The Rise And Fall Of '60s Counterculture* (Canongate, 2008)

Peter Doggett, *You Never Give Me Your Money, The Battle For The Soul Of The Beatles* (Vintage, 2010)

Sean Egan, *Rolling Stones And The Making Of Let It Bleed* (Unanimous, 2005)

Martin Elliott, *The Rolling Stones, Complete Recording Sessions, 1962–2012* (Cherry Red Books, 2012)

Marianne Faithfull (with David Dalton), *Faithfull* (Michael Joseph, 1994)

Marianne Faithfull (with David Dalton), *Memories, Dreams & Reflections* (Fourth Estate, 2007)

Ben Fong-Torres, *Hickory Wind, The Life & Times of Gram Parsons* (Omnibus Press, 1991)

Fred Goodman, *Allen Klein: The Man Who Bailed Out The Beatles, Made The Stones, And Transformed Rock & Roll* (Mariner, 2016)

Bill Graham & Robert Greenfield, *Bill Graham Presents: My Life Inside Rock And Out* (Delta Books, 1992)

Joe Hagan, *Sticky Fingers, The Life & Times Of Jann Wenner And Rolling Stone Magazine* (Canongate, 2017)

Richard Havers, *The Stones In The Park: The Summer of '69 And The Making Of The Greatest Rock And Roll Band In The World* (Haynes Publishing, 2009)

Richard Havers, *The Rolling Stones: On Air In The Sixties* (Virgin, 2017)

David Hepworth, *Uncommon People, The Rise And Fall Of The Rock Stars* (Black Swan, 2018)

Clinton Heylin, *Bootleg! The Rise & Fall Of The Secret Recording Industry* (Omnibus Press, 2003)

Glyn Johns, *Sound Man: A Life Recording Hits With The Rolling Stones, The Who, Led Zeppelin, The Eagles, Eric Clapton, The Faces...* (Plume, 2014)

Norman Jopling, *Shake It Up Baby!: Notes From A Pop Music Reporter, 1961–1972* (Rock History, 2015)

Phil Kaufman & Colin White, *Road Mangler Deluxe* (White Boucke Publishing, 1993)

Nick Kent, *The Dark Stuff: Stories From The Peatlands* (Penguin, 1994)

Al Kooper, *Backstage Passes And Backstabbing Bastards: Memoirs Of A Rock'n'Roll Survivor* (Billboard Books, 1998)

Shawn Levy, *Ready, Steady, Go! Swinging London And The Invention Of Cool* (Fourth Estate, 2002)

Mark Lewisohn, *The Beatles – All These Years, Volume 1: Tune In* (Little Brown, 2013)

Dora Loewenstein & Philip Dodd (Eds), *According To The Rolling Stones* (Weidenfeld & Nicolson, 2003)

William Manchester, *The Glory And The Dream: A Narrative History Of America 1932–1972* (Michael Joseph, 1975)

George Melly, *Revolt Into Style: The Pop Arts In Britain* (Penguin, 1970)

Barry Miles, *The Rolling Stones: A Visual Documentary* (Omnibus Press, 1994)

Philip Norman, *Mick Jagger* (HarperCollins, 2012)

Andrew Loog Oldham, *Stoned* (Vintage, 2001)

Mark Paytress, *The Rolling Stones, Off The Record* (Omnibus Press, 2003)

Keiron Pim, *Jumpin' Jack Flash: David Litvinoff And The Rock'n'Roll Underworld* (Vintage, 2017)

Perry Richardson, *The Early Stones: Legendary Photos Of A Band In The Making 1963–1973* (Secker & Warburg, 1993)

Geoffrey Aquilina Ross, *The Day Of The Peacock, Style For Men 1963–1973* (V&A Publishing, 2011)

Robert Santelli, *Aquarius Rising: The Rock Festival Years* (Delta, 1980)

Joel Selvin, *Altamont, The Rolling Stones, The Hells Angels And The Inside Story Of Rock's Darkest Day* (Dey Street Books, 2016)

Paul Trynka, *Sympathy For The Devil: The Birth Of The Rolling Stones And The Death Of Brian Jones* (Bantam Press, 2014)

Max Weinberg (with Robert Santelli), *The Big Beat: Conversations With Rock's Great Drummers* (Billboard, 1991)

Dick Weindling & Marianne Colloms: *Decca Studios And Klooks Kleek: West Hampstead's Musical Heritage Remembered* (The History Press, 2013)

Simon Wells, *Butterfly On A Wheel: The Great Rolling Stones Drug Bust* (Omnibus Press, 2012)

Bill Wyman & Ray Coleman, *Stone Alone: The Story Of A Rock'n'Roll Band* (Viking, 1990)

Bill Wyman & Richard Havers, *Rolling With The Stones* (Dorling Kindersley, 2002)

For everything you need to know about the Rolling Stones, the following website proved invaluable: Nico Zentgraf's Rolling Stones database is awesomely comprehensive: www.nzentgraf.de.

For up-to-date news: www.stonesnews.com; iorr.org.

And if you are in London, check out Paul Endacott's bus tours of the Rolling Stones' London: www.60sbus.london.

Further afield, contact Philip Jump c/o www.badlands.co.uk, who is happy to show the curious around Brian Jones' Cheltenham.

Acknowledgements

It's a mighty long way down rock'n'roll, as someone else sang in a different time. This journey took me all over, from Altamont to Berkhamstead; Chelsea to Clapham; Cheltenham to Hartfield. Actually, that's not quite true – I never did get to California, but spent many happy hours in Gloucestershire, Hertfordshire and Sussex. Throughout, I was in good company, so sincere thanks go out to…

Keith Altham, Steve Blacknell, Chas Chandler, Fred Dellar, Daryl Easlea, Martin Elliott, Dr Cherilyn Fenech, David Fricke, Lon Goddard, Philip and Mary Morton, Richard Morton Jack, Rosemary Morton Jack, Andy Neill, Helinda Anne Perry, Andy Rawll, Tony Russell, Paul Sexton, David Sinclair, David Stark, Geoff Summerton and Chris Welch. Visit Chris's new website for a tantalising glimpse of life as a sixties music journalist: www.chriswelchonline.com.

Inestimable thanks to Philip Jump, Mark Lewisohn and Simon Wells, who gave up their time to shepherd me round.

Special thanks to John Sugar, Stones fan par excellence, and for getting me to Gate 5, Section 109, Seat 297 at the Olympic Park on May 22, 2018! Ditto Bernard Doherty and Alexandra Sutton.

Thanks to David Barraclough, Lucy Beevor and Imogen Gordon Clark for realising this book.

And of course, my dear wife Sue… so many journeys, so many memories…

As an only child, I would like to dedicate this book with deep affection to my cousins Margaret, Roger, Lisa, Carol, Ian, Louise, Susan, Madeline and Adrian.

And to the next generations…

In England: Colin, Catarina and Olivia Lusk; Simon and Eleanor Lusk; Jamie, Simon, Chloe, Halle and Ivy; Henrietta, James, Thomas and Lucy Hillman; Joanna, Matt, Hannah and Samuel Fairless; Dan, Ana and Cara Cooke. In Canada: Sara and 'Little' Peggy; Jack, Zoe and Luke Duchek; Emma and Luke Jeffrey; Sam and Evangeline Honeyman; and Alexander Benoit.

In Australia: Andrew and Amanda. One day, long after I am gone, may they enjoy the majesty that is 'You Can't Always Get What You Want' and relish *Let It Bleed* on disc or 'in a format yet to be invented'.

In Memoriam

Scott Appel, John Bauldie, Sean Body, Bill Caddick, Roy Carr, Carol Clerk, Stuart Colman, Karl Dallas, my cousin Alastair Davison, Tom Dobson, David Ferguson, Debbie Geller, John Gill, Stephen Grater, Richard Havers, Chris Hunt, Tony Ireton (who didn't much like music, but was my oldest friend), Steph Jones, Anthea Joseph, Steven Jump, Dave Laing, Barry Lazell, my cousin Malcolm Lee, Ian MacDonald, Paul Mason, Pierre Perrone, Kelly Pike, John Platt, Mark Rye, David Sandison, Bob Shelton, Mark Smith, Gael Whelan, Bob Woffinden, Big Pete and Jonah... Too long a list... They were friends and colleagues who all loved their music. They were all taken far too soon...